REVENUE SYSTEM IN POST-MAURYA AND GUPTA TIMES

Revenue System in Post-Maurya and Gupta Times

DWIJENDRA NARAYAN JHA

With a Foreword and an Afterword by

VISHWA MOHAN JHA

MANOHAR

2020

First published 1967
Reprinted 2020

ISBN 978-93-90035-22-9

Published by
Ajay Kumar Jain *for*
Manohar Publishers & Distributors
4753/23 Ansari Road, Daryaganj
New Delhi 110 002

Printed at
Replika Press Pvt. Ltd.

To the memory of

Hem Chaturvedi (d. 2011)

Roman Equivalents of Nāgarī Letters.

अ a	ऋ ṛ	क् k	च् c
आ ā	ए e	ख् kh	छ् ch
इ i	ऐ ai	ग् g	ज् j
ई ī	ओ o	घ् gh	झ् jh
उ u	औ au	ङ ṅ	ञ ñ
ऊ ū			
ट् ṭ	त् t	प् p	य् y
ठ् ṭh	थ् th	फ् ph	र् r
ड् ḍ	द् d	ब् b	ल् l
ढ् ḍh	ध् dh	भ् bh	व् b
ण् ṇ	न् n	म् m	श् ś

ष् ṣ	Anusvāra	ं	ṁ
स् s	Visarga	ः	ḥ

CONTENTS

FOREWORD

In a time of innovation all that is not new is pernicious.[1]

I was delighted when the idea of reissuing Professor D.N. Jha's half-a-century old (1967) book, *Revenue System in Post-Maurya and Gupta Times* (*Revenue System* in short) was mentioned to me, and readily set upon the task of writing a foreword to it. I was delighted because the republication could become an occasion for sending out more than one important message, as it would allow me to revisit the historiographical context in which the volume first saw the light of day, as well as to reflect upon the contemporary conjunctures of historical thinking and practice in which it does so again.

The volume, any more than the even more ancient *Contributions to the History of the Hindu Revenue System* (1929) by U.N. Ghoshal (*Contributions* in short), has not dated, for it has not been superseded, for the simple reason that the subject has ceased to interest researchers for the past several decades. Its arguments and evidence continue as a result to hold the field, for all the vast potential of further and deeper research. As the issues have fallen into a wholly unmerited – unexplained at the very least – neglect and consequent desuetude, the phrase 'revenue system' itself has gone out of vogue. Titles matter, and well-wishers suggested a catchier, more market friendly one for this reissue. We had to demur. A major purpose of the reissue is to underline the undiminished relevance of the old theme. Revenue system – collection and distribution of social wealth – was arguably a leading organizing principle of ancient and early medieval economies of

1. Louis Antoine Léon de Saint-Just, 'Report to the National Convention' (10 October 1793).

India; and, after all, *Revenue System in Post-Maurya and Gupta Times* is no *Carracks, Caravans and Companies.*[2]

THE CONTEXTS: THEN AND NOW

To a whole range of the leading lights, economic history was still something of a novelty – often anything but a welcome one – at the time the *Revenue System* was first published. The first thing that more than one reviewer noted about the work, perhaps with some impatience, was the branch of history it belonged to. The total number of titles 'dealing primarily *or in part* with aspects of the economic history of ancient India' since Ghoshal's *Contributions*, of which Jha's was the latest, had crossed thirty, noted one reviewer.[3] Another started with the book's bibliography to find 'some 20 books on ancient India devoted wholly to economic history', and, probably going by the same source, could locate the revival of 'the fashion' from the mid-1950s after its beginning and early vogue in the (late) 1920s and early 1930s; though welcoming the book in question, he could not help seeing it as 'yet another indication that the flood is reaching full spate with no signs of abating'.[4]

However, it was in the pages of the *Journal of American Oriental Society* that the real damage was done to the young scholar's doctoral publication in a near summary dismissal by the venerable Ludwik Sternbach, especially in the following remark: 'It is an expansion of Chapter VII of Vol. III of P.V. Kane's *History of Dharmaśāstra* from where the author extensively derived his

2. This title of Niels Steensgaard's magnificent study was found too unviable and, for its almost immediate reprinting by University of Chicago, had to give way to *The Asian Trade Revolution of the Seventeenth Century: The East India Companies and the Decline of the Caravan Trade*; for the commercially repelling 'carracks' no room was to be there even in the subtitle!
3. Gokhale 1968: 1603, emphasis added.
4. Trautmann 1968. Of the reviewers, J.W. Spellman alone recognized the untapped potential and great promise of this field of enquiry in an unduly, if characteristically, hard-hitting review of the book (Spellman 1968: 638-40).

knowledge.'[5] The time has come to refute the rashness of this judgement. If there is an expansion in thirteen chapters, along with thorough documentation with hundreds of citations, of a sixteen-page piece, then that must set it qualitatively apart from the original inspiration. The fact remains that there is no such relation between Kane's and Jha's works. This is perhaps best seen by a look at the connection there is between the two. Jha consulted the first three volumes of the *History of Dharmaśāstra*, abbreviating it as *Hist. Dharm*. Of the seven references to Kane that I have been able to trace,[6] *none* refers to Chapter VII of Volume III. Actually, in this chapter on the King's Treasury or public finance, Kane does not so much as distinguish between the periods of early India, citing *Manu*, *Mānasollāsa*, and the *Rājataraṅgiṇī* together, and has no use whatsoever for the *Contributions*, the acknowledged real influence on our *Revenue System*.

While others saw it as one more addition to an old lot, a discerning Romila Thapar would isolate it on more than one count, as one of its own kind. Here was a historian, she noted, who was not particularly charmed by 'empires and large kingdoms' but astute enough to make 'a period of political fragmentation' his starting point; who was reconstructing 'a system of an inequitable distribution of the tax burden'; who was suggesting a rise in tax burden in the Gupta period; and so on.[7] Implicitly, in other words, it marked a break in the continuum.

That would have also been the self-perception of the author as a member of the new Marxist history pioneered by D.D. Kosambi and R.S. Sharma. It came out clearly in an essay on trends and prospects in the economic history of India (up to AD 1200) that he co-authored with Sharma, where several criticisms of the nationalist historians' writings on economic history were made.[8] However, there the *Revenue System* does not figure as an exemplar of the

5. Sternbach 1969: 823.
6. Jha 1967: 2 fn2 (Kane, vol. II part 1); 16 fn47 (vol. III); 90 fn33 (vol. III); 124 fn8 (vol. II part 1); 128 fn26 (vol. II part 2); 139 fn1 (vol. III), and; 141 fn23 (vol. III).
7. Thapar 1968.
8. Sharma and Jha 1974: 51-62.

new departure, and no such claims are expressed as such in the book. So where exactly does *Revenue System* stand in the literature on early Indian economic history?

An answer may promptly be found in the extensive surveys of early Indian historical writings, as to not only how, as part of the new Marxist historiography, it stood out from the previous economic histories, but also how it has been displaced by new concerns in consciously post-Marxist narratives (i.e. *post* the Marxist historians of early India, rather than Marxism as such, in which little interest is taken by the post-Marxist historians). As answers go, it may not be the correct one.

One of the answers is that it is only since the late 1950s, following the ground-breaking works of Kosambi and Sharma that landownership and revenue system came to be studied in earnest by a large number of historians. All that the earlier historians – there is a specific reference to the works of N.C. Bandyopadhyaya, K.M. Gupta, Pran Nath, U.N. Ghoshal and A.N. Bose – did was to 'essentially compile … the incidental material', mostly from literary sources and only 'sporadically supplementing it with inscriptional evidence, with varying degrees of success'.[9] The compilation of 'the incidental material', it is elaborated, was 'mere collection of data on land types, varieties of land measures, crops, revenue terms or the theoretical position of the *varṇas*'.[10] As the discussion progresses, it also becomes clear that the literary sources were of one particular kind, hardly representative of the whole range, while the sporadic epigraphic supplementing was not exactly illuminating, the result hardly spectacular. It was only 'on the basis of brahmanical literature' that these nationalist historians painted their pictures of a happy and content ancient India, marked among other things by 'absence of oppressive taxation';[11] or else, for the same end, they

9. Sahu 1997: 1.
10. Ibid.: 3.
11. Ibid.: 2.

'mixed up evidence from smṛiti[12] literature and inscriptions'.[13] In fine, as 'the analysis and explanation of agrarian life within incorporative concepts was unknown and the peasant was, more often than not, missing in the discussions', true understanding was 'lost in the maze of descriptive details cutting across time segments [i.e. devoid of any chronological sense]'.[14]

This binary of Marxist histories 'since the later part of the 1950s' (which studied revenue system, landownership and the rest in proper conceptual frameworks) and the 'earlier' nationalist histories (which 'essentially' and all too uncritically compiled assorted data on crops, revenue terms, land measures, and the like) is all overturned by the other answer. Now the proposition is that 'aspects such as landownership, agriculture and the revenue system' came to be studied by historians such as Bandyopadhyaya, Nath and Ghoshal, in course of developing a critique of colonial writings.[15] Then K.M. Gupta, K.A. Nilakanta Sastri and A. Appadorai 'laid the foundations for the study of land system and society in south India': the first doing it in a 'traditional' (?) manner; the second 'largely [i.e. not sporadically] on the basis of inscriptional evidence', and; the third by 'drawing on the chronicles of travellers and epigraphic material [without mixing it all up]'.[16] A.N. Bose, who in the first interpretation is one among all these pre-Kosambi compilers of economic miscellany, is now seen to be writing excellent economic history before Kosambi and Sharma!

Through a combined use of the Jātakas, Smṛitis and epigraphic and numismatic evidence A.N. Bose provided an excellent description of north Indian rural economy. Thematically he covered almost the same ground

12. I use *ṛi*, not *ṛ*; *cha*, not *ca*; and *sha*, not *ṣa* in transliterating Indic words here, modifying for the sake of consistency also the quotes by other authors (though not the reference titles). In an unpublished article (entitled 'Chewing the Cud') that I wrote a few years ago, I have given reasons for my preference for this earlier system of transliteration that used to be normally followed, at least in India, in Indological studies.
13. Ibid.: 53 n166.
14. Ibid.: 3.
15. Ibid.: 2.
16. Ibid.

as that of the earlier historians, but he seems to have been influenced by Marxism. In his work there is an awareness of the exploitative social relations in early historical India.[17]

Both the answers cannot be correct at the same time. Yet, as will be evident from the references, it is in one and the same write-up (which is otherwise fairly coherent and always lucid) that both sets of arguments are to be found together – all intermingled, with individual statements from one found cheek by jowl with those from the other.

This lumping together of mutually inconsistent chains of arguments is symptomatic of a pervasive state of the discipline. There has been a progressive loss of touch with the works of bygone generations, so much so that it is possible to believe in all kinds of things about them – a few of these perceptions may be real, it is their juxtaposition with the fanciful rest that is the pointer. A due appreciation of Jha's *Revenue System* calls for giving his predecessors their due.

We may begin with Jha's own perceptions. We hardly find there any of the prevalent self-congratulatory beliefs in the ongoing revolutionary phase of all-round innovation in historical thinking and research. To be sure, Jha does distance himself from his predecessors in forthright terms, and is indeed candid to the point of being harsh, even acerbic, in his judgements on others. S.K. Maity's brief treatment of the revenue system of the Guptas is 'perfunctory', the better-appreciated detailed study of Mauryan public finance by M.H. Gopal suffers from anachronisms, and even the pioneer Ghoshal is stated to have 'dismissed' too briefly the important theme which Jha has set out to cover in over 200 pages (p. 1).[18] There are also statements about the historical method in the *Revenue System*: placing the 'greatest reliance' on epigraphic evidence (p. 7), keeping in mind the prescriptive nature of the legal texts (p. 2), and sundry other issues, e.g. 'the contradiction between the revenue terminology and its actual content' (p. 44). In fact, the reviewers agreed in their appreciation for Jha's cautious approach,

17. Ibid.
18. The reputation he continues to live up to was thus acquired quite early!

but neither they nor Jha himself thereby assert that he is the first person to have done so, or one of an emerging school of pioneers. 'Dr. Jha', Ludo Rocher observed,'has set himself a number of methodological criteria which should help him using his sources objectively', e.g. not 'to read modern ideas and institutions in the *Arthaśāstra*';[19] this was however to be understood as a criticism specifically of the work of M.H. Gopal, with no claim to blazing a new trail.[20] Jha's bark is in fact worse than his bite. The numerous discussions of the views of Maity suggest an acknowledgement that would scarcely be accorded to a 'perfunctory' work; and the dismissal did not mean that Ghoshal did not do a proper and much valued job, but that his was only a chapter-long treatment of a vast subject.

Significantly, however, an element of exaggeration was beginning to creep in quite early, as in the following reviewer's remark: 'Dr Jha has used epigraphical evidence more widely than is usually the case in such studies.'[21] Not the same as the author's own statement about placing more reliance on inscriptions than on the other sources, and easily contradicted by a reference to the *Contributions* (a major source for D.C. Sircar's *Indian Epigraphical Glossary*), impressions such as this (i.e. from earlier sporadic uses to a regular employment of epigraphical data in the post-nationalist historiography) have been gathering strength in regular renewals, though hardly borne out by the evidence. The artificial historiographical divides thus created have overlain and buried underneath the actual ones.

19. Rocher 1972: 288.

20. On the fundamental dissimilarity of modern principles of taxation with those in early India, Jha provides a useful corrective to Ghoshal too (pp. 25-7): '... the similarity between ancient Indian approach to taxation and the modem principles of public finance is only superficial for in their implications the two differ widely' (p. 27). However, he does not, quite correctly, accuse Ghoshal of reading modern ideas in the past.

21. Thapar 1968: 195.

Uncovering a Nationalist Fault Line

Jha, it would seem, cannot help referring to all kinds of financial oppression of the masses by the state in his book (e.g. 30-2, 44, 47, 67-9). Is it perchance here that we have a Marxist counter-narrative to the nationalist portrayals of the cloud-cuckoo-land that was ancient India? Yes, it is, but only with huge doses of allowances, for the actual historiographical contrasts are far less stark, far more complex than anything that has been said on the matter.

So far from arguing 'absence of oppression' in ancient India, Ghoshal's *Contributions* is replete with references to it. Jha can state confidently that the *bali* tax in the Jātakas was 'often … oppressive' (p. 44), without discussion, because this had already been well established by Ghoshal: 'References are accordingly found in the Jātakas to the oppressive imposition of *bali* by the king, not to speak of the exactions and tyrannies of the tax-collectors (*bali-sādhakas* or *niggāhakas*), whose name passed into a synonym for importunate demand.'[22] 'Some prevalent forms of oppression upon merchants' in the *AŚ* are detailed by Ghoshal,[23] followed by those of other kinds, and there is a threadbare discussion of the Junagadh Inscription of Rudradāman as '*a concrete illustration*[24] of the items of oppressive taxation mentioned in the Arthaśāstra'.[25] And so on and so forth.

It is possible to detect nationalism in the *Contributions* nonetheless. It is to be kept in mind here that nationalism is nothing if not competitive (except in the historical conjunctures when one

---

22. Ghoshal 1930: 25. Ghoshal, however, thinks it to have been the name of the chief revenue demand by the state (ibid.), while Jha sees it as the term for additional cesses, citing a longer list of references (p. 44 fn62) only one of which overlaps Ghoshal's (Ibid.: 108 nn4, 6). Here is an important unsorted difference between the two.
23. Ghoshal 1929: 88-9.
24. Emphasis added. Here is one opportunity, out of countless others, to disabuse ourselves of the belief that it was only in the post-nationalist historiography that there occurred the 'shift from the presentation of the theoretical position as enunciated in the normative texts to efforts at understanding rural life as it was actually lived' (Sahu 1997: 3).
25. Ibid.: 189.

nationalism becomes the liberating force for others). As to the *AŚ* provisions, the nationalist defence – nationalist because no other purpose of the comparison is discernible – was that the state in ancient India was not alone in oppressing its subjects: Kauṭilya's references 'may be fitly matched with the methods of financial oppression known to the other countries of the East as well as the West, of antiquity as well as modern times.'[26] But having brought in the comparison, the historian's conscience in Ghoshal overcame the nationalist urge to equally emphasize that the Indian evidence surpasses anything anywhere else for its immorality ('adopting every species of force and fraud'), in 'the methods of unabashed appropriation of temple treasures' and in 'exploitation of popular religious beliefs in the interest of the State treasury'. This last item about the exploitation of religious beliefs in the *AŚ* was to be famously elaborated by Sharma[27] and celebrated by fellow travellers like Debiprasad Chattopadhyaya.[28] The Marxist may or may not have taken the leaf out of the Nationalist's book: it is difficult to say pending further research. Undoubtedly they were on the same page.

Likewise for the incidence of forced labour. Its wide prevalence as a great potential source of oppression is underlined in the *Contributions*, and, it is recognized that both 'references in the general literature and concrete examples from the history of the Himalayan States' would show it to have been precisely that; in comparative terms, much like the eighteenth-century French *corvée*.[29] However, there were other references too, where forced labour in early India would appear to be 'as mild in its operation as the English Statute labour',[30] and certainly much milder than its Chinese counterpart. One piece of evidence is the frequently-used adjective *utpadyamāna* ('as it may arise') for forced labour. Interpreting it as 'as it becomes due', he argues that this 'evidently

26. Ibid.: 131.
27. Sharma, 'Religion and Politics in the Arthasastra of Kautilya', in Sharma 1959, Chapter XI.
28. Chattopadhyaya 1993: 181-4.
29. Ghoshal 1929: 285.
30. Ibid.: 285-6.

shows that it could be levied only on specific occasions',[31] and so was not arbitrary and oppressive. And from the fact that Xuanzang 'declares the burden of forced service in one place to be non-existent, and in another place to be limited',[32] he concludes: 'Evidently, it was very mild as compared with the Chinese rule of personal service from twenty to fifty days in the year.'[33] In conclusion, Ghoshal does not use one set of evidence to contradict or suppress the other, but, quite unexceptionably, sees in their difference temporal and spatial variation: 'its nature seems to have varied at different times and places.'[34]

At this point, a critical difference of the Marxist history begins to emerge. Jha interprets *utpadyamāna* in the opposite manner, and, gathering some further support from the *Kāmasūtra*, concludes as follows:

> The element of oppression may have been rendered stronger in the Gupta period, when the king's right to demand impressed labour was transferred to the donees who were the recipients of land grants. [The term] … means that the donee was entitled to the privilege of getting free labour as the occasion arose. … It seems that forced labour included all conceivable kinds of work, for which any special occasion was not needed. (p. 69)

It is to be noted that in so doing Jha was following Sharma, who had argued in *Indian Feudalism* that the phrase enabled 'the grantees … to determine the occasion for forced labour at their discretion.'[35]

In those nationalist times, intermediaries of any kind, whether revenue farmers or zamindars, were considered evil and parasitic exploiters of peasantry. So one yardstick of the well-being of the rural masses was the extent of the absence of these intermediaries. Ghoshal used this criterion to compare and contrast the lot of the ancient Indian peasantry with that of the Muslim-period one, to the advantage of ancient India.

---

31. Ibid.: 218.
32. Ibid.: 226-7.
33. Ibid.: 227.
34. Ibid.: 285.
35. Sharma 1965: 49.

> On the whole, then, it appears that *throughout the longest period* of its history in ancient times Assignments played a relatively unimportant part in the agrarian system of Northern India, and the king's revenue officers as a rule dealt directly with the cultivators. Of farmers of the land-revenue our authorities practically make no mention, almost the only authentic example of their existence being found in the records of the Maitrakas of Gujarat. Truly, then, the dictum summing up *the essence of the agrarian system in Moslem India*, namely, that the farmer and the assignee were normally the masters of the peasant's fate, would not apply to ancient period.[36] (Emphases added)

Speaking mainly of north India, Ghoshal does note the importance of Assignments from the seventh century onwards – when according to 'the high authority' of Xuanzang, 'the practice of granting Assignments to officers of all grades was well established' – up to eleventh century. But he believed that the practice fell away in the twelfth century, and the evidence during the long duree of pre-seventh-century ancient India was sometimes tenuous and uncertain, but largely in the negative. The total absence of the evidence of Assignments from Megasthenes to Faxian was especially striking: 'When the veil of obscurity is next lifted up before our eyes towards the close of the fourth century before Christ and, again, at the beginning of the fifth century of the Christian era, we find Megasthenes and Fa Hian testifying to the existence of direct relations between the Government and the cultivators, while Assignments are not even noticed by them.[37]

Ghoshal was concerned only with secular grants ('Assignment'), setting little score by the plethora of religious ones. His authority for the reference to Assignments and revenue farming being 'the essence' of the agrarian system of the Muslim times is W.H. Moreland who however was not prepared to pass any blanket judgement on either: 'Neither institution is inherently bad; both must be judged according to their conditions, and, most of all, their duration.'[38] But his argument about the shortness of tenure being the bane of the assignment system would have favoured Ghoshal's

36. Ghoshal 1930: 74.
37. Ibid.: 73.
38. Moreland 1929: 205.

thinking, by which logic pre-Islamic system of 'clan-monarchies' and of course religious grants would be the most beneficial for peasantry.

In course of describing the revenue systems from the Gupta period onwards, Ghoshal had to concentrate perforce on the testimony of religious land grants, which he did with the usual competence and thoroughness. In the process he routinely refers many times to instances of oppression in the countryside (e.g. the 'list of oppressors from whose visit a village is exempted in the Nowgong grant of Balavarman of the tenth century A.C.').[39] Nowhere through his numerous references to oppression and oppressors in the land-grant inscriptions (overwhelmingly religious) does he ever pause to discuss the issue of financial oppression, as he would so impressively with reference to the *Arthaśāstra*, Junagadh Inscription, and the Jātakas. This was *the* blind spot of the historian.

The Marxian perspective could not but remove these blinkers. Ghoshal had noted probably more often than Jha the references to the billeting of soldiers, or the *chāṭas* and *bhaṭas*, in the inscriptions. Going by the known record of such people from other places and times, a moment's reflection would have suggested to Ghoshal what he left for Jha to point out: 'an important source of oppression seems to have been the billeting of royal agents and soldiers in the villages' (p. 32.); 'they may have been probably in the habit of collecting oppressive extra impositions and realising illegal taxes for their own benefit' (p. 33). Following *Indian Feudalism*, it is in the following that one may locate the decisive breach with the nationalist historiography: '... land grants ... tended to increase the burden on peasants and thus served to accelerate the process of social polarisation. ... The brāhmaṇas were liberally rewarded for their work, but at the cost of the lower *varṇas* who worked as peasants in the villages' (p. 137).

On the critical point of overall conclusion, however, nationalism did manage to get the better of the historian, not in his *Contributions* but in his *Agrarian System*. After all this scrupulous and rigorous discussion of the evidence on people's oppression, Ghoshal can

39. Ghoshal 1929: 224; also 243-4 fn2, 245 fn3, 248.

reduce it all to an observation that is made only 'sometimes' in our sources and does not refer to 'the actual condition of the people' (*contra* his own, already-cited references to the 'concrete illustration' from the Junagadh record and the 'concrete examples [of tyrannical forced labour] from the history of the Himalayan States'). Even more ironically, for the sake of argument, the nationalist can conveniently condemn the masses of this indigenous evidence as inferior to the foreigner's facile testimony, to conclude as follows: 'If, then, the ancient records sometimes refer to oppressive burdens of the land-revenue and other charges, it can be said with truth that the glimpses which the observations of the foreign travellers furnish into the actual condition of the people generally indicate a happy and contented peasantry.'[40]

The fuller story of the prevalent condition of people as portrayed in pre-Marxist, generally nationalist, histories of early India is even richer and more complex than is seen here in the case of Ghoshal. That has to be left for some other occasion. It is also time we paid attention to the nationalism of the Marxist historians of India; among other things, it was deeply humanist and truly Indian, never tainted by biases of creed, caste or region. It is clear all the same that historians of all hues worked under the same broad umbrella of economic history. Right after his *Contributions* (1929), the (Hindu) nationalist U.N. Ghoshal delivered five lectures on and published them as *The Agrarian System in Ancient India* (1930), just as the (Indian) Marxist R.S. Sharma, no sooner had he delivered the lectures on *Indian Feudalism* in 1964, than he organized a seminar on the history of land revenue in India in 1965.[41] Ghoshal makes no secret of his debt to the work of Moreland (*The Agrarian System of Moslem India*, 1929), and while Irfan Habib was to break much new ground, it was to be done under the same topic of

40. Ghoshal 1930: 80. In what was to become his typical style of compressing references in the foot/end-notes for the sake of conciseness, he refers us to the two contrasting sets of evidence in two notes (ibid.: 114-15 nn 27-8). They are rather poor summaries of his own findings in the *Contributions*.
41. R.S. Sharma, ed., *Land Revenue in India: Historical Studies* (Motilal Banarsidass: Delhi, 1971).

agrarian system. In fact, revenue system (as the predominant mode of surplus appropriation) and control[42] of assets including land control (representing production relations) are the essentials of any (post-tribal) economic structure, the very warp and woof of an economic fabric. It is not so much in shifting themes of study as in the variations upon the same themes that the historiographical shifts need to be located. There were new concerns and concepts (surplus production and class formation, for instance) that changed the face of economic history; even so they stayed within, or had no quarrel, in principle, with the old rubrics of agrarian or revenue system.

A New Economic History

Sometime after 1985, a new economic history began to develop, largely as a fallout of the celebrated feudalism debate[43] as well as some allied controversies in the economic history of the earlier period. In its painstaking attempts to chart new territory and break fresh ground, it has sought to move away from this common frame of reference, only to land, despite itself, into a theoretical no-man's-land as it were.

Initiated (I think) by B.D. Chattopadhyaya, this new economic history is inspired and remains heavily influenced by his writings. The perspectival issues have accordingly been discussed mostly with reference to early medieval north India, but on the larger canvas of Early India. It begins by noting a series of limitations, real and imagined, of the existing economic histories, which are stated to suffer from a deeply flawed understanding of the 'evolution and consolidation of the agrarian foundations of Indian society' on account of their 'unchallenged' assumption of a homogeneous Indian reality, built around 'generalizations from the perspective of

42. Legally ownership, but the law may not always have been the reality. The distinction between 'effective control' and 'legal ownership' (Cohen 1978: 34-5) is particularly important for early medieval India with multiple levels (and therefore meanings) of control and ownership.
43. Conducted brilliantly but also, in no mean measure, in professional bad taste (selective citation and criticism, petty bickering, gossip, and worse, even obstructing/refusing publication).

Gangetic northern India'.[44] In one detailed statement on the alternative outline of early Indian economy,[45] 'agrarian space' – whether 'rural settlements' or 'agrarian regions' – is the main theme as well as the general context in which other themes are to be studied. These are iron technology, irrigation, and expansion of agriculture resulting in the formation and expansion of settlements, ultimately the formation of agrarian regions (with due attention to forests, tribals, and pastoralists). Much of all these would belong to the category of productive forces, but *is not conceptualized as such.*

It is in the realm of distribution of the produce that this new history is seen at its most vulnerable. In a healthy bid to look for what others neglected, it ends up discarding not just what had been achieved, but the very framework and categories in which distribution of produce is to be studied. Two illustrations should suffice. First, little note is taken of the state as the most important appropriator of social surpluses, of taxation and its redistribution as the dominant forms of produce distribution. In other words, that the land systems of all kinds came together under the revenue systems of overarching states is altogether missed. Second (which is a corollary of the first), instead of adding new dimensions to, and enriching and refining the existing accounts of lord-peasant relations, it seeks to dispense with the twofold distinction, which amounts to dispensing with the categories of the landlord and the peasant. *In place of* a class of intermediaries/landlords created by means of land-grants and lording it over a mass of subject peasantry, the granting of land rights is now to be studied for royal legitimation *only* and not for land relations *also*; groups within peasantry are to be studied at the expense of the peasantry as a group, not in addition to it, even as the category of landlords or intermediaries dissolves into so many categories of 'elite groups'.[46] And the groups were to be studied in terms of their identity marks – as *mahattaras*, *gāvuṇḍas* and the like – rather than in economic terms (smallholders, sharecroppers, rich peasantry, etc.): the economic criteria of

44. Sahu 1997: 3.
45. Ibid.: 8-39, 43-57.
46. Chattopadhyaya 1995: 336.

differentiation are largely absent even in the programmatic discussions of this new history. There is no reference whatsoever to any kind of relationship, economic or otherwise, between the 'elite groups' on one hand and the peasantry on the other, evidently for no better reason than the fact that these were the staples of the old historiography. A discussion of theories of landownership here and a reference to forced labour there give little clue as to how they might relate to each other, or to the other items under discussion. There has inevitably been a falling apart of economic history into so many segments. The resulting disarray has taken several forms, most painfully in the ordering and presentation of digested materials in textbooks, which has tended to be fitful at best, marked by the severest of omissions at worst.

'A GLOSSARY OF TERMS'?

At the time Ghoshal struck out on his enquiries, knowledge of the revenue system of early India was nearly non-existent.[47] Well-read in the general-theoretical and historical literature on taxation (e.g. Edwin Seligman's *Essays in Taxation*) and with the work of Moreland before him, he was well aware of the wide compass of such a study. Given the nature of the sources, however, his 'principal concern', he notes, 'has been to find out the precise meanings of the large array of technical terms'.[48] That was to be the starting point, the groundwork preparatory to writing economic history proper. Interpretation of terms has remained a major burden of all subsequent studies, right up to our *Revenue System*.

The complaint is that they all have remained stuck at the starting point. Their very substantial achievements are not to be

---

47. We reproduce the following from the *Imperial Gazetteer of India* (1901) that was quoted by him as the standard scholarly opinion about the pre-Mughal revenue system in India: 'In its primitive form the land-revenue was that portion of the cultivator's grain-heap which the state annexed for public use, and this crude method of realising the bulk of the State income appears to have been practically the only method in force throughout the greater part of India until the 16th century of our era.' (Ghoshal 1929: 275 fn1.)
48. Ghoshal 1929: x.

doubted, but the perception is that in all these works 'discussions of taxation tend to become glossaries of terms'[49]: 'Considered as a glossary of economic terms', rather than as a study of revenue system as such, 'this book [by Jha] does break new ground'.[50]

A re-reading would show this impression to be doubly mistaken. A good part of the blame for the mistakes however must rest with the authors themselves. As they emphasized the enormity of their preoccupation – explaining the probable import of a myriad of revenue terms, a good many of them confined in their incidence to inscriptions alone[51] – and forgot to explain the rest and the overall nature of their work, the observers got the impression that they had done little else. As we might say in current parlance, they did not 'market' themselves properly enough, and got short-sold as a result!

The first oversight in seeing it as a mere compilation of revenue terms pertains to those parts of the work where significant generalizations about the working of the revenue system are made for which no such (or not much) semantic exercise was required: principles of taxation; ownership of land; modes of assessment and quantum of revenue demand; an entire chapter on 'immunities'; most of the discussions on oppressive taxation and forced labour, and; the really provocative argument of crucial if generally unnoticed historiographical import,[52] that there was an increase in revenue

49. Trautmann 1968: 675.
50. Spellman 1968: 639.
51. Or, when they occur in literature, the meanings are clearly inapplicable to the epigraphic contexts, e.g. *chāṭa*.
52. The harping in those charged times on all of ancient India as a Golden Age could at times test the patience of even the more considerate of scholars, who sought relief in the discovery of the *AŚ*. In introducing R.G. Bhandarkar's *A Peep into the Early History of India*, H.G. Rawlinson thus vented himself: 'Chandragupta's vast and complicated bureaucracy was organized upon most efficient lines, but those who look upon India's past as Golden Age, would do well to consider the oppressive tyranny and the cruel severity of the whole system' (Rawlinson 1920: iii.). It was by contrasting this India of the *AŚ*, with its numerous restrictions and oppressive taxation and much else that was so undesirable, with that of Faxian, when people could happily move about without restrictions and did not feel the iron hand of the state that had been the lot of their ancestors, that Vincent Smith, followed by others, reconstructed his image

demand through the post-Mauryan and Gupta periods. Given the obscurity, for instance, about common ownership of land, with 'the legal literature ... provid[ing] no direct evidence of common ownership' (p.12), it is a critical find that from time to time the epigraphic material has thrown up some strong hints, with little terminological ambiguity, about the existence of communal ownership of land, e.g. the grant of land by a 'corporation of elephant-riders' (p. 11 fn21) and the gift of a village by the people of Nasik (p. 12).

Second, the meaning of a term is never discussed for its own sake in any of these works; it is done only in course of developing some important aspect of the revenue system. One good example has already been discussed, i.e. the implication of *utpadyamāna*. Likewise, two very different kinds of agrarian structure would emerge from the two different interpretations of that all-important Gupta and post-Gupta period set of revenue terms, *udraṅga* and *uparikara*. If we go along with Ghoshal, Mauryan kind of state farms remained quite important even in these later centuries;[53] if

---

of the Gupta Age as a Golden Age (Smith 1919: 154-6). Current discussions of the Gupta Period as a Golden Age are altogether innocent of its basis in a contrast with Kauṭilya's India as well as its advocacy by people like Vincent Smith.

The hypothesis of the upward curve of taxation from the post-Mauryan period onwards strikes at this basis. The curve did not stop at the Gupta period. In the aforementioned 1964 seminar on land revenue in India, the combined conclusion of an essay by Jha (1971) and another by B.P. Mazumdar (1971) was 'the growth and rise in ground taxes during the period from 200 B.C. to 1200 A.D.', presented as such on the book's blurb. This indeed is the overall impression that is conveyed by comparing the early set of inscriptions with the early medieval one. The impression however needs to be subjected to a more critical enquiry. It is significant that, while presenting a most detailed enumeration of taxes and obligations first 'in earlier epigraphs' and then 'in later epigraphs', with the qualification that the listings are not exhaustive, Sircar should commit himself to just this: 'That the tax burden on the early Indian villagers was heavy is *more clearly indicated* by medieval records than by those earlier in date' (Sircar 1969a: 66. Emphasis added).

53. Ghoshal 1929: 210-11, 213, etc. The implications of his interpretation are repeatedly made explicit in his *Agrarian System* (Ghoshal 1930: 45, 51,

Jha is to be believed, it was all a case of private cultivators paying some kind of taxes (pp. 53-6, 82, 171-2). In either case the interpretive exercise was on no occasion intended to be mere glossarial, prior to doing history proper.

This brings me to the final couple of points that I should like to close this essay, and open my next one, with. First, the inescapable importance of terminological analyses for historical reconstruction holds true for not just revenue system but all kinds of history, social, religious and the rest: they must always accompany, instead of preceding, a very extensive range of source-based enquiries into early history, at least for a long, long time to come. In fact, the empirical surefootedness of any investigation in early India based on primary research that treats as unproblematic the given meanings of key terms in the written sources must be regarded as prima facie suspect. Second, equal attention must also be paid to an area of vast promise, which is becoming more and more untapped with time: our great historiographical heritage. Given the state of the discipline in a number of its branches that I am familiar with, a regular reference to previous authorities is likelier to be rather worthwhile than a waste of time. There is a paradox in our twofold plea: the given is not to be taken at face value but to be evaluated afresh and, if necessary, problematized; yet, when we seek to find a way, we will do well to look for and review alternative paths charted by others in the past – other than the given one – and see if it helps. I hope the paradox is explained adequately as I expatiate on these points in the Afterword, in the appended essay on the *Arthaśāstra*.

To conclude, the reprint of the *Revenue System* is intended to underline the continuing relevance of the subject and the effort, as well as to make it more widely accessible than is the case at present. The occasion may also be feted for what it represents, i.e. the need for recovering and building up on all that remains valuable, even as one must of necessity throw out the historiographical bathwaters. For the critical eye, there will be many more points to

---

52, 79), as 'State-owned lands cultivated by tenants in the villages' (ibid.: 52).

discover and appreciate (not necessarily in concurrence) in Professor Jha's work than it has been possible to indicate in the foregoing. All credit and thanks are due to Shri Ramesh Jain of Manohar for his sustained and keen interest in bringing it out in the present avatar, and also to Shri Siddharth Chowdhury for helping to improve my text.

Atma Ram Sanatan Dharma College,
New Delhi
December 2019

VISHWA MOHAN JHA

ACKNOWLEDGEMENTS

This work substantially represents my thesis accepted by the Patna University in 1964 for the degree of Doctor of Philosophy. Professor R. S. Sharma, Head of the Department of History, Patna University, took pains to go through the entire work in its manuscript stage and made valuable suggestions on many points. Of his time and talents he gave unstintingly and his exacting standard of scholarship has contributed much to the present work. Dr. Yogendra Mishra, Professor and Head of the Department of History, Patna College, Patna, was kind enough to supervise the progress of my work and help me in various ways. I do not know how to express my gratitude to the late lamented Professor D. D. Kosambi, Poona, who ploughed through the manuscript before it was sent to the press but did not live to see it in print.

Writing any book, good or bad, is always difficult; it would have been more so in my case but for my friends whom I exploited often with indecent pertinacity. Among the important victims are Dr. (Mrs.) S. Jaiswal, Shri Brajadulal Chatterjee, Sri Govind Lal Vyas, Pandit Rajeshwar Jha, Dr. Bambahadur Mishra, Dr. Abhay Kant Choudhary, Shri Laliteshwar Prasad, Shri Basudeo Narain, and Shri P. N. Sahay. I also wish to thank Shri B. K. Pandeya for preparing the index.

Lastly, my thanks are due to Shri S. K. Bhattacharya, Proprietor, Punthi-Pustak, Calcutta, who took up the publication of this work, and to Shri A. K. Munshi, Manager, Pooran Press, Calcutta, who expeditiously saw it through the Press.

PATNA 1967 D. N. J.

ABBREVIATIONS

Ait. Br.	*Aitareya Brāhmaṇa.*
Amar.	*Nāmaliṅgānuśāsanam* of Amarasiṁha.
AO	*Archiv Orientalni.*
Āpastamba.	*Āpastamba Dharmasūtra.*
AŚ	*Arthaśāstra.*
ASR	*Annual Reports of the Archaeological Survey of India.*
ASWI	*Annual Reports of the Archaeological Survey of Western India.*
Bṛhaspati.	*Bṛhaspati-smṛti.*
BSOS	*Bulletin of the School of Oriental and African Studies.*
Baudhāyana.	*Baudhāyana Gṛhyasūtra.*
CII	*Corpus Inscriptionum Indicarum.*
Div.	*Divyāvadāna.*
Ed.	Edited by
EI	*Epigraphia Indica.*
GOS	Gaekwad Oriental Series.
Hist. Dharm.	P. V. Kane, *Histry of Dharmaśāstra.*
HOS	Harvard Oriental Series.
HRS	U. N. Ghoshal, *Contributions to the History of Hindu Revenue System.*
IA	*Indian Antiquary.*
IC	*Indian Culture.*
IHQ	*Indian Historical Quarterly.*
Indian Historiography.	U. N. Ghoshal, *The Beginnings of Indian Historiography and Other Easays.*
JA	*Journale Asiatique.*
JASB	*Journal of the Asiatic Society Bengal.*

Jāt.	*Jātaka.*
JBBRAS	*Journal of the Bombay Branch of the Royal Asiatic Society.*
JBORS	*Journal of the Bihar & Orissa Research Society.*
JBRS	*Journal of the Bihar Research Society.*
JESHO	*Journal of the Economic & Social History of the Orient.*
JNSI	*Journal of the Numismatic Society of India.*
JORM	*Journal of Oriental Research,* Madras.
JPTS	*Journal of Pali Text Society.*
JRAS	*Journal of the Royal Asiatic Society of Great Britain and Ireland.*
JUB	*Journal of the University of Bombay.*
Kāmandaka.	*Kāmandakīyanītisāra.*
Kātyāyana.	*Kātyāyanasmṛtisāroddhāra.*
Kumāra.	*Kumārasambhava.*
Lüders' List.	*Lüders' List of Brāhmī Inscriptions.*
Mbh.	*Mahābhārata.*
Mālavikā.	*Mālavikāgnimitra.*
Manu.	*Mānava Dharmaśāstra (Manusmṛti).*
Milinda.	*Milindapañho.*
Nārada.	*Nāradasmṛti.*
NS	New Series.
pt.	Part
PTS	Pali Text Society.
Raghu.	*Raghuvaṁśa.*
Ṛtu.	*Ṛtusaṁhāra.*
Śāk.	*Abhijñānaśākuntalam.*
Śat. Br.	*Śatapatha Brāhmaṇa.*
SBE	Sacred Books of the East.
Sel. Ins.	D. C. Sircar, *Select Inscriptions bearing on Indian History and Civilisation.*

ŚP	*Śānti Parva.*
Tr., trans.	Translated by, translation
Vasiṣṭha.	*Vasiṣṭha Dharmaśāstra.*
Viṣṇu.	*Vaiṣṇava Dharmaśāstra* (*Viṣṇusmṛti*).
Yāj.	*Yājñavalkyasmṛti.*
ZDMG	*Zeitschrift der Deutschen Morgenlandischen Gesellschaft.*

CHAPTER I

INTRODUCTION

U. N. Ghoshal was the first to have made a serious study of the revenue system of ancient India. His famous book *The Contributions to the History of Hindu Revenue System,* published in 1929 from Calcutta, is a piece of pioneer research on the subject. This work covers the period from the Vedic age to *c.* A.D. 1200, and hence its treatment of the post-Maurya and Gupta periods is far from exhaustive and adequate. In fact the book devotes the maximum space to the Maurya period because of the ready availability of the Arthaśāstra material, whereas the Scythian and the Gupta periods are dismissed in about thirty-six pages. Atindra Nath Bose also in his *Social and Rural Economy of North India* (*c.* 600 B.C.-A.D. 200)[1] assigns a chapter to the land revenue and allied charges, but his study is based mainly on the pre-Maurya sources and the *Arthaśāstra,* and does not take us farther than *c.* A.D. 200. The treatment of the subject in *The Economic Life of Northern India in the Gupta Period* by S. K. Maity, published in 1957, is perfunctory, and some source materials have not been understood in their historical perspective. The first adequate study of the revenue system of a shorter period, however, was made by M. H. Gopal, whose *Mauryan Public Finance* was published in 1935. In the present work we have tried to follow up the inquiry undertaken by Gopal, avoiding his temptation to read modern ideas and institutions in the *Arthaśāstra.* We have confined our study to the period from the fall of the Mauryas in 185 B.C. to the break-up of the Gupta empire in A.D. 550.

The sources of the present study are principally legal and literary writings and epigraphic records. Among the legal texts of our period, the law-books of Manu, Viṣṇu, Nārada, Yājña-

1. The book was published in two volumes from Calcutta in 1942-45.

valkya, Bṛhaspati and Kātyāyana are the important ones.[2] Some of the obscure passages of these lawgivers have often been interpreted with the help of commentaries, but we have been cautious in accepting the commentators' interpretation, because they belong to a very late period. Since the *Smṛtis* are in the nature of legal precepts, they may often describe things as should have been and not as they actually were in practice. But they become more or less reliable sources of information when corroborated by other contemporary materials. The idealised picture as available from the law-books is greatly modified by the *Jātakas* and other religious writings as also by the Brāhmaṇical literary works of the period, and, above all, by epigraphic records.

The *Jātaka* stories, nearly 550 in number, are varied in their character and often furnish valuable information about some aspects of the revenue system of the period to which they belong. The existing *Jātaka* is merely a commentary and not the original canonical text. Each *Jātaka* consists of *paccupanna-vatthu* (the story of the present), relating in prose the occasion of the Buddha's telling the story, *atīta-vatthu* (the story of the past), speaking of one of the former births of the Buddha, *gāthās* which generally belong to the 'story of the past' but very often also to the 'story of the present,' *veyyākaraṇa* (short commentary) which explains the *gāthās* word for word, and *samodhāna* (connection) in which Buddha generally identifies the personages of the story of the present with those of the past. The antiquity of most of the *gāthās*, belonging as they do to the Buddhist canon, goes back to a very early period. This is also supported by their language, which is more archaic than that of the prose narrative of the present and the past.[3] For our purpose the prose portions of the *Jātakas* are more important. In the *Gandhavaṁsa*[4] the authorship of the prose narratives in the form of commentary is ascribed

2. We have accepted the dates of these lawgivers as suggested by Kane. Vide the chronological table in *Hist. Dharm*, II. Pt. I. pp. xi-xii.
3. Winternitz, *A History of Indian Literature*, II, p. 119.
4. *JPTS*, 1886, p. 59.

to Buddhaghoṣa (5th century A.D.), which has, however, been questioned on good grounds by Rhys Davids[5] and Burlingame.[6]

On the other hand, it has been assumed by some scholars that the extant *Jātaka* stories offer us a picture of the narrative literature and the conditions of civilisation at the time of the Buddha or of a still earlier period.[7] But this view cannot be accepted without question. The archaeological evidence testifies to the fact that the Buddhist birth stories became familiar only from the 2nd and 1st centuries B.C. The reliefs on the stone walls around the *stūpas* of Bharhut and Sanchi depict scenes from the *Jātakas,* including those which are narrated only in prose. This is borne out by the fact that in Bharhut the titles of some of the *Jātakas* are written above the reliefs.[8] These precious monuments prove that a number of narratives, which are sometimes also found in the existing *Jātaka* commentary, were in the 2nd (perhaps even the 3rd) century B.C. technically called Jātaka and were regarded as Bodhisatta stories.[9] From this it may be inferred that some of the birth stories were perhaps so popular two or three centuries before Christ as to suggest a still greater antiquity for them.[10] But this should not mean that the entire bulk of the *Jātaka* literature belongs to the time of the Buddha. Winternitz is of the view that for the great mass of the verses no greater antiquity than the 3rd century B.C. can con-

---

5. T. W. Rhys Davids, *Buddhist Birth Stories,* I Introduction, p. lxiii.
6. E. W. Burlingame, *Buddhist Legends,* HOS, Vol. 28, pp. 49, 59ff.
7. Bühler, *On the Origin of the Indian Brāhma Alphabet,* Strassburg, 1898 ; Fick, *The Social Organisation in North-East India in Buddha's Time,* Calcutta, 1920 ; Mrs. Rhys Davids, "Notes on Early Economic Condition in North India", *JRAS,* 1910, pp. 59ff ; R. L. Mehta, *Pre-Buddhist India,* Bombay, 1939.
8. A list of the 27 or 29 *Jātakas* of the Bharhut stūpa, which have been identified so far, is given by Rhys Davids, *Buddhist India,* p. 209, and Hultzsch, *JRAS,* 1912, p. 406.
9. Winternitz, *op. cit.,* p. 121.
10. Warmington (*Commerce between the Roman Empire and India,* p. 77) points out that the fables of Babrius, and of Phaedrus, who belongs to the earlier half of the 1st century B.C., also contain *Jātaka* stories.

scientiously be urged, certainly not proved, and much of the prose assuredly belongs to the Christian era.[11]

The post-Mauryan date of the *Jātakas* appears all the more plausible in view of the fact that the stories are often permeated with the atmosphere of flourishing trade and commerce. It emerges from a study of the *Jātakas* that the worth of every marketable commodity, from a dead mouse and a day at the festival, up to all kinds of fees, pensions, fixed loans, stored treasures and income, is stated in figures of a certain coin and its fraction. In fact the *Jātaka* literature reveals a society having the full use and enjoyment of plentiful coinage, which may be symptomatic of very brisk mercantile activities.[12] Thus it has been rightly suggested that the *Jātakas* represent a state of society which provided suitable conditions for trade, perhaps during the Sātavāhana period.[13] Although the finds of punchmarked silver and copper coins, coupled with a large number of iron objects, assigned to the period of the North Black Polished Ware (*circa* 600-250 B.C.), clearly point to the definite beginnings of urban life and the rise of trade and commerce in much earlier times,[14] the *Jātaka* literature gives the impression of an economy which is far more advanced than the rude beginnings of city life known from the excavations at Hastinapura and Katra in Mathura. Therefore the picture of the economic life that obtains in the *Jātakas* may be taken to reflect, to a certain extent, the condition of the Sātavāhana or the post-Maurya period, when maritime trade between India and the Roman empire assumed fairly big dimensions. So far as traditions regarding political events are concerned they may refer to pre-Maurya times, but the description

---

11. Winternitz, *op. cit.*, pp. 121-22. Cf. Fiser according to whom the third, fourth and fifth volumes of the *Jātakas* can be generally considered as parts that have assumed their present shape in a period posterior to the majority of the simple stories of the first and second volumes (*AO*, XXII. p. 249).
12. In connection with the remuneration of officers, we have shown that the *Jātakas* refer to them as being paid in terms of money.
13. Kosambi, *An Introduction to the Study of Indian History*, pp. 259-60.
14. Sharma, *Śūdras in Ancient India*, p. 85.

of social and economic life reflects the state of affairs in which the *Jātakas* were finally compiled, a generalisation which is true of the *Mahābhārata* also. Since, however, the *Jātakas* admittedly incorporate much of the older tradition, we have used them as supplementary evidence.

There is, however, not much controversy about the dates of other Buddhist works such as the *Milindapañho*, the *Divyāvadāna*, the *Mahāvastu*, the *Avadānaśataka* and the *Lalitavistara*, etc., all of which are generally assigned to the post-Maurya period. Although these works do not yield much information on the revenue system of the period, they sometimes help us in interpreting other sources in their historical background.

We may also mention a few *kāvyas* of post-Maurya times. The *Gāthāsaptaśatī*, commonly attributed to the Sātavāhana king Hāla, is a collection of seven hundred Prākṛta verses dealing mainly with different aspects of rustic love. It does not throw much light on the revenue system, but it enables us to follow the gradual changes in the office of the village-headman. The *Buddhacarita* and *Saundarananda-kāvya* of Aśvaghoṣa, a contemporary of Kaniṣka,[15] are both written in the *kāvya* style and belong to the same class of ornate court poetry. The former is the first actual epic of the Buddha, created by a poet and the second, connected as it is with the life story of the Buddha, amplifies, in particular, those scenes and episodes which receive scanty attention, or none at all, in the *Buddhacarita*. A few passages in these works refer to the terms *kara* and *bali*, which we have discussed at their proper places.

In the Gupta period, however, we have comparatively more literary records, which are of some use to us. The most important are naturally those of Kālidāsa, whose *Mālavikāgnimitra*, *Vikramorvaśīya*, *Abhijñānaśakuntala*, *Ṛtusaṁhāra*, *Meghadūta*, *Raghuvaṁśa* and *Kumārasaṃbhava* need no introduction. These works mainly refer to conditions of opulence and plenty, and contain useful references to the economic life of the time. The *Mudrārākṣasa* of Viśākhadatta and *Mṛcchakaṭika* of Śūdraka also supplement our knowledge of the subject.

---

15. Winternitz, *op. cit.*, p. 257, n. 1.

Apart from the above-mentioned sources, we have often drawn upon several technical works of the period. The *Mahābhāṣya* of Patañjali, who belonged to the second century B.C., is a commentary on the Aṣṭādhyāyī of Pāṇini and hence is not expected to be of much service in the reconstruction of revenue history; but it has been utilised by us at some places. The *Kāmasūtra* of Vātsyāyana, assignable to the Gupta period, deals mainly with the Hindu erotics, but touches on several other aspects of Hindu social life and throws some light on the nature of forced labour, which formed an important source of revenue to the state. The *Bṛhat-saṁhitā* of Varāhamihira (A.D. 505-587) is a highly technical work on astrology, but contains some useful data about the effects of the contemporary system of taxation. The most important of the works of the present category, however, is the *Nāmaliṅgānuśāsana,* popularly known as *Amarakośa,* a lexicon compiled some time in the Gupta period. We have made a good use of this work in connection with the interpretation of certain revenue terms.

The travel accounts of foreigners also deserve our attention. No ambassador like Megasthenes is known to have come to India on a political mission during our period, but the account left by the Chinese traveller Fa-hsien, who came to India during the reign of Candra Gupta II and visited Madhyadeśa in A.D. 405-411, is of some value for our study. Since he came on a religious pilgrimage to India, he said little about the general state of the country, and part of whatever little he said is wrong. For example, it is doubtful whether Buddhism held the predominant position he would lead us to believe. The evidence of the coins and inscriptions shows that the rulers were non-Buddhists, and that Buddhism must, by this period, have long passed its zenith.[16] Fa-hsien probably passed most of his time in studying in the various monasteries and saw little of the everyday life of the country. This is clear from his erroneous observations. His statement about the absence of drinking in the Gupta period is definitely a case of misrepresentation. Thus Fa-hsien's report

16. Maity, *op. cit.,* p. 6.

cannot be accepted as true unless corroborated by the indigenous sources. The same is true of the account of Hsüan Tsang, who visited this country during the time of Harṣavardhana.

In the present work greatest reliance, however, has been placed on the inscriptions, whose provenance and chronology are almost certain except in a few cases. However, the available epigraphic material in North India during post-Maurya and Gupta times is not adequate to answer all the questions we would like to raise. The Śaka-Kuṣāṇa Kharoṣṭhī records of the post-Maurya period from North-Western India are not of much use to us. Similarly, the inscriptions from the Mathura region of the time of the Kuṣānas do not contain any land grant and hence are not of any substantial help in the reconstruction of the revenue history of the time. Land grants, which mention the names of revenue official and units, and sources of revenue, are first available in the Sātavāhana kingdom, which extended into Northern India. The Sātavāhana territory represents the area where the South merges into the North and vice versa, and hence the Sātavāhana grants of land, possibly reflect, in considerable measure, the revenue conditions prevailing in the North.

In the Gupta period, although we have several land charters from Eastern India, their number in the kingdom of the Vākāṭakas, the Parivrājaka Mahārājas and the Maitrakas is greater. The Vākāṭaka kingdom covered mainly parts of Central India, the Western Deccan, some portions of Gujarat and thus stretched well beyond the Vindhyas, and the Parivrājaka Mahārājas ruled over some parts of Central India. The Maitrakas of Valabhī ruled over the entire Saurāṣṭra region and some parts of Gujarat proper. Thus we have not only taken account of the epigraphs strictly belonging to North India but also those of the upper Deccan. The inclusion of these records in our sources has rendered it possible to present a connected history of the revenue system and enabled us to appreciate certain local variations in the fiscal organisation.

Although most sources of our study have been tapped by previous scholars, we have tried to interpret and co-relate them in such a manner as to present a clear and full picture of the revenue system of post-Maurya and Gupta times. An attempt has been made to bring out the salient features of the fiscal organisation of this period. In treating the sources of king's revenue and the machinery for their administration it has been our objective to establish, wherever possible, a link with the past and to point out the departure from it.

CHAPTER II

LAND OWNERSHIP AND KING'S RIGHT TO TAXES

In order to appreciate the basis of royal taxation in ancient India, it is necessary to consider the king's position in relation to land : in other words, whether land was owned by the village communities, by private individuals or by the king himself.

According to Campbell[1] and Maine[2] the traditional village communities exercised joint ownership of land. The Maliya Copper-plate of Dharasena II[3] is interpreted by Fleet to suggest some sort of corporate ownership. This charter records the grant of 100 *padāvartas* of land in Śivakapadraka known as the holding of the cultivator Botaka.[4] Fleet translates *padraka* as common land, on the authority of H. H. Wilson[5] according to whom *padar* (i.e., *padr*) is explained as "common-land, land adjacent to a village left uncultivated." This interpretation of *padraka*, however, appears to be untenable. The suffix *padra*, which is derived from $\sqrt{}$*pad*, itself means a village, or a place of habitation, besides a road in a village, the earth or a name of a district.[6] Sankalia[7] points out that a Kṣatrapa inscription dated A.D. 181[8] mentions Rasopadra*grāma*. He adds that in many later inscriptions—those of Traikūṭakas, Kaṭacuris, Maitrakas of Valabhī and others —*padra* occurs with *grāma*. He, therefore, rightly suggests that

1. Campbell, *Modern India* (London, 1852), p. 92.
2. H. S. Maine, *Village Communities in East and West* (London, 1890), pp. 91-94.
3. *CII*, III, no, 38, p. 170 and n. 3.
4. *Ibid.*, ll. 22-26.
5. H. H. Wilson, *Glossary*, p. 286.
6. Monier-Williams, *Sanskrit-English Dictionary, s.v. padra.*
7. Sankalia, *Studies in the Historical and Cultural Geography and Ethnology of Gujarat*, p. 51. Cf. K. M. Gupta, "Land system in accordance with Epigraphic Evidence," *IA*, LI, p. 73.
8. *Sel. Ins.*, p. 176, 1. 4.

padra did not connote a village ; it had become a part of the village, the suffix *padra* indicating, when compounded with the name proper, a place of habitation in, around, or on a road leading to a village. In our opinion, therefore, *padraka*, appended to Śivaka in the Maliya Copper-plate of Dharasena II, has nothing to suggest joint ownership. Besides, it is mentioned in the record itself that the land in Śivakapadraka is known as the holding of Botaka. If *padraka* is taken to mean a common-land, how could the holding belong to an individual as is stated in the charter ?

Again, from a land transaction for religious purpose in East Bengal,[9] Pargiter has tried to prove some sort of joint ownership during Gupta times. The remarkable fact, this record conveys, is that land could be purchased only after the unanimous approval of the leading men of the district as well as the common-folk (*prakṛtayaḥ*).[10] Basak argues, "If we assume that the lands belonged to the state why could it not alienate them without the consent or approval of the people's representatives, the *mahattaras* and the businessmen (*vyavahārins*)[11] of the province and the district, and sometimes even the common folk ? One way of answering these questions may be that these lands belonged not to the state but to the whole village or village-assemblies, and hence their transfer could not take place without the consent or approval of the latter".[12] The view of Basak is also supported by Majumdar.[13] Basak's argument, however, is not convincing, for the fact of alienation of land and the introduction of a new owner were evidently matters which concerned the whole village and the consent of the village through its leading men was considered important. Moreover, the importance of neighbours and elders in boundary disputes is recognised by the law-books. Thus Manu ordains that the decision concerning the boundary marks of fields, wells, tanks, of gardens and houses depends upon

9. *IA,* XXXIX, p. 214.
10. The Copper-plate inscription of Dharmāditya, *IA,* XXXIX, p. 195.
11. The word *vyavahārin* has been wrongly translated as businessman.
12. *AMSJV,* III, Pt. 2, pp. 486-487.
13. Majumdar, *Corporate Life in Ancient India* (Calcutta, 1922), p. 186.

the evidence of the neighbours.[14] A passage of Yājñavalkya[15] may be cited to the same effect. Similarly, according to Nārada,[16] in all quarrels regarding landed property or boundaries, the decision rests with the neighbours, the inhabitants of the same town or village, other members of the same community, and the senior inhabitants of the village. Bṛhaspati[17] also recognises the importance of neighbours and senior inhabitants in settling boundary disputes, though according to him, in default of witnesses and boundary marks, even a single man, agreeable to both parties, might fix the boundaries.[18] Kātyāyana states that when a dispute between two men arises as to fields, houses, ponds, wells, gardens and dams, the evidence of neighbour who dwells on the border (*sāmanta*) is the deciding factor in all these matters.[19] He adds that in the absence of witnesses *sāmantas* (neighbouring villagers), *maulas* (who were at first *sāmantas* but later migrated to another country), *vṛddhas* and *uddhṛtas* are in order the means of decision.[20] The role of neighbours and elders is considered important because they perhaps knew well the titles, boundaries etc., of the land in question. There is, therefore, nothing unusual if the village elders or the common folk, referred to in the above charter, were consulted in transacting a land sale; and in our opinion, the transaction recorded in the above epigraph does not indicate communal ownership.

There are, however, a few inscriptions which bear traces of joint ownership of land. An epigraph[21] from the Nasik region,

---

14. *Manu,* VIII, 262.
15. *Yāj.,* II. 154.
16. *Nārada,* XI. 2.
17. *Bṛhaspati,* XIX, 26.
18. *Ibid.,* 33.
19. *Kātyāyana,* verse 734.
20. *Ibid.,* verse 737.
21. *Lüders' List,* no. 1142; cf. Nagardhana Plate of Svāmirāja (*EI,* XXVIII, no. 1, 11. 4-8) which mentions a grant of land by the corporation of elephant-riders. The ownership exercised by a corporation or guild, however, need not be the same as in the above instance.

belonging to the post-Maurya period, records the gift of a village by the *Nāsikakas* which has been translated as 'the people of Nasik'. Since the village is donated by a group of donors, mentioned as *Nāsikakas,* it is possible that they perhaps exercised joint ownership over the village in question. According to another inscription Āmrakārdava, the grantor, "having prostrated himself in an assembly of five" (*pañca-maṇḍalyāṁ praṇipatya*) gave the village of Īśvaravāsaka. It seems that by paying homage he sought the consent of the assembly of five. The word *pañca-maṇḍalī,* Fleet suggests, "is the same as the *panchait,* panchayet or Panch, of modern times, the village jury of five (or more) persons convened to settle a dispute by arbitration, to witness and sanction any act of importance etc. This practice may be taken to be a survival of communal ownership.[23] In view of the above, the consent of the elders in land transactions, as is mentioned in the charter from East Bengal,[24] was at best a survival of old tribal common ownership; but in any case, there is nothing to show that it had remained anything more than a formal affair during our period.

The legal literature, though it provides no direct evidence of common ownership, frequently refers to individual holdings and enjoyment of land. The germ of the concept of private ownership of land is contained in the idea of first occupation which underlies the popular maxim of Manu : "The field belongs to him who first removed the weed and the deer belongs to him who first wounded it."[26] The aphorism of Manu refers perhaps to that stage of development when land was not scarce, i.e., the pressure of population on land was not so much as to cause its scarcity. The prevalence of such a condition in certain parts of the country may be inferred from a passage of the *Milindapañho*[27] which

---

22. The Sanchi Stone inscriptions of Candra Gupta II of the year 193, *CII,* III, no. 5, 1. 6.
23. *Ibid.,* p. 32, n. 5.
24. *Supra.*
25. *Manu,* IX. 44.
26. *Ibid.*
27. *Milinda.,* p. 219.

refers to "an individual who clears the forest and takes other steps to make the land suitable for cultivation." Evidently, in those parts of the country where land was scarce, it may have been possible to enjoy the fruits of land without any interference, despite the absence of any legal title, though possession in this case was "fundamentally different from the notion of permanent dominium".[28]

In those parts of the country, however, where conditions were slightly advanced and demand for land had increased, Manu's analogy of deer and land lost its validity. First occupation was no longer considered a criterion of valid possession, so that the lawgivers suggest another mode of legal acquisition of land. According to Bṛhaspati[29] he who had occupied land quite unopposed and uninterrupted for a period of thirty years could not be deprived of such property. It was also lost to the former owner by such forbearance. Further, according to the same lawgiver when enjoyment of property extending over three generations descended to the fourth, it became legitimate possession and a title was not necessary.[30] A passage from Nārada[31] may be cited to the same effect.

Despite their recognition of simple possession of long standing as a criterion of ownership, the jurists themselves lay much emphasis on its insufficiency and lay down that ownership is not possible without legal title. Yājñavalkya[32] states that enjoyment (*bhoga*) acquires validity when it is accompanied by a clear title (*āgamena viśuddhena*), and is not valid without the same. Brhaspati[33] holds a similar view. Nārada[34] adds that he, who can plead possession without being able to produce any legal title, must be considered a thief, and the ruler of the land should inflict upon him the punishment ordained for a thief. It has

28. Vinogradoff, *Historical Jurisprudence*, I, p. 328.
29. *Bṛhaspati*, VII. 27-28.
30. *Ibid.*, 54, 60.
31. *Nārada*, I. 96.
32. *Yāj.*, II. 28.
33. *Brhaspati*, VII. 24-26, 30.
34. *Nārada*, I. 86-87.

been pointed out by Maity[35] that this rule is contradicted by Nārada and Bṛhaspati themselves, both of whom recognise simple possession of long standing as evidence of ownership.[36] But what he considers to be a contradiction can be easily explained. Probably the lawgivers' idea of simple possession of long standing as a criterion of ownership might have prevailed in those parts of the country which were not developed, but at the same time legal title was considered a desideratum in other parts where conditions were comparatively less primitive.

That the ancient Indians were acquainted with individual holdings of land is further substantiated by the various modes suggested by the lawgivers for acquiring property. Gautama,[37] who is assigned to a period earlier than that under review, lays down that a person becomes owner (*svāmī*) by means of inheritance, purchase, partition, acceptance and finding. Similarly, Manu[38] states seven legitimate modes of acquiring wealth, viz., inheritance, finding or friendly donation, purchase, conquest, lending at interest, performance of work (or performance of service for others) and acceptance of a gift from the virtuous. Nārada[39] maintains that property obtained by inheritance, gifts made out of affection, and what had been obtained with a wife (as her dowry) are the three kinds of pure wealth for all classes without distinction. Ghoshal[40] has rightly pointed out: "While some authorities have in view the ownership of things, others refer only to the more general idea of their acquisition. Nevertheless, they imply in either case the association of the essential qualities of ownership (viz., sale, gift and bequest) with the possession of property."

One might here argue that since the jurists refer to the mode of acquiring property in general and do not refer to land in particular, the assumption that land was acquired through the above

---

35. Maity, *op. cit.*, p. 12.
36. *Supra.*
37. *Gautama,* II. 1.
38. *Manu,* X. 115.
39. *Nārada,* I. 51-54.
40. Ghoshal, *The Agrarian System in Ancient India,* p. 87.

mentioned methods cannot be accepted without question. But at a time when economy was pre-eminently agricultural, the law-givers might have meant by property in general landed property too. Besides, Bṛhaspati[41] specifically mentions that immovable property (*sthāvara*) is acquired in seven ways, i.e., by learning, by purchase and mortgage, by valour, by marriage, by inheritance and by succession to the property of the kinsmen without issue. Equally important is the fact that two of Bṛhaspati's seven classes of documents are concerned with the gift and sale of landed property.[42] Thus it appears that individual landholdings were quite in vogue and the land-holder had a general right to enjoy his land at pleasure.[43]

Coming to the epigraphic evidence, which may be taken as faithful reflection of the practice of a particular period, an inscription from Nasik records the gift of a field by one Mugudāsa.[44] Another epigraph[45] from the same place mentions a gift of a land by Uṣavadāta who had bought the same from a brāhmaṇa. The Junar inscriptions[46] supply significant instances of private transfers of land and of the gift of small units of agricultural land, occupied by private individuals. But these are not secular land deeds; nor has any secular sale or transfer deed of the period survived. The absence of any record of the sale or gift of land for non-religious purpose may mean two things : either, the right to dispose of one's land, which was in theory recognised by the jurists, was in practice limited to religious grants and gifts; or the secular sale or transfer deeds have not survived perhaps because

---

41. *Bṛhaspati,* VII. 23.
42. *Ibid.,* VIII. 6-7.
43. Cf. Buddhaghoṣa according to whom a property concerning which another has arrived at the state of doing whatever he likes, without incurring punishment or blame, is said to belong to another. Vide *The Expositor* (Tr. of the *Aṭṭhasālinī* by Maung Tin), p. 129.
44. *Lüders' List,* no. 1130.
45. *EI,* VIII, no. 8(10), 1.4.
46. *Lüders' List,* nos. 1163, 1167. One inscription mentions the gift of a field measuring 15 *nivartanas* in the Puvanada village by a certain Palapa (*ASWI,* IV. p. 96, no. 20).

they were written on perishable materials such as palm-leaves or cloth.[47]

All these, however, need not be taken to mean the prevalence of full-fledged private ownership[48] the scope of which seems to have been limited. The one great limitation on the landholder's right over his land may be said to have arisen out of the enormous increase of royal authority. Already during the time of the Mauryas, the imperial authority was keenly felt in the major part of the Indian sub-continent. And though in post-Maurya times some sort of political disintegration had set in, the institution of kingship came to be divinised. The Kuṣāṇa rulers adopted the title *devaputra* in post-Maurya times as can be inferred from its mention in 21 Brāhmi (according to *Lüders' List*) and 3 Kharoṣṭhī (according to Konow's list) inscriptions.[49] The theoretical justification for the use of this epithet came to be provided by a near contemporary Mahāyānist Buddhist text, *Suvarṇaprabhāsottamasūtra,* according to which thirty-three gods contributed to the substance of the king.[50] Although the law-books do not use the term *devaputra* (son of God) for the king, Manu states that the king is vested with the respective attributes of eight gods.[51] He adds that even if a child the king should not be disregarded, for he functions as a great divinity in the form of a human being.[52] Similar idea finds expression also in the *Śānti Parva* which represents the original king to be descendant of God.[53] Thus in the post-Maurya period not only did the Kuṣāṇa rulers assume the title of *devaputra,* but also the theorists of the time helped in the divinisation of kingship. This, in turn, may have put a check on the private ownership of land.

---

47. For references see *Hist. Dharm.*, III. p. 308.
48. For more arguments in favour of private ownership see Jayaswal, *Hindu Polity* (Bangalore, 1955), pp. 329 ff. For the criticism of Jayaswal's arguments see Ghoshal, *Indian Historiography*, pp. 158-166.
49. R. S. Sharma, *Political Ideas and Institutions*, p. 174.
50. *JA*, 1934, pp. 3-4.
51. *Manu*, VII. 7.
52. *Ibid.*, VII. 8.
53. *ŚP*, chapter 59.

The King's right over land is substantiated by a host of Gupta inscriptions, which record the donations of plots of land as well as entire villages, often with total exemption from taxes which otherwise went to the king's coffers.[54] It is argued that land grants may have meant only the transfer of and exemption from revenues which the ruler received, and not the transfer of ownership.[55] This may have been true of many land grants, but there are nearly half a dozen, if not more, inscriptions—from the Valabhī region—referring to actual transfer of ownership. In the Palitana plates of Dhruvasena[56] dated A.D. 525-26, it is stated that one hundred and forty *pādāvartas* of land which previously belonged to the householder Īśvara was given to another person. A few more records of this ruler testify to similar transaction of land.[57] Another inscription[58] from the same region mentions that one hundred and thirty *pādāvartas* of land held by a certain Gokṣa was granted by the king to another person. Thus it appears that the king could—and he actually did—alienate land from the private landholders and introduce new owners, thus superseding the rights of individual landholder. This may mean that an individual proprietor exercised only a qualified ownership over his land, the king being its ultimate lord in which capacity presumably he levied taxes from the people.

It may, however, be urged that the writings of the period often look upon taxes as king's wages for the service of protection. In the *Baudhāyana Dharmasūtra*,[59] the king is stated to be an official receiving the revenue as his fee for the service of protection. According to Vasiṣtha the particular duty of a king is to protect all beings.[60] Elsewhere he states that the king

54. For references see Maity, *op. cit.*, pp. 16-17.
55. Lallanji Gopal, "Ownership of Agricultural Land in Ancient India," *JESHO*, IV, pp. 151 ff.
56. *EI*, XI, no. 9(1) 11. 16-19.
57. *Ibid.*, no. 9 (2, 3, 4).
58. The Palitana plates of Dharasena II of the Gupta year 252, *Ibid.*, no. 5, 11. 24-28.
59. *Baudhāyana*, I. 10. 18. 1.
60. *Vasiṣtha*, XIX. 1.

who rules his subjects justly shall take 1|6 of the crops, presumably as his wages.[61] Manu also states that the king who even after taking various kinds of royal taxes from his subjects does not protect them soon goes to hell.[62] Even the theory of the king's ownership of soil in Manu has to be buttressed with that of the king's duty of protection, when it is required to justify the king's claim to one-half of the treasure-trove and the output of mines.[63] The *Mahābhārata* expressly states that the king is to maintain peace and justice, and receive the 'sixth part' as his wages. Furthermore, a king, who fails to protect or administer properly, is regarded as a thief stealing the 'sixth part' unrighteously. This explains why the epithet *baliṣaḍbhāgataskara* is repeatedly applied in the *Mahābhārata* to unrighteous kings. Similarly, the lawgiver Nārada[64] declares the king's revenues to be his fee for the protection of his subjects. So strictly is the notion of the king's responsibility for protection carried out to its logical conclusion that the law-books often require him to make good the equivalent of the stolen property that he has failed to recover.[65]

The Buddhist attitude as reflected in the *Divyāvadāna,* which is dated about the third century A.D., is almost identical with the Brāhmaṇical one. It is related in one of its stories how the two good ministers of a king admonish him in the following strain : "Kingdoms, O lord, are like flowers and fruit trees ; just as flourishing plants and fruit trees being properly nourished yield flowers and fruits at the proper season, so the kingdoms being protected yield taxes and revenues".[66] A similar view is embodied in the *Mahāvastu,*[67] a Buddhist work of post-Marya times. All

61. *Vasiṣṭha,* I. 42.
62. *Manu,* VIII. 307. Manu puts much emphasis on the king's duty of protection (vide *Manu,* VII. 2, 35).
63. *Manu,* VIII. 39; HRS. p. 18.
64. *Nārada,* XVIII. 48. Cf. *Yāj.,* (I. 335) who states that the king takes the sixth part of the virtuous deeds (of his subjects) by protecting them with justice. He adds that if he takes taxes without protecting them, half their sins go to him (I. 337).
65. Cf. *Gautama,* X. 47 ; *Viṣṇu,* III. 67 ; *Manu,* VIII. 40 ; *Yāj.* II. 36.
66. *Div.,* pp. 562-63.
67. *Mahāvastu,* I, pp. 358-59.

these reveal one basic idea that taxes were levied in exchange of the services rendered by the king or the state.[68] The *Catuḥśatikā* of Āryadeva also expresses the idea that the king is the servant of the people and taxes constitute his wages for protection.[69]

The notion that the king is the servant of the people who pay his wages in the form of taxes, however, is often contradicted by the lawgivers themselves as well as by the general literature of the Gupta period. At one place Manu, who has been cited earlier, as a champion of the wages-theory of taxation, says in unambiguous terms that the king is entitled to his share of treasure and minerals because he is the lord of all.[70] This view is more clearly expressed by Kātyāyana, who belongs to the Gupta period, and according to whom the king claims taxes because he is the lord of all.[71] The idea of the king's supreme lordship of the land seems to have had considerable popular appeal in the Gupta period, for Kālidāsa represents the king as enjoying the earth much as Indra enjoys the heaven.[72] The significance of the root *bhuj* is wide but in this context the word is precise, with a distinct implication of that particular type of enjoyment which is thought

---

68. The doctrine of the relation of taxation to protection is thought of great importance in Hindu political theory. P. N. Banerjee claims that the conception of the king as the servant of the state was one of the basic principles of political thought in Ancient India (*Public Administration in Ancient India,* pp. 72-73). Similarly, D. R. Bhandarkar thinks that according to the Hindu notion the king never wielded an unqualified power, but was looked upon as merely a public servant though of the higher order (*Carmichael Lectures,* Pt. I, pp. 122-23). Cf. B. K. Sarkar, *Political Institutions and Theories of the Hindus,* p. 183.

69. *Catuḥśatikā* p. 461, quoted by Bandopadhyaya, *Development of Hindu Polity and Political Theories*, p. 210.

70. *Manu,* VIII. 39.

71. *Kātyāyana,* Verses 16-17.

72. *divaṁ marutvāniva bhokṣyate bhuvaṁ digantaviśrāntaratho hi tatsutaḥ*
ato'bhilāṣe prathamaṁ tathāvidhe manobabandhānyarasān vilaṅghya sā
Raghu, III. 4.

of in our country as the highest type.[73] Moreover, the king is called *bhūvallabha*, the Earth's beloved, and when he is called *deśavarādhipa* we can be sure that the country is visualised as choosing him as if in a *svayaṁvara*.[74] In other words, the king's relationship to the Earth is thought of as sexual. One of the plainest illustrations of this relationship can be had from Kālidāsa who refers to Aja as enjoying the Earth which is like a newly married bride.[75] In the *Harṣacarita* also, the Earth is represented as sitting comfortably in the king's knee.[76] In the *Kathāsaritsāgara*, which is a late work, we come across stories that relate the Earth declaring herself the wife of a particular king.[77] Later inscriptions also testify to the supposed sexual relationship between the king and the Earth. In a South Indian epigraph of A.D. 904, for instance, we are told that (while acting as his elder brother's viceroy) Vijayāditya treated the Earth with the respect due to a sister-in-law.[78] In the role of a royal spouse, the Earth is obviously the king's maintainee and the enjoyed one. According to Derret, it will be, however, unnatural to imagine that the husband enjoys his wife, as it were, in right of wage.[79] Thus it sounds unrealistic to think that the king, who was the supreme lord of the land, received taxes from his people as wages. Nor does the notion of taxes as wages in return of protection seem to have been applicable to the actual working of the revenue system, for history does not provide a single instance of a king who did not claim taxes from his subjects if he failed to protect and govern them successfully. However, the lawgivers' emphasis on revenues as being the king's wages and their reticence about his relationship

---

73. Derret, "Bhu-bharana, Bhu-pālana, Bhu-bhojana," *BSOAS.*, XXII. p. 112.
74. *Loc. cit.*
75. *Raghu*, VIII. 7 ; cf. *Ibid.*, VIII. 3.
76. *Harṣacarita*, VI, *utsaṅge bhuvā........*
77. Penzer (Ed.), *Ocean of Story* (Tawney's English translation of the *Kathāsaritsāgara*), IV. 175-6 ; VI. 194.
78. *Epigraphia Carnatica*, XII, Nanj. 269, pp. 225-6. For further references of similar nature see Derret, *op. cit.*, pp. 112-13,
79. Derret, *op. cit.*, p. 112,

as suggested by the metaphors may have been, to a large measure, due to their efforts to minimise a feature with which public were all too familiar and which tended to impede their inculcation of the *śāstra's* chief lesson, namely that, 'divinity' or not, the king must not consider himself a superhuman being and must concentrate on his duties towards his dependants and not upon the delights which his position may afford.[80] Nevertheless the law-books and literary records of the Gupta period suggest no existence of a fairly strong school which supports royal taxation on the ground that the king is the owner of land.

80. *Ibid.*, p. 116.

CHAPTER III

PRINCIPLES OF TAXATION

The advantages which a king may have enjoyed by virtue of his being the ultimate lord of the land seem to have been considerably offset by certain admirable principles of taxation embodied in early Indian sources. Despite the supreme position of the king, the law-books affirm that taxes should not be arbitrary. There appears to have existed an awareness among the lawgivers that uncertainty of any kind about the levy of taxes is troublesome both to the state and the taxpayer. This perhaps explains why our sources often fix the amount of land revenue and other payments. Kauṭilya[1] ordains that taxes on commodities intended for sale should be prescribed once for all. Manu lays down that taxes should be realised in accordance with the *śāstra.*[2] A passage from the *Mahābhārata* can be cited to show that by levying taxes not sanctioned by the *śāstra* a king is said to wrong himself.[3] The term '*śāstra*' implies the fixed rate and other incidents and rules out uncertainty and arbitrariness. Evidently, this is in line with Adam Smith's second canon of taxation according to which taxes ought to be certain and not arbitrary; and the time of payment, the quantity to be paid etc., ought to be clear and plain to the contributor and every other person.

An important feature of the tax-maxims of the ancient Hindus seems to be the idea of reconciling the needs of the state with the ability of the people to pay taxes. A rule expressed

---

1. *AŚ,* II. 12; cf. *Śukra,* IV. 2,214. Kauṭilya also lays down rates for land revenue and allied charges (*infra*).
2. *Manu,* VII. 80.
3. *ŚP,* 72. 15.

practically in identical terms in the *Śānti Parva,*[4] and in Manu[5] indicates that taxes should always be fixed in such a way that the king himself and the producer may participate in the result. The negative side of this rule is expressed in a passage of the *Śānti Parva*[6], according to which the king should not, by his thirst, destroy his own foundations as also those of others and that he should avoid those acts which may lead the people to hate him. Manu adds that the king by destroying his own substance causes suffering to himself as well as to others.[7] The logical consequence of the above stated dictum is expressed at one place by Manu,[8] according to whom even if a king is in financial straits, he should not take what ought not to be taken, nor even though he is affluent should he relinquish his just dues, be they ever so small. All this seems to presume that the state revenues ultimately depend upon the production of wealth by individuals, and that whatever tends to diminish the latter is bound to react upon the former.[9]

The relation between taxation on the one hand and the people's ability to pay on the other is often illustrated in our sources by homely similes and metaphors. Thus the king, we are told by Kauṭilya,[10] should pluck the ripe fruits from his garden, but should not take unripe fruits which cause provocation, lest this should bring about his own ruin. Bhīṣma also states in the *Śānti Parva*[11] that just as a person desirous of milk never obtains any by cutting off the udders of a cow, so a kingdom afflicted by improper means never yields any profit to the king; just as a person who treats a cow with tenderness obtains milk, so does the king who rules his kingdom by proper means derive advantages from it; the earth, being properly protected by the king,

4. *Ibid.,* 88. 15.
5. *Manu,* VII. 127.
6. *ŚP,* 88. 16
7. *Manu,* VII. 139.
8. *Ibid.,* VII. 171-172.
9. *HRS,* p. 20.
10. *AŚ,* V. 2.
11. *ŚP,* 72. 16-19.

yields grain and cash to him as a gratified mother yields milk to her child. Similar ideas are repeated elsewhere in the *Śānti Parva*. We are told, for instance, when the calf is allowed to suck, it grows strong and is able to endure fatigue, but when the cow is milked too much the calf cannot do any work ; so in a kingdom drained too much, the subjects fail to achieve anything worth-while.[12] Similarly according to Kāmandaka[13] the king should act like a milkman and florist in matters of realising taxes from the people. This view is also embodied in the *Pañcatantra,* which states that the gardener plucks fruits and flowers but does not harm the trees and the bee sucks the honey without damaging the flower ; so also the king should collect taxes but should not cause any suffering to his subjects. For one who kills the goat can at best get one meal and one who feeds it well can get milk for several years.[14]

The lively similes and metaphors quoted above seem to suggest that although taxation subserves the essential needs of the king or the state, instead of destroying the source of the subsistence of the people, taxation should leave enough for them to carry on. This has been compared with Sismondi's third canon according to which "taxation should never touch what is necessary for the existence of the contributors".[15]

Closely connected with the above is the principle of moderation, which has received much emphasis in the contemporary sources. In the opinion of Manu,[16] just as the leech, the calf and the bee take their food little by little, so should the king take moderate annual taxes. This is repeated in the *Śānti Parva,*[17] according to which the king should tax his kingdom like a bee gathering honey from plants and act like the leech drawing blood mildly. We are further told that he should conduct himself towards his subjects like a tigress in matters of carrying her cubs,

12. *Ibid.,* 88. 18-20
13. *Kāmandaka,* V. 84.
14. *Pañcatantra,* I. 242-243.
15. Bastable, *Public Finance,* p. 416.
16. *Manu,* VII. 129.
17. *ŚP,* 89. 4ff.

touching them with her teeth, but never piercing them therewith. He should suck his kingdom by mild means in the fashion of a mouse which, though possessed of sharp teeth, cuts the feet of sleeping animals without letting them become conscious of it. The king should add to taxes on his subjects like a person gradually increasing the burdens of a young bullock. All these popular similes boil down to the dictum that taxes should be levied by slow, almost imperceptible degrees and not in a lump. This anticipates in some measure Sismondi's fourth canon of taxation that it "should not put to flight the wealth which it strikes"[18]—a rule which presupposes that the people's ability to pay taxes should receive sufficient consideration.

The apparent resemblance between the Hindu approach to taxation and the modern canons however, calls for a careful scrutiny. An important feature of the ancient Indian principles of taxation is the idea that taxes are the wages for the protection of the people by the king.[19] According to Ghoshal[20] and others the reciprocal relation between taxation and protection enunciated in the ancient Hindu texts is a striking anticipation of the so-called fee theory of taxation which was widely accepted among Western political theorists of the 17th and 18th centuries such as Grotius, Pufendorff, Hobbes, Locke, and Rousseau, though it took a definite shape only in Adam Smith who says : "The subjects of every state ought to contribute toward the support of the government, as nearly as possible, in proportion to the revenue which they respectively enjoy under the protection of the state. The expenses of the government to the individuals of a great nation are like the expense of management to the joint tenants of a great estate, who are all obliged to contribute in proportion to their respective interests in the state".[21] It is clear that according to this maxim taxation is a price for protection rendered by the state, and the idea appears to be a natural complement

18. Quoted in *HRS,* p. 23.
19. *Supra.*
20. *HRS,* p. 273
21. Adam Smith, *The Wealth of Nations,* E. Cannan (Ed.), (Newyork, 1904), II, p. 310.

to the contract theory. In other words, the modern fee-theory or benefit theory of taxation seems to have its basis in the contract theory of the origin of the State. The Hindu lawgivers also seek to establish that theoretically taxes are the wages for the service of protection rendered by the king and this has obviously some resemblance with the principle adumberated by Adam Smith.

Most of the earlier European writers, who argued in terms of protection, concluded in favour of proportional taxation; and Adam Smith himself, except in one or two passages, was its chief exponent. Generally it was held that the need for protection be measured in proportion to income and wealth, or in some cases, in proportion to expense.[22] There is, however, nothing in our sources to suggest that such considerations as increase in wealth, income or expense played any significant role in the assessment of revenue. The law-books, of course, prescribe varying rates of 1|6, 1|8, 1|10, or 1|12 of produce of the soil, but the sentiment in favour of the rate of one-sixth seems to have been fairly strong[23] so that the proportion to which the king was entitled appears to have been more or less constant. Whatever difference, however, exists in the rates prescribed in our sources, is perhaps due to the varying degree of fertility of soil, and not due to the corresponding rise or fall in an individual's income. Nor is there any indication that the principle of proportional taxation was followed in regard to the assessment and realisation of commercial taxes, for which the rates prescribed in the law-books are mostly constant.[24] Thus there is nothing to show that taxes rose and fell according to the increase and decrease in expenses. In other words, the idea of proportion which is a natural corollary to the modern fee-theory of taxation seems to have been unknown in ancient India.

In his statement quoted above, Adam Smith introduces us to the idea that taxes should be imposed according to the ability of

---

22. Musgrave, *The Theory of Public Finance* (McGraw-Hill Press, 1961), p. 65.

23. *Infra.*

24. For the discussion of these rates see Chapter IV.

the taxpayer, which is popularly known as the ability-to-pay theory in modern economics. In the Elizabethan poor law and in the early legislation of the American colonies too, the term 'ability-to-pay' referred to property. With the progress of industrial society and the development of a monetary economy there followed a successive shift in emphasis to income rather than property as an index of ability to pay; and in Adam Smith also there is a clear recognition of the fact[25] He, however, advises that wages and necessities which compose the real subsistence income should be exempted from taxation and thus distinguishes the real subsistence income from the taxable one. The ancient Indian law-books, which prescribe rates of taxation, indicate that with regard to land revenue a certain portion (generally one-sixth) of the produce of the soil went to the state exchequer. Although the jurists might have made—and as has been shown elsewhere they actually made an attempt to shift the burden of taxation on profits, strictly speaking, it does not mean any clear differentiation between the taxable and the non-taxable income of an individual. In the light of these facts, it appears that the similarity between ancient Indian approach to taxation and the modern principles of public finance is only superficial for in their implications the two differ widely.

The basic policy of the lawgivers, however, seems to have been to theoretically ensure the safety of the people from financial oppression, which has been condemned by them in clear terms. Realising what ought not to be collected is, thus, mentioned by Kauṭilya[26] as one of the causes leading to the impoverishment of the subjects. He further states that when the subjects are rendered poor they become greedy, and when greedy they become disaffected and voluntarily go over to the side of the king's enemy or destroy their own king. Manu[27] is of the opinion that among all modes of purification, purity in the ac-

25. Musgrave, *op. cit.*, p. 94.
26. *AŚ*, VII. 5. This is striking particularly in view of the fact that elsewhere Kauṭilya recommends certain very oppressive measures to swell the treasury.
27. *Manu*, V. 106.

quisition of wealth is the best. Elsewhere he tells us that the king who thoughtlessly oppresses his subjects is soon deprived of his kingdom and life.[28] He adds that as the lives of living beings perish by emaciation of their bodies, so do the lives of kings perish by oppressing their kingdom.[29] That the oppression was censured is further reflected in a verse of the *Śānti Parva,*[30] which states that the king whose subjects are always stricken with anxiety or laden with taxes and overwhelmed with all sorts of evil is defeated by his enemies. The king is further advised never to fill his treasury by acting unfairly or from covetousness[31] At one place in the *Śānti Parva*[32] Yudhiṣṭhira is enjoined to punish and dismiss those officers who realise from the subjects more than what is due, and to appoint others who will take only what is due. No less clear is the view of Yājñavalkya,[33] according to whom the king who seeks to increase his treasury with wealth extracted by unjust means from his realm loses the same in no time and meets destruction along with his relatives. Kātyāyana also censures financial tyranny over the people. According to him the king who acts without greed is blessed with sons, and his domains and treasury proper.[34] The negative side of this injunction is contained in the following verse where we are told that the king, who unjustly takes taxes, fines, share of crops and tolls from his kingdom, incurs sin.[35] Thus it appears that theoretically at least the position of a taxpayer was favourably defined in matters of paying taxes to the king.

That principles discussed above could not always have been idle theories can be inferred from several post-Maurya and Gupta inscriptions, which suggest that normally perhaps the kings followed the precepts of the lawgivers and refrained from

---

28. *Ibid.*, VII. 111.
29. *Ibid.*, 112.
30. *ŚP,* 137. 105.
31. *Ibid.*, 71. 13.
32. *Ibid.*, 89. 22.
33. *Yāj.*, I. 340.
34. *Kātyāyana,* verse 18.
35. *Ibid.*, verse 19.

tyrannising over the people. In one of the Nasik Cave inscriptions of the first century A.D., it is said of Gautamīputra Śātakarṇi that he was one "who never levied nor employed taxes but in conformity with *dharma*" (*dharmopajitakaravi-niyogakaraṣa*).[36] In the second century A.D. flourished another illustrious ruler, the Mahākṣatrapa Rudradāman, whose Junagadh Rock inscription testifies to the fact that he built the dam of the Sudarśana lake without oppressing the inhabitants of towns and country (*paura-janapadaṁjanam*) by taxes (*kara*), forced labour (*viṣṭi*) and benevolences (*praṇaya-kriyā*) but by spending a vast amount of money from his own treasury.[37] Coming to the Gupta period, an inscription of the Parivrājaka Mahārāja Saṁkṣobha (A.D. 518-19) describes his father, the Mahārāja Hastin, as one "who sought to govern properly the kingdom."[38] Similarly, of Droṇasiṁha, a ruler of the Maitraka dynasty of Valabhī, it is said in the Maliya Copper-plate (A.D. 571-72) of Dharasena II that he had as his law the rules and ordinances promulgated by Manu and other sages.[39] The same record describes Guhasena, a famous ruler of the Maitraka line, as one whose title to *rājan* was befitting, as he had pleased the hearts of his subjects by properly protecting them according to the rules prescribed in the *Smṛtis*.[40] More references of a similar nature are available in the records of the same dynasty, and this may imply that the Maitraka rulers perhaps followed the rules laid down in the law-books.

The description of kings as following the rules of the *Smṛtis*, recorded in the above-mentioned epigraphs, may have been nothing more than a kingly vaunt. In fact, no contemporary epigraph that we know of speaks anything evil about the ruler of the land. It is, therefore, not improbable that the epithets, such as 'religious', 'pious' and 'follower of the *śāstras*', may have been largely eulogistic in intent and purpose or simply conventional.

36. *EI*, VIII, no. 8(2), l. 5.
37. *Ibid.*, no. 6, ll. 15-16.
38. *CII*, III, no. 25, ll. 8-9.
39. *Ibid.*, no. ll. 4-6.
40. *Ibid.*, l. 12. l. 12.

On the other hand, if the rules laid down by the jurists were followed in practice, in certain cases they could lead to highly burdensome tax measures. Manu, for instance, compares the king, who takes, taxes to the sun that draws water (in order to return it in the form of rains).[41] A similar idea is expressed by Kālidāsa, who describes king Dilīpa as receiving taxes from his subjects for their own welfare like the sun who extracts water in order to render it back a thousandfold.[42] This may by implication mean that a king is entitled to take as much from his people as he likes because he is capable of giving proportionate dividends in return. Although we do not come across any historical instance of a king who may have used such an idea to bad ends, the possibility of *Smṛti* rules being misinterpreted and abused cannot be altogether ruled out. Furthermore, Nārada is of opinion that as pure and impure water become alike on their junction in the ocean, even so (all) property acquired by a king becomes pure in his hands.[43] In other words, this one injunction of Nārada, if followed by a ruler, can smash all the humanistic, benevolent and enlightened principles of taxation, which we have discussed above, and which have been glorified by many modern scholars.[44] What is worse, a greedy ruler could receive sanction for his oppressive measures from such passages and could yet claim to have governed according to the *Dharmaśāstras*.

Probabilities apart, our sources often refer to actual instances of financial oppression of the subjects. The *Yuga Purāṇa* states that the Śakas will be avaricious.[45] A *Jātaka* reference proves that the tax-collectors (*niggahakas*)[46] were perhaps an over-zealous lot and became a byword for importunate demand.[47] It is stated in the *Bhūridatta Jātaka* that at the instance of their

41. *Manu*, IX, 304-305. Cf. *Kāmandaka*, V. 74.
42. *Raghu.*, I. 18.
43. *Nārada*, XVIII. 45.
44. *HRS*, *pp.* 272 ff ; Ganguli, *IHQ*, II, p. 129.
45. *arthalubdhāśca te sarve bhaviṣyanti mahābalā*, *Yuga Purāṇa*, p. 37, 1.135.
46. *Jāt.*, VII, p. 212.
47. *Ibid.*, IV, p. 362.

king they plundered the wealth of cultivators like fearless robbers.[48] In one *Jātaka* they are referred to as eating the cooked food of the taxpayer and killing a calf for skin.[49] In the *Dūta Jataka,* a king is said to have drained his country of its gold by his exactions,[50] while the *Mahāpiṅgala Jātaka* refers to Mahāpiṅgala, the king of Banaras, as crushing his subjects like sugarcanes in a mill.[51] In one *Jātaka,* we come across a gloomy picture of relentless extortions that would preclude the nemesis. It is stated that kings shall accumulate wealth by crushing their subjects like sugarcanes in a mill and by taxing them to utmost ; and unable to pay taxes, the people shall flee from villages, towns and the like, and take refuge in the borders of the realm.[52] A similar picture is available in another *Jātaka* story, which relates that the kingdom of Kampilla was deserted by the people for oppressive taxation. Men are said to have gone to forest with their families. Others remained indoors at night but fled to forests on daybreak, fencing their homes with thorn branches.[53] Although financial oppression of this magnitude cannot be said to have been usual, that it was not altogether unlikely can be guessed from a story of the *Divyāvadāna,* in which two evil ministers advise the king in the following strain : "Seasamum, O Lord ! does not yield oil unless it is made to dry, torn to pieces, oppressed and pressed ; so also, O king, is the kingdom".[54] Evidently such an argument may have had dangerous implications resulting in all kinds of royal tyranny over the people. Nor could such an idea have been an idle one, for Varāhamihira also refers to the possibility of the oppression of the subjects by the rulers and their officers.[55]

The probability of the depopulation of an area because of

---

48. *Ibid.,* VI, p. 212.
49. *Ibid.,* V, p. 106.
50. *Ibid.,* IV, p. 224 ; cf. Ibid., III, p. 319.
51. *Ibid.,* II, p. 240.
52. *Ibid.,* I, p. 399.
53. *Ibid.,* V, p. 98 ff.
54. *Div.,* pp. 562-563.
55. *svanṛpatiparacakrapīḍitā manujāḥ, Bṛhat Saṁhitā, III, 15* ; *apasavye narapatitaskarāvamṛdaiḥ prajānāśah, ibid.,* V. 44.

excessive taxation is also hinted at in a passage of the *Arthaśāstra*.[56] The same contingency is indicated by the *Śānti Parva*, which warns that the king is to see that the agriculturists of the kingdom do not leave it through oppression[57] The *Viṣṇu Purāṇa* also contemplates a similar probability in cases of famine and heavy taxation.[58] Although historical instances of population migration due to burdensome taxation during our period are lacking, the two spurious Copper-plates of Samudra Gupta indicate the possibility of the villagers oppressed with taxes migrating into tax-free villages.[59]

An important source of oppression seems to have been the billeting of royal agents and soldiers in the villages. Some Sātavāhana land grants record donations of lands which were exempted from the entrance of royal officers; nor were they to be disturbed by them.[60] This privilege is mentioned in the Basim plate of the Vākāṭaka Vindhyaśakti II as *abhaḍappāvesa*,[61] which has been taken by Mirashi to mean an immunity from the entrance of soldiers[62] (*bhaḍa*=*bhaṭa* meaning soldier). Several Vākāṭaka land grants, however, mention the term *abhaṭachhatra-prāveśya*,[63] which has been explained as "not to be entered by regular soldiers and umbrella-bearers".[64] On the other hand, several inscriptions of other contemporary dynasties, ruling in Central or Western India, often bear the compound *acāṭabhaṭaprāveśya*,,[65] in which

56. *AŚ*, VII. 5.
57. *ŚP*, 126.9.
58. *durbhikṣakarapīḍābhirativopadrutā janāḥ* |
godhūmānnayavānnādhyāndeśānyāsyanti duḥkhitāḥ ||
—*Viṣṇu Purāṇa*, VI. 1. 38.
59. *CII*, III, no. 60 ; *EI*, XXV, no. 9.
60. *Sel. Ins.*, p. 192, 1.4.
61. *EI*, XXVI, no. 20, 1.22.
62. *Ibid.*, p. 155.
63. *Ibid.*, *XXII*, no. 27, 1.20 ; XXIII, no. 14, 11.30-31 ; XXIV, no. 10, 1.21 ; no. 37(B), 1.20 ; XXVI, no. 21, 1.25 ; XXVII, no. 16, 11. 28-29 *CII*, III, no. 55, 1.26, etc.
64. *EI*, XXII, p. 175.
65. *Ibid.*, XVI, no. 4, 1.6 ; XIX, no. 21, 11. 9-10 ; XXI, no. 20, 1.8 ; *CII*, III, no. 22, 1.16; no. 26, 1.8; no. 28, 11.9-10 etc.

case *cāṭa* may be the same thing as *chhātra* of the Vākāṭaka records. Bhagwanlal Indraji interprets *cāṭabhaṭa* as *cāṭān prati bhaṭān*, "soldiers against robbers"[66] But the alternative forms of the expression referred to above, suggest that *cāṭa* is not governed by *bhaṭa*. Bühler is of opinion that *cāṭabhaṭa* means irregular and regular soldiers;[67] and Fleet concurs with this view.[68]

Some writers have sought to explain *cāṭa* as flatterer, deriving the word from the Sanskrit *cāṭu*, meaning flattery.[69] Pran Nath, however, thinks that *cāṭa* is the same thing as *cara*,[70] to which the *Arthaśāstra*[71] refers either in the sense of a spy or a policeman. The police function of the *caras* may be inferred also from a passage of the *Śānti Parva* according to which they should be stationed in the markets, parks, places of assembly, streets and gardens, since they were responsible for public security.[72] *Bhaṭas*, on the other hand, are generally taken to mean soldiers. The *Amarakośa*[73] uses *bhaṭa* as a synonym of *sainya* (soldiers). The Surat plates of Vyāghrasena also make it clear that the *cāṭas* and *bhaṭas* acted partly as police and partly as military, and were perhaps appointed to arrest robbers and persons guilty of high treason.[74] But their mention in the land grants may as well mean that either the village folk had to pay some contribution of money or supplies to them when they halted at or passed through villages, or, that they were connected with the collection of revenue. In either case they may have been probably in the habit of collecting oppressive extra impositions and realising illegal taxes for their own benefit.

The cruelty and avarice of the *cāṭas* and *bhaṭas* perhaps account for the popular dislike for them. Yājñavalkya[75] men-

66. *IA*, IX, p. 175, n. 41.
67. *Ibid.*, V, p. 115 and note.
68. *CII*, III, p. 98, n. 2.
69. *EI*, XI, p. 176.
70. *Economic Condition of Ancient India*, p. 65.
71. *AŚ*, II. 35.
72. *ŚP*, 69.11-13.
73. *Amar.*, II. 8.62.
74. *EI*, XI, no. 21, 11.10-11.
75. *Yāj.*, I. 335.

tions them together with thieves and record-keepers (*kāyasthas*). The *Śabdakalpadruma* quotes an unknown *Smṛti* passage which means that whatever is given to *cāṭas* bears no fruit.[76] According to Bāṇa also, the *cāṭas* and *bhaṭas* were hated by the country people on account of their cruelty and greed. At one place he describes them as talking and laughing with the slaves and servants of the nobles after taking plenty of grain from the fields;[77] and at another, he writes that the poor grumbled at the cruelty and ill treatment received at their hands.[78] Similarly, in the *Mṛcchakaṭika* a friend of the hero remarks in Prākṛta that "even the most daring and wicked will not dare to go to a place where the *cāṭas*, courtiers etc., reside".[79] It is, therefore, no wonder that the brāhmaṇa donees were protected from these officials by a special clause of the charters, which sought to prohibit their entrance into the donated area.[80]

To sum up, so far as the theory goes, the principles of taxation as described in our sources, seem to be quite sound, and reveal a fairly advanced stage of financial thinking, considering the time when they were formulated. But we should not think that these principles were rigorously observed in all cases. As we have already indicated, there are instances to show that there were cases of breaches also.

76. *cāṭacāraṇadāseṣu dattaṁ bhavati niṣphalam, Śabdakalpadruma*, p. 2909.
77. *Harṣacarita* (Nirnayasagar Press, 1937), p. 205.
78. *Ibid.*, p. 211.
79. *Mṛcchakaṭika* (Bombay Sans. Series, Vol. I), Act. V, p. 223.
80. We are reminded of the *publicanis* of Rome who were connected with tax-collection. Even Cicero recognises explicitly the irreconcilable conflict between their interests and those of the provincials; he admits likewise the selfish and ruthless conduct of the former. It was a popular feeling of the Romans in the first century B.C. that the *publicanis* were a nuisance and that it was the duty of every honest administrator to combat them (Rostovtzeff, *The Social and Economic History of the Hellenistic World*, II, p. 965).

CHAPTER IV

LAND REVENUE

Though our sources enunciate certain admirable principles of taxation, they are mostly silent about the rules and methods of assessment. The *Arthaśāstra*,[1] which belongs to an earlier period, is the only work which, in connection with the duties of the *samāhartā* (collector-general) and his staff of officers, gives sufficient data regarding the assessment of land revenue. Thus one of the duties of the *gopa* (officer in charge of 5 or 10 villages) is stated to be to prepare various registers, such as those of boundaries and village fields, uncultivable lands, and of transfers. He is further required to compile what may be called census lists of dwelling houses, to specify therein whether the houses are taxable or tax-free, and to state the taxes charged upon them severally under the heads of cash payment, unpaid labour, tolls and fines.[2] The *Arthaśāstra*[3] further provides for the deputation of inspectors by the *samāhartā* in the selected villages, where he is to check up and report on the various heads of revenues assessed on the dwelling houses and the remissions granted to them. It, therefore, follows that in Maurya times land revenue

1. *AŚ*, II. 35.
2. *Ibid.* In the Roman Empire also, the periodical census furnished lists of the living inhabitants with an estimate of their wealth, so that they could be arranged in classes and their tax could be assessed. This census list distinguished between the various categories of land : fields under cultivation, plantation of vines or of olives, woods and pastures. Moreover, homes and other buildings were also included in the list, together with movables, furniture, slaves, and even cash savings, all this being regarded as an extension of the landed property, since the incidence of the tax was upon the land itself and not upon its possessor (Victor Chapot, *The Roman World*, pp. 95-96).
3. *Ibid.*

and the connected charges were probably assessed upon the individual holdings of the villagers.

Land revenue appears to have been normally charged on individual holdings in the Maurya period, but collective assessment on whole villages was not unknown. Kauṭilya[4] mentions *piṇḍakara* under the heading *rāṣṭra* (country parts). This term is explained by his commentator Bhaṭṭasvāmin as comprising taxes levied from whole villages. Evidently it stood for a lump assessment upon villages as distinguished from principal land tax which was assessed on individual holdings of land.

In post-Maurya and Gupta times *piṇḍakara* or any other term of similar import is not mentioned in our sources, which implies the absence of collective assessment of any tax on an entire village. The older practice of charging revenue on individual holdings, however, seems to have continued in our period. This can be inferred from the Sātavāhana land charters, which record gifts of plots of land in specified villages.[5] The fact that in these instances the granted fields were to be enjoyed by individuals may suggest that to a certain extent the assessment of land revenue was made upon individual holdings.

The land grants of the Gupta period testify more clearly than the earlier ones to assessment on individual holdings of land. The two charters[6] belonging to the region of modern Indore—one of the Mahārāja Svāmidāsa (c. A.D. 386-387) and the other of the Mahārāja Bhuluṇda (c. A.D. 426-427)—record donations of lands in favour of the brāhmaṇas. Since the holdings of individual cultivators were sought to be donated here, it may suggest that villagers were separately assessed for land revenue. Similarly, an undated inscription of the Parivrājaka ruler Hastin,[7] who ruled in the Baghelkhand region of Central India, records the gift of half of the village of Dhavasandika. At least two other epigraphs of the Parivrājaka Mahārājas refer to a portion of a village or

4. *AŚ*, II. 15.
5. *Lüders' List*, nos. 1162, 1163, 1164, 1166, 1167, etc.
6. *EI*, XV, no. 16 (1 & 2).
7. *grāmārddho*, CII, III, no. 29, 1. 8.

portions of two different villages forming the object of gift.[8] Again several documents of the Maitrakas mention the king's gift (along with the royal dues therefrom) of fields or wells or both, lying in the extremities of specified villages and forming in many cases the holdings (*pratyāya*) of the cultivators whose names are mentioned. Thus in the Goras Copper-plates (A.D. 643) of Dhruvasena II a field consisting of three pieces and measuring 100 *pādāvartas* in the village called Bahumūla is granted. The record states that the field was to the north of the field of Devī. Another field of 100 *pādāvartas,* donated in the same .record, is described as having the *brahmadeya* field of Sthavira in its west and the holding of Kuṭumbī Kuhuṇḍaka in the north.[9] All this may imply that the villages concerned were not assessed collectively but with reference to individual holdings.

How far individual holdings of land were assessed on the basis of their measurement is a question which cannot be satisfactorily answered. In the *Kāma Jātaka,*[10] it is related that when the royal officers (*rājakammikas*) came to the village to measure the fields, the *seṭṭhī* asked the prince, who, after renouncing his claim to the throne in favour of his younger brother, had come to live with the former's family, to write to the king for remission of the *bali*. Ghoshal[11] points out that in this case the measurement of land is immediately associated with the *bali* assessment, and this may imply the prevalence of a standard or average rate of the government demand for a known unit-area, which could be applied for assessment of the individual holdings. The *Kurudhamma Jātaka*[12] refers to the pious hesitation of the *rajjuka*

8. *IA,* VIII, pp. 8, 28.
9. Diskalkar, "Some Unpublished Copper-plates of the rulers of Valabhi", *JBBRAS,* I (N.S.), pp. 51-52; for similar references see *IA,* I, p. 16; VII, p. 70; VIII, p. 301.
10. *Jāt.,* IV, p. 109.
11. Ghoshal, *Agrarian System in Ancient India,* p. 25.
12. *Jāt.,* II, p. 376, Pāṇini also refers to a systematic survey of agricultural land undertaken by special officers called *kṣetrakaras,* corresponding to the *rajjugahaka amaccas* of the Buddhist sources (vide R. S. Sharma, "Stages in Ancient Indian Economy," *Enquiry,* No. 4, p. 22).

ammacca (surveyor) that the king will be a loser if the stick of the measuring rope is pitched on this or that side of a crab hole situated just at the boundary of a field. This also may suggest that the king's share was fixed after measurement. The *Arthaśāstra* corroborates, though indirectly, the importance of measurement in the assessment of land tax in so far as it refers to the ascertainment of total areas of fields by numbering cultivated and uncultivated plots.[13] Besides, Kauṭilya definitely mentions the standards by which land was measured.

The post-Maurya sources too mention certain standards of linear measurement, though they do not make any direct reference to assessment according to the area of land. The *Arthaśāstra* gives a fairly detailed list of linear measures, most of which are mentioned in the sources of our period.[14] Thus Patañjali mentions *aratni*[15] and *vitasti*,[16] among other units such as *akṣa*,[17] *pāda*,[18] *prādeśa*[19] and *diṣṭi*.[20] Coming to the epigraphic evidence, several land grants of the Sātavāhana period refer to the areas of donated fields in the *nivartana* measure,[21] which occurs in the *Arthaśāstra* as well.[22] In the Gupta period we come across certain measurements which are generally not known from earlier sources. Thus in the eastern part of the Gupta empire, a system of land measurement with units known as *aḍhavāpa, droṇavāpa,* and *kulyavāpa,* seems to have been common; while in the Vākāṭaka and Maitraka documents, a measurement called *pādāvarta* is frequently referred to in connection with the areas of

13. *AŚ.*, II. 35.
14. *Ibid.*, II. 20.
15. *Mahābhāṣya*, I, 1. 14, p. 25, 1. 5.
16. *Ibid.*, V, 2. 37, p. 378, 1. 13.
17. *Ibid.*, I, 2. 45, p. 220, 1. 2.
18. *Ibid.*
19. *Ibid.*, I, 4. 84, p. 346, 1. 23.
20. For detailed discussion of land measurement units of post-Maurya and Gupta times see Maity, *Economic Life of Northern India*, pp. 35-43 ; Bose, *Social and Rural Economy*, II, pp. 278-281 ; Pran Nath, *op. cit.*, pp. 79-80.
21. *EI*, VIII, no. 8(4), 1. 3 ; no. 8(5), 1. 9 ; *Lüders' List* no. 1162, etc.
22. *AŚ*, II. 20.

fields and tanks.[23] Another land measure mentioned in the Vākāṭaka land grant is known as *bhūmi*.[24] Since the system of measurement varied widely in different parts of the country, there were evidently local standards which may have been adhered to by government officers. In none of the above records do we get any reference to assessment on the area of land, though they refer to measurement units. There is, however, a solitary Vākāṭaka record which mentions *rajuka*[25] as its writer. If *rajuka* be taken as a settlement officer, as is commonly believed, the possibility of assessment on the basis of the area of land cannot altogether be discounted.

A study of the rate of land tax, as prescribed in our sources reveals that often the quality of land may have been an important consideration in assessing land revenue. Gautama,[26] who probably belongs to the pre-Maurya period, prescribes three distinct rates, viz., 1|6, 1|8, and 1|10. The commentator Haradatta takes these rates to apply to different types of soil.[27] Kauṭilya mentions an income called *ṣaḍbhāga*, which perhaps refers to land revenue.[28] In another place, the *Arthaśāstra* records the expression *dhānyaṣaḍbhāga*, i.e., one-sixth of the grain grown as being taken by the king. This, however, does not mean that Kauṭilya recognises the uniform rate of 1|6 in all cases. Elsewhere[29] Kauṭilya himself states that upland and lowland are to be recorded separately by the *gopa*. While laying down the rules for extraordinary revenue he further contemplates unhusked grain to be assessed at 1|3 or 1|4 of the crop of rich soils which are independent of rainwater, but soils of intermediate and inferior qualities are evidently assigned lower rates.[30] Among the law-

23. For reference see Maity, *op. cit.*, pp. 31-38.
24. The Chammak Copper-plate of Pravarasena II, *CII*, III, no. 55, l. 18.
25. *EI*, XXIV, no. 10, l. 34. For discussion *infra*.
26. *Gautama*, X. 24.
27. Haradatta on *Gautama*, X. 24.
28. *AŚ*, II. 15; for identification of *ṣaḍbhāga* and *bhāga* see below.
29. *Ibid.*, II. 35.
30. *Ibid.*, V. 2.

givers of our period, Manu[31] ordains that a king can take 1|6, 1|8, or 1|12 of the crops. This passage is quoted in the *Vīramitrodaya*, where it is remarked that the option laid down is based on the varying fertility of the soil and the consequent greater or less labour involved in cultivation.[32] Bṛhaspati[33] lays down the rates of 1|10, 1|8 and 1|6 on *khila* land, on the land exposed to the rainwater, and on the crops harvested in *vasanta* respectively. *Khila* land may be taken as cultivable waste[34] the cultivation of which may entail more than the usual cost. Similarly, lands exposed to the dangers of rainwater make a rich harvest uncertain, and the crops harvested in the spring season are least subject to risks. Perhaps in view of these considerations Bṛhaspati prescribes three distinct rates of land tax, which are the same as laid down by Gautama.

Land tax may have been assessed at rates in keeping with the varying fertility of the soil, but most of the authorities mention the rate of 1|6. Manu, who has been quoted earlier as advocating three different rates, states at one place that the king who affords no protection and yet receives the sixth part of the produce takes upon himself all the sins of his people.[35] Both Viṣṇu[36] and Nārada[37] mention 1|6 to be the usual rate of land revenue. It is repeatedly stated in the *Śānti Parva*[38] that the king is entitled to 1|6 of the produce. The rate of 1|6 seems to have been so deeply associated with popular sentiment that the king is often known by the appellative *ṣaḍbhāgin*.[39] A similar attitude is reflected in the works of Kālidāsa who states that the king can claim 1|6 of the produce of land from the people.[40] He further

31. *dhānyānāmaṣṭamo bhāgaḥ saṣṭho dvādaśa ava vā Manu,* VII. 130.
32. Vide G. N. Jha, *Notes on Manusmṛti,* pt. 2. p. 466.
33. *Bṛhaspati,* 1. 43.
34. Maity, *op. cit.,* p. 24.
35. *Manu,* VII. 308.
36. *Viṣṇu,* III. 24.
37. *Nārada,* XVIII. 48.
38. *Supra.*
39. *AŚ,* II, 15 ; *Viṣṇu,* III. 22 ; *Nārada* quoted above ; *ŚP,* 69. 24, 72. 10.
40. *Raghu.,* II. 66.

tells us that the ascetics living in the forest pay the sixth part of their penances;[41] and he refers to them as placing 1|6 of the rice collected by them on the bank of the river to be taken by the royal officers.[42] Thus it seems that the rate of 1|6 was perhaps normally prevalent, though of course variations may have been admissible.[43]

Although 1|6 seems to be the theoretically accepted rate, the account of Megasthenes suggests that in spite of the injunctions of Kauṭilya the Mauryan land tax was much higher. Ghoshal has taken Megasthenes' statement as quoted by Diodorus to mean that the cultivators ordinarily paid 1|4 of the produce to the Mauryan state.[44] In other words, the testimony of the Greek ambassador may imply that the normal rate of land revenue in his time was equivalent to the rate prescribed by the Indian jurists for emergencies of the state.

The relatively high rate of Mauryan land revenue is also attested to by the Rumindei Pillar inscription of Aśoka, which records the royal order that the village Lumbini, by virtue of its being the birth-place of the Buddha, is made liable to 1|8 of the *bhāga* (*aṭṭhabhāgiya*) and exempted from *bali*. Ghoshal rightly points out that the fact that this concession was made by Aśoka for the holiest place of his faith suggests that not only was complete remission of the land revenue not thought of in the Maurya period, but that its principal branch was fixed sufficiently high to make its reduction to the ratio of 1|8 amount to a very great favour.[45] It appears that although in theory Kauṭilya prescribes 1|6 as the normal rate of land tax, in practice the ratio was much higher; and not less than 1|4 if the Greek testimony is accepted. We do not, however, know whether in the post-Maurya and Gupta period there was a similar discrepancy between theory

41. *Śāk.*, II. 13.
42. *Ibid.*, (Nirnayasagar Press), p. 76.
43. Curiously enough the land charters nowhere directly lay down the rate of land tax to be realised from the villagers, although such terms as *aṣṭabhāgika* and *dharmaṣaḍbhāga* give some indirect idea.
44. *HRS*, p. 168.
45. *Ibid.*, p. 171.

and practice. It is curious that the contemporary inscriptions do not give any indication of the rate of land tax, although the occurrence of the expression *dharmasaḍbhāga* in several Gupta epigraphs may suggest that the rate of 1|6 was in vogue. This may mean that the king's normal grain share was realised at lower rates in Gupta times than in the Mauryan days.

Equally pertinent and no less controversial is the question whether land tax was levied on the gross income or on the profit of the cultivator. With regard to tax on merchants our sources implicitly indicate an attempt to shift the burden of taxation on the net profit,[46] but the lawgivers nowhere explicitly state that land tax was assessed on the agriculturists' profit. Kullūka explains a passage of Manu quoted above to mean that the king's share is to be estimated on the increase upon the capital employed. Medhātithi and Govinda are concurrent, and Nandana even more clearly states : "In every case, the share is on profit made after deducting expenses." But as the commentators belong to a later period their interpretation of the *Smṛti* passages may not apply to the period under study. Among the contemporary sources the *Śānti Parva*[47] broadly recognises the criteria of income and expenditure in determining the king's share, though, strangely enough, other sources of our period do not seem to suggest that land tax was assessed on the cultivator's profit. It is, however, not improbable that there may have existed a broad recognition of the fact that taxes should fall on the profit and not on the capital, though how far this principle was observed specifically in relation to land tax is largely a matter of speculation.

The main item of land revenue appears to have been the customary royal share of the agricultural produce sometimes known as *bhāga*. As the designation of a specific tax on land, the word *bhāga* first occurs in the *Arthaśāstra*.[48] At one place it is mentioned as an independent term along with *bali*, *kara*, etc. under the heading *rāṣṭra;* at another[49] it forms a part of

46. *Supra.*
47. *ŚP*, 120. 9.
48. *AŚ*, II. 6.
49. *Ibid.*, II, 15.

ṣaḍbhāga, which is mentioned with *bali, kara* etc. under the same general heading. Therefore, "*bhāga* undoubtedly means the king's customary share of the produce normally, though not universally, amounting to 1|6th."[50] Kṣīrasvāmin,[51] the 12th century commentator of the *Amarakośa,* also quotes the view of the *Arthaśāstra* to define *bhāga* as the king's 1|6th share of produce.

Bhāga seems to have been the principal tax on land in post-Maurya and Gupta times. In the Junagadh inscription of Rudradāman the royal treasury is said to have been filled with *bali, śulka* and *bhāga,* and the Sudarśana dam is said to have been built without oppressing the people with *kara, viṣṭi* and *praṇaya.* Since the latter three taxes are referred to as oppressive, *bhāga,* which is not mentioned as such, perhaps stands for the main item of land revenue, i.e., king's normal grain share. The inscriptions of the Gupta period recording grants of land to the brāhmaṇas frequently refer to the donee's exemption from *bhāgabhogakara*[52] among the other levies. Fleet[53] considers the term *bhāgabhoga* to be one expression meaning "enjoyment of taxes or shares". The two words, however, are sometimes used in the reverse order and recorded as *bhogabhāga.*[54] If we construe this term in the same manner as Fleet does the first, it would mean "share of the enjoyment". But really speaking, this term is a compound formed by two independent words, *bhoga* and *bhāga,* and hence it indicates two separate taxes. Therefore Sircar's[55] explanation of the *bhāga* of inscriptions as the royal share of the produce may be nearer the truth.

Another fiscal expression, *bali,* occurs in early Indian sources. It is the oldest Indo-Aryan term for the royal revenue.

---

50. U. N. Ghoshal, "Some Hindu Fiscal Terms Discussed", *Proceedings of Fourth Oriental Conference,* II, p. 205.
51. *rājagrāhyaḥ ṣaḍbhāgādiḥ,* Kṣīrasvāmin's comm. on *Amar.* II, 8. 28.
52. *CII,* III, no. 26, 1. 9 ; no. 27, 1. 11 ; no. 28, 1. 17, etc.
53. *Ibid.,* p. 254, n. 4 ; p. 120, n. 1.
54. *Ibid.,* no. 39, 1. 68 ; no. 40, 1. 12 ; no. 41, 1. 14, etc.
55. *Sel. Ins.,* p. 372, n. 7 ; of., *EI,* XV, pp. 293ff ; Majumdar, *History of Bengal,* 1, p. 277.

In the *Ṛgveda* it is the king's due both from his subjects and from conquered kings.[56] Macdonnell and Keith,[57] however, suggest that *bali* was from the very beginning of the nature of a tax not depending solely upon the free will of the subjects. In fact, it is hardly likely that even a kingdom of the primitive tribal type of the early Vedic age could subsist on purely voluntary contributions. In any case, in the period of the *Brāhmaṇas, bali* seems to have been known as a compulsory contribution payable by the subjects;[58] and if ever voluntary it was, in the later period it may have remained so only in name. We may here add that in ancient Assyria also the term "gift" was used for regular taxes for a long time in spite of the fact that the subjects were compelled to make these payments.[59] It is not unlikely that in ancient India there continued for some time the contradiction between the revenue terminology and its actual content.[60]

With the gradual development of revenue nomenclature and the emergence of new items of taxation, the word *bali* appears to be all the more intriguing in its connotation. *Bali* as used in the *Arthaśāstra* is essentially of the nature of a petty cess over and above the king's normal share of the produce,[61] whereas in the *Jātakas*[62] the term often means additional and oppressive cesses.

Unlike the *Jātakas*, the *Milindapañho* mentions *bali* as an emergency tax from which the four chief ministers are declared free.[63] This may imply that the import of the term had undergone some change in post-Maurya times. But the Junagadh inscription of Rudradāman[64] (A.D. 150), which is the only inscription of our period recording *bali* in the sense of a tax, does not corroborate the view incorporated in the *Milindapañho*. The

56. Cf. HRS, pp. 4-5.
57. *Vedic Index*, II, 62.
58. *Ait. Br.*, VII, 29.
59. Olmstead, *History of Assyria*, p. 516.
60. R. S. Sharma, *Political Ideas and Institutions*, p. 132.
61. Ghoshal, "Some Hindu Fiscal Terms Discussed", *op. cit.*, p. 203.
62. *Jāt.*, I. pp. 199, 339; II, p. 240; III, p. 9; V, p. 98.
63. *Milinda.*, p. 146.
64. *EI*, VIII, no. 6, l. 14.

mention of *bali* in the *Milindapañho* in the sense of an emergency levy cannot be taken to be a local variation because the area of composition of the work, and Junagadh, where the inscription of Rudradāman is found, are quite near to each other. Nor does any other source take *bali* to mean an emergency impost. It is, therefore, not unlikely that the use of *bali* in the sense of an emergency tax in the *Milindapañho* is a case of misrepresentation.

The *bali* of the inscriptions has often been taken to mean a religious tax. Thus Thomas[65] interprets the term as mentioned in the Rumindei Pillar inscription of Aśoka to mean some kind of religious cess. Maity[66] also takes it to be a religious tax on the ground that the word occurs in the land grants of the Gupta period along with *caru* and *sattra* which are two important sacrificial rites. The inscription of Rudradāman, where *bali* occurs in the sense of tax, records it with other fiscal terms such as *śulka* and *bhāga*. The epigraphs of the Gupta period, however, invariably treat *bali* as one of the five sacrificial performances, the four others being *caru, sattra, vaiśvadeva* and *agnihotra*. Thus *bali* in this context cannot mean any tax. What is more important, it does not figure in the list of taxes from which the donees were generally exempted in the Gupta period and later times.

Bali is mentioned as tax mostly in legal and literary writings, which often ignore *bhāga* in its technical sense. In connection with the rate of land tax Viṣṇu[67] and Manu[68] refer to *bali* and not to *bhāga*. Similar is the case with the rājadharma section of the *Mahābhārata*.[69] Aśvaghoṣa[70] also mentions *bali* in the sense of regular land tax. Bṛhaspati[71], who probably belongs to

65. Thomas, *JRAS.*, 1909 p. 467. For further discussions by Charles Lyall and K. A. Nilkanta Sastri, see *JRAS*, 1908, pp. 850-51 and *IHQ*, XX, pp. 285-287 respectively.
66. Maity, *op. cit.*, p. 61.
67. *Viṣṇu*, III. 22-23.
68. *Manu*, VII. 130.
69. *ŚP*, 69: 24 ; 72. 10.
70. *Buddhacarita*, II. 44 ; *Saundaranandakāvya*, II. 33.
71. *Bṛhaspati*, *āpaddharma* section, verse 20.

the Gupta period, refers to *bali* in the same sense. At one place in the *Mahāvaṁśa*, a work of the Gupta period, the levy of *bali* is said to be very essential, which may imply that it was perhaps the basic land tax.[72] In the *Amarakośa*,[73] assignable to about the 5th century A.D., the term is used as a synonym of *śulka* and *kara* in the general sense of tax. From all this it appears that the *bali* of the *Dharmaśāstras* and general literature is identical with the *bhāga* of the inscriptions.

Kara is another form of revenue known from our sources. As a fiscal term *kara* appears to have been unknown to the earlier literature, but in the *Arthaśāstra* and the law-books it is of frequent occurrence. In a passage of Manu[74] it is differently interpreted by various commentators. According to Medhātithi *kara* means gifts of commodities (*dravya-dānam*) and according to Sarvajñanārāyaṇa a fixed gold payment on land (*bhūminiyataṁ deyaṁ hiraṇyam*). Rāmacandra interprets the term as contribution in the form of grass, wood, etc. (*gulmadāyādikam*), and Kullūka takes it to denote contribution from villagers and townsmen either monthly or in *Bhādrapada* and *Pauṣa* (*grāmapuravāsibhyaḥ pratimāsaṁ vā bhādrapauṣa niyamena grāhyam*). According to Rāghavānanda, however, *kara* is a monthy payment by villagers (*grāmavāsibhyaḥ pratimāsikam*). The last two interpretations are very much in accordance with Bhaṭṭasvāmin's explanation of the term in his commentary on Kauṭilya.[75] Bhaṭṭasvamin understands *kara* to mean "the annual tax paid during the months of *Bhādrapada, Vasanta* and the like".[76] With it may be connected the definition of *kara* in the *Arthaśāstra* text quoted by Kṣīrasvāmin,[77] i.e., it is a charge upon all movable and immovable articles. *Kara* thus

72. *Mahāvaṁśa*, XXVIII. 4.

73. *Amar.*, II. 8. 28.

74. *Manu*, VII. 307.

75. *AŚ*, II. 15.

76. *karaḥ prativarṣadeyaḥ bhādrapadikavasantikādyupādānam*, comm. on AŚ, II. 15, *JBORS*, XI, Pt. 2, pp. 83-84.

77. *pratyakaṁ sthāvarajaṅgamādideyaḥ karaḥ*, comm. on *Amar.*, II. 8. 28.

may have been of the nature of a periodical tax levied more or less universally from villagers, and it may have been realised over and above the king's normal grain share. This is corroborated by the Junagadh inscription of Rudradāman[78] (c. A.D. 150) where the king's treasury is said to have been filled by *baliśulkabhāgaiḥ*, while the Sudarśana dam is said to have been built without oppressing the people with *kara*, forced labour (*viṣṭi*) and benevolences (*praṇaya*). The use of *bali* at one place and *kara* at another seems to indicate that both cannot stand for tax in general. In other words, *kara* appears to have been an oppressive impost and therefore different from, and over and above, the general land tax.

Literary, and particularly epigraphic, sources indicate that *kara* was a general tax. Aśvaghoṣa[79] takes the term in the broad sense of taxes. In the Allahabad *praśasti* of Samudra Gupta, *kara* is used in the sense of tax in general.[80] Again, the spurious Gaya Copper-plate of Samudra Gupta[81] provides that the taxpaying (*karada*) cultivators and artisans should not be allowed to settle in a certain gift village. The mention of artisans as taxpaying (*karada*) may indicate that *kara* is used to denote all the taxes, including those paid by the cultivators as well as the artisans. Likewise in the land grants *akaradāyī*[82] denotes one who is exempt from taxes in general. Some of the records bear expressions such as *sarvakaraparihāraiḥ*,[83] *sarvakarasametaḥ*[84] and the like, which may simply imply that *kara* comprised all taxes. On the other hand, in an inscription[85] *kara* stands for all kinds of contributions

78. *EI*, VIII. no. 6, ll. 15-16.
79. *Saundaranandakāvya*, II. 27.
80. *CII*, III, no. 1, l. 22.
81. *Ibid.*, no. 60, l. 13.
82. *Ibid.*, no. 55, l. 26.
83. *EI*, XXIV, no. 9, l. 14.
84. *Ibid.*, XXIII, no. 18, l. 10. Other expressions of similar import used in the inscriptions are *sarvakaradānasametaḥ* (*CII*, III, no. 81. l. 22), *sarvakaravisarjjitaḥ* (*Ibid.*, no. 41, l. 9), *sarvakaratyāgaḥ* (*Ibid.*, no. 29, l. 97). The word *kara* in these compounds bears the sense of tax in general.
85. *CII*, III, no. 26, l. 9.

other than land revenue (*bhāga*) and *bhoga*, and yet in another[86] it excludes *śulka*, *bhāga*, *bhoga*, and *hiraṇya*. Elsewhere it has been pointed out that the Smṛtis mention *kara* also in the sense of a tax on merchant's profits.[87] Hence the term *kara* is used indiscriminately in both general and specific senses in varying contexts, and it is difficult to ascribe any definite meaning to it. It seems to have been some kind of land revenue, but its exact nature cannot be determined.

Like the above-mentioned items of land revenue, *hiraṇya* appears in most of the early Indian sources. The *Arthaśāstra*[88] refers to it as a branch of king's revenue. Kauṭilya[89] tells us that the *samāhartā* (collector-general) should prepare a written record (*nibandha*) specifying *inter alia* the contributions payable by the villagers severally and collectively under the heads of grain, domestic animals, *hiraṇya*, forced labour and so forth. Curiously enough, however, the *Arthaśāstra*[90] does not include *hiraṇya* in its regular list of constituents of the body of income (*āyaśarīram*) which suggests that in the Maurya period it was an irregular levy. The *Arthaśāstra*, however, definitely lays down a rate for its realisation. Thus in the traditional story of the origin of kingship recorded by Kauṭilya, the people having chosen Manu as their king, undertake to contribute 1|6 of the crops, 1|10 of merchandise as well as *hiraṇya* as his share. In a similar context the *Mahābhārata*[91] prescribes 1|10. Though Patañjali states that *hiraṇya* makes a king wealthy, he does not use the term in the sense of any specific land tax, let alone the question of fixing any rate of payment in this connection. But in the law-books of the post-Maurya period *hiraṇya* definitely figures as an item of king's regular revenue; and Viṣṇu[92] and

86. *EI*, I, no. 11, 1. 15; *Ibid.*, VII, 22, 1. 15.
87. *Infra.*
88. *AŚ*, I. 13.
89. *Ibid.*, II. 35.
90. *Ibid.*, II. 6.
91. *ŚP*, 67. 23.
92. *Viṣṇu*, III, 25.

Manu[93] prescribe its rate at 1|50. From the Gupta period onwards, the land grants, with the possible exception of the Vākāṭaka charters, mention this term in the list of revenues from which the donees are stated to have been exempted. But they do not give us any clue as to the rate at which *hiraṇya* was paid to the state. In any case, we can be sure that in our period it constituted an important and established item of royal income.

The term *hiraṇya* in the contexts referred to above, however, has been variously interpreted by different scholars. The word as occurring in the *Arthaśāstra* has been translated simply as gold.[94] The *hiraṇya* of the law-books is sometimes taken as gold and sometimes either as a tax on the hoard or a tax on the capital of the annual income.[95] But in view of its high value, it is highly improbable that peasants paid taxes in gold. According to still another explanation, *hiraṇya* refers to the right of the state to the gold and probably to other mines as well. None of the above interpretations, however, appears tenable. In the *Smṛti*[96] texts *hiraṇya* is usually joined with *paśu* (domestic animals), and it figures as a recognised source of revenue in the same context as the crops, trees, roots, fruits, flowers, leaves, grass and so forth. *Hiraṇya*, therefore, according to Ghoshal may be said to have belonged to the groups of taxes relating to the simple agricultural and industrial products of a village.[97] We may add that in the land grants it is often conjoined with *bhāgabhogakara*[98] which, as has been shown elsewhere,[99] means king's normal grain share and the miscellaneous contributions by the agricultural class. Similarly, in some cases the term occurs together with *dhānya*, which means the king's share of the crops.[100] *Hiraṇya*, therefore, appears to have been a tax on agricultural products.

---

93. *Manu*, VII. 130.
94. Shamasastry, *Arthaśāstra* (Tr.), seventh edition, p 158.
95. N. C. Bandopadhyaya, *Kauṭilya*, pp. 139, 140.
96. Manu and Viṣṇu quoted above.
97. *HRS*, p. 61.
98. *CII*, III, no. 27, l. 11 ; no. 28, l. 17 ; no. 29, l. 14, etc.
99. For *bhāga* see above, for *bhoga* see below.
100. *Infra*.

The clue to the proper interpretation of the term, Ghoshal rightly points out, is furnished by certain conditions of land revenue prevalent in later times. In the medieval period payments of the land revenue before the reform introduced by Todar Mall were made in kind, but certain classes of crops (called *zabti*) were always assessed in cash on the ground that it was very difficult to divide them into shares.[101] Ghoshal, therefore, makes a reasonable guess that *hiraṇya* was a tax of this nature, more precisely a tax in cash levied upon certain special kinds of crops as distinguished from the tax in kind which was charged upon the ordinary crops.[102] Sircar also endorses this view.[103] It may be pointed out that we have reference to a tax on certain agricultural products, realised in cash. An inscription dated A.D. 592 states that the tax for a sugarcane plantation within a specified area (*vāṭa*) was 32 silver coins, though it was only 2½ silver coins if the field belonged to a religious donee.[104] It is further stated in the same record that the tax for an *alla-vāṭa* was half the amount prescribed above. *Alla* is the Prākṛt form of Sanskrit *ardraka*, ginger, and *alla-vāṭa* may possibly mean 'a ginger plantation' Thus taxes on certain types of products were paid in cash, and no wonder if *hiraṇya* was a tax levied on commercial crops.

Although several Kauṭilyan items of land revenue seem to have continued down to the Gupta period, the case is different with irrigation tax (*udakabhāga*) which was one of the revenue heads of the Maurya state,[105] which constructed reservoirs, filled with water, either perennial or drawn from other sources.[106] There is a conspicuous lack of consolidated evidence in regard to irrigation in post-Maurya and Gupta times; and the scattered references that we get do not point to anything like irrigation levy (*udakabhāga*) which the Maurya state had been realising.[107] Nor

---

101. *HRS*, p. 61.
102. *Ibid.*, p. 62
103. *Sel. Ins.*, p. 372.
104. *EI*, XXX, no. 30, 1.20.
105. *AŚ*, II. 24.
106. *Ibid.*, II. 1.
107. *Ibid.*, II. 24.

does it figure in the long list of taxes from which brāhmaṇas or grantees were exempted in the post-Maurya[108] and Gupta inscriptions.

The absence of irrigation tax in our period might have been at least in part due to the fact that the state generally ceased to bear the main responsibility for irrigation and consequently could not claim any cess for that reason.[109] Manu's injunction against the seizure of houses, tanks, orchards, and fields by others may mean that tanks were owned and constructed by individuals for irrigational purposes.[110] Manu ordains that amongst other things selling one's own tank, garden, wife or child is a sin to be expiated by penance.[111] Again, Nārada states that if a man were to repair a dike without the permission of its owner, he would not be entitled to profit out of it.[112] Thus the law-books seem to suggest some kind of individual ownership of irrigation tanks, dams, reservoirs etc., which, in turn, means that irrigation might have been to a certain extent an individual concern. Dion Chrysostom (c. A.D. 50-117) also informs us that in order to convey water from large and small rivers in India the local inhabitants made many channels.[113]

That the individual initiative perhaps played a considerable part is borne out by a number of inscriptions from the Śaka-Kuṣāṇa period. The Mount Banj inscription[114] of the year 102, the Paja inscription of the Year[115] 111 (A.D. 27) and the Peshwar Museum inscription No. 21[116] record private donations of wells, and the undated Karnal inscription[117] and Kaladana inscription

---

108. R. S. Sharma, *Proc. of the Indian History Congress*, 1957, p. 63.
109. *Ibid.*
110. *Manu*, VIII. 264.
111. *Ibid.*, XI. 62
112. *Nārada*, XI. 20. cf. *Yāj.*, II. 157.
113. Oratio, XXXV; 434, McCrindle, *Ancient India as described in Classical Literature*, p. 175.
114. *CII*, II, pt. 1, p. 55.
115. *Ibid.*, p. 63.
116. *Ibid.*, p. 155.
117. *Ibid.*, p. 179.

of the year 113[118] mention gifts of tanks by private individuals.[119] The Tusam Rock inscription,[120] which palaeographically belongs to the fifth century A.D., records the construction of two reservoirs, for the use of God Viṣṇu, by an Ācārya Somatrāta. Besides, some kind of cooperative effort in the sphere of irrigation can also be gleaned from our sources. Manu's injunction[121] against a villager who fails to do his best in repairing breach in the embankment of water courses implies cooperative efforts by the villagers for the construction of embankment, irrigation works etc., under the aegis of the state.[122] Sources are mostly silent on this point, though some Śaka inscriptions refer to the gift of wells and tanks by *sahayaṇa*,[123] a word whose actual import is uncertain. Sten Konow takes this term to mean some kind of association or fraternity, though he has not been able to make any suggestion about its nature.[124] Whatever may be its meaning, it is clear from a passage of Bṛhaspati[125] that in the Gupta period guilds looked after irrigation dams.

All this, however, should not mean that the state entirely ceased to bear responsibility for irrigation. The Hathigumpha inscription[126] of Khāravela, the Junagadh inscriptions of Rudra-

118. *Ibid.*, p. 65.
119. Though most of these epigraphs refer to North-Western India the provenance of some similar records indicates that wells, tanks, reservoirs etc., were often gifted out in most parts of Northern India. Vide *Lüders' List* No. 82 which refers to Mathura, and the Gunda Inscription of the Kṣatrapa Rudrasimha, dated A.D. 181 (*EI*, XVI, no. 17(1) 11. 4-5) which mentions a place in north Kathiawad region.
120. *CII*, III, no. 67.
121. *Manu*, IX. 272.
122. Sharma, *op. cit.*, p. 63.
123. *CII*, II, pt. 1, pp. 22, 29, 54 etc.; *EI*, XIX, no. 33, 1. 4. A variation of *sahayaṇa* is recorded in some epigraphs as *sahayara* (CII, II, pt. 1, p. 79).
124. *CII*, II, pt. 1, p. 22.
125. *Bṛhaspati*, XVII, 11-12.
126. *EI*, XX, no. 7, 1. 3.

dāman,[127] and of Skanda Gupta[128] among others testify to the royal initiative in this sphere. It appears, however, that the state spent its resources only on the implementation of comparatively bigger projects, beyond the means of an individual. Thus with limited state initiative in the sphere of irrigation in our period, there remained perhaps no justification for any regular irrigation levy (*udakabhāga*) of the Maurya period.

The disappearance of the Mauryan *udakabhāga* in our period need not necessarily mean a fall in the burden of taxation. For unlike the terms discussed above, we come across certain fiscal expressions such as *uparikara* and *udraṅga,* which are mentioned only in the inscriptions from the Gupta period[129] onwards and do not occur in any of the pre-Gupta sources. According to Fleet[130] the word *uparikara* is derived from *upari* or *upri* and means "a tax levied from the cultivators who had no proprietory rights in the soil". In the inscriptions, however, the word is recorded invariably with *udraṅga,* and this has led Ghoshal to suggest that the two fiscal terms are used antithetically. He thus explains *udraṅga* as a tax levied from the permanent tenants and *uparikara* as a tax imposed on the temporary ones.[131] He associates *uparikara* with the Marathi word *upri,* which means a cultivator not belonging originally to a village, but residing and occupying land in it, either upon a lease for a stipulated term of years, or at the pleasure of the proprietor. The evidence for this, it has been suggested, is very tenuous, since the Marathi language developed ten centuries after the date of our inscriptions, and it is rash to draw

127. *Ibid.,* VIII, no. 6, ll. 9-16.

128. *CII,* III, no. 14, l. 17.

129. *CII,* III, no. 21, l. 12 ; no. 22, l. 16 ; no. 23 ; l. 7 ; no. 26, l. 8 ; no. 29, l.9 ; no. 31, l. 8 ; no. 38, l. 26 ; *EI,* VIII, no. 28, l. 17. Senart thinks that *sakarukara* of a Sātavāhana grant (*EI,* VII, no. 7 (14), l. 3) is the natural equivalent of *sodraṅga soparikara.* This view, as Senart himself recognises, is wholly conjectural, although there is nothing improbable in the *udraṅga* and *uparikara* taxes going back to the Sātavāhana period (*HRS,* pp. 188-189).

130. *CII,* III, p. 98, n. 1.

131. *HRS,* p. 210.

conclusions from such feeble linguistic evidence.[132] The same is true of Fleet's interpretation. Moreover, in most of the land grants two terms occur together, and if *uparikara* and *udraṅga* mean taxes on temporary and permanent tenants respectively, it would imply that a certain piece of donated land was cultivated both by permanent and temporary tenants simultaneously which obviously seems absurd. Of course, in the case of village grants[133] the presence of both types of tenants cannot be altogether discounted, but in the case of charters which record the grant of pieces of land[134] with the assignment of *uparikara* and *udraṅga* this could not have been possible. Nor is there any independent evidence to show that the government used to impose any extra special taxation on temporary and permanent tenants. There is besides no reason why the state records should distinguish the tax paid by the permanent tenants from that obtained from the temporary ones.[135]

Barnett rejects the view of Ghoshal, and suggests that *uparikara* is something like the Tamil *melvaram*,[136] i.e., crown's share of the produce. Accordng to Altekar,[137] on the other hand, *uparikara* is identical with *bhoga* which consisted of contributions in the shape of articles of provisions.[138] Both the contentions, however, appear erroneous in the context of the Gupta evidence. In the Karitalai Copper-plate inscription of the Mahārāja Jayanātha dated A.D. 493-94,[139] the terms *uparikara* and *udraṅga* occur as also the expression *bhāgabhogakara*. Therefore *uparikara* can neither be quated with *bhāga*, the crown's share of produce which is indicated by *melvaram* in Tamil, nor with *bhoga*. Since *upari* in Sanskrit, Hindi and Bengali means

132. Maity, *op. cit.*, p. 61.
133. *CII*, III, nos. 21, 22, 23, 26, etc.
134. *Ibid.*, no. 38.
135. Alterkar, *Rāshtrakūṭas and their Times*, p. 216.
136. *JRAS*, 1931, p. 165.
137. Altekar, *op. cit.*, p. 216.
138. For *bhoga* see below.
139. *CII*, III, no. 26, 11. 8-9.

'upon' or 'extra',[140] it perhaps has led Sircar[141] to explain *uparikara* as an 'extra cess'. But it must be acknowledged that none of the explanations so far offered is conclusive. The interpretation of the term bristles with difficulty, particularly because of the conspicuous reticence of the literary sources on the subject.

It is equally difficult to interpret the term *udraṅga*, which like *uparikara* occurs only in the land grants and not in the literature of the period. Bühler,[142] first of all, pointed out that the *Śāsvatakośa* gives for *udraṅga* the equivalents *uddhāra* and *udgrantha*; following this source, Fleet[143] takes *udraṅga* to mean the share of the produce usually collected for the king. But we have already noted that sometimes *udraṅga* and *bhāga*, which probably means the regular land tax, occur in one and the same grant,[144] and therefore it is not likely that the former could mean king's own usual grain share. Ghoshal,[145] on the other hand, interprets *udraṅga* as a tax on permanent tenants and has been supported by Sircar[146] in this contention. But the explanation is untenable for the reasons given above. Maity offers two alternative explanations. According to the first, *udraṅga* may have been an anomalous derivative of the Sanskrit word *udaka* and thus may have meant something like a water tax.[147] But, as has been shown above we have no independent evidence to prove the prevalence of anything like water tax in the Gupta period. According to another explanation given by Maity,[148] *udraṅga* may be the samething as *draṅga* which according to the *Rājataraṅgiṇī*,[149] a later work, is a watch-station, and the term may have stood for a police tax levied on the district for the main-

140. Maity, *op. cit.*, p. 62.
141. *Sel. Ins.*, *p.* 266n.
142. *IA*, XII, p. 189, n. 39.
143. *CII*, III, pp. 97-98. Altekar is also of the view that *udraṅga* meant *bhāga*, the normal land tax (Altekar, *op. cit.*, p. 216).
144. *Supra.*
145. Ghoshal., *op. cit.*, p. 210.
146. *Sel. Ins.*, p. 371, n. 5
147. Maity, *op. cit.*, p. 62.
148. *Ibid.*
149. *Rājataraṅgiṇī* (Stein's trans.), II, pp. 291-92.

tenance of the local police station. This view is more or less endorsed by Puspa Niyogi.[150] It is difficult to say anything with certitude either in favour or against the plausibility of this explanation. Probably, like *uparikara, udranga* also may have been a levy over and above the usual grain share, though any attempt to determine its exact nature will only be conjectural unless some fresh evidence is forthcoming.

The land grants of the Gupta period sometimes mention several other terms such as *halikākara,*[151] *ditya,*[152] *meya,*[153] or *tulyameya*[154] and *dhānya,*[155] none of which is referred to in any source other than the contemporary epigraphs. No indication is available in earlier or contemporary sources about the meaning of *halikākara,* which is recorded only in two land charters of the Ucchakalpa ruler Sarvanātha,[156] who seems to have ruled in the Baghelkhand region in the last part of the fifth century and the early part of the sixth. Ghoshal suggests that *halikākara* may mean a tax on ploughs.[157] What, however, may have been the precise nature of a tax on ploughs is not possible to ascertain. Maity opines that the above-mentioned term may connote an extra tax imposed upon the area which could be cultivated by one plough.[158] Although *hali* as a measure of land does seem to be the likely object of a special tax, there is evidence to imply that in later times land was sometimes taxed according to its area.[159] On the other hand, we know that plough taxes were levied from the people down to Mughal times.[160] Even though taxes on

150. Puspa Niyogi, *Economic History of North India,* p. 187.
151. *EI,* XIX, no. 21, l. 10; *CII,* III, no. 30, l. 13.
152. *EI,* no. 13, l. 6; XI, no. 21, l. 11
153. *CII,* III, no. 60, 1. 12 ; *EI,* II, no. 30 1. 8 ; IV, no. 16, 1. 9 ; IX no. 53, 1. 9 ; X, no. 16, 1. 15.
154. *EI,* VII, no. 22, l. 15
155. *Ibid.,* XXXI, no. 35, l. 12; no. 39, l. 21; *CII,* III, no. 38, l. 26.
156. The Sohawal Copper-plates of the year 191, *EI,* XIX, no. 21; l. 10. The Khoh Copper-plates of the year 197, *CII,* III, no. 30, l. 13.
157. *HRS,* p. 213.
158. Maity, *op. cit.,* p. 63.
159. *Cambridge History of India,* IV, p. 450.
160. *Ibid.,* p. 454.

ploughs and on the area of cultivation may have been in vogue in later times, this cannot be taken to suggest conclusively that *halikākara* stood for either. The exact meaning of the term, therefore, appears to be uncertain.

The word *ditya*, which occurs in the Surat plates of the Traikuṭaka king Vyāghrasena, literally means "that which is to be given".[161] The expression is recorded in the inscriptions as *sarvadityaviṣṭiparihārena* meaning exemption from all dues and forced labour. This may mean that *ditya* may have denoted all taxes except forced labour. In other words, the expression appears to have a very wide connotation.

The term *meya*, which is mentioned in some Eastern as well as Central Indian epigraphs of the Gupta period, is generally followed by the term *hiraṇya*. In the Madhuban Copper-plate inscription of Harṣa,[162] however, the term is recorded as *yathāsamucitatulyameyabhāgabhogakara*. *Tulyameya* here may be treated as an adjective of *bhāgabhogakara*, and the entire expression may thus mean the king's normal revenue in kind that can be weighed and measured. But in the Gupta records *meya* does not occur along with *bhāgabhogakara* which makes it likely that *meya* was a substitute for a general land tax known as *bhāga*.

The term *dhānya* also appears to have denoted the general land tax. Most land grants mention *dhānyabhogakara* in place of *bhāgabhogakara*, which shows that *dhānya* occurs in place of *bhāga*. The Kurud plates of Narendra, of the year 24, palaeographically assignable to tre 5th century A.D., however, record *dhānya* with *bhoga* and *bhāga*.[163] Again, a grant of the Maitraka ruler Dharasena II bears the expression *sadhānyabhāgabhogahiraṇyādeyaḥ*.[164] This may be taken to imply a distinction between *bhāgabhoga* on the one hand and *dhānya* on the other. Ghoshal suggests that probably *dhānya* was a fixed contribution in kind while *bhāga* a share of the produce.[165] The expressions

161. *EI*, XI, no. 21, l. 11.
162. *EI*, VII, no. 22, l. 15.
193. *EI*, XXI, no. 35, l. 12.
164. *IA*, VII, p. 72.
165. *HRS*, p. 219.

dhānya, meya and *ditya,* however, do not appear together in our inscriptions, which may imply that all the three carry more or less the same connotation, though *ditya* may have had a comparatively wider application.

It would appear from the foregoing discussion that several fiscal terms indicating taxes on land in the *Arthaśāstra* continued to be in use down to the Gupta period, though their precise meaning in the context of changing times may not be clearly understood. Thus such taxes as *bhāga, kara* and *hiraṇya* of the *Arthaśāstra* find mention not only in the *Smṛtis* but also in the land grants of the later period. On the other hand, terms like *piṇḍakara* and *udakabhāga* do not occur in the later sources, which may to a certain extent preclude the possibility of their existence in the Gupta period.

Certain new land revenue terms such as *uparikara, udraṅga* and *halikākara* appear for the first time in the Gupta period. In addition to these there may have been several other taxes in existence at that time, because the enumeration of taxes in the contemporary inscriptions is usually followed by the word *ādi* or *ityādi* (etcetra). We may add that in a few Pallava charters donees are granted land with eighteen *parihāras,* though all of them are not enumerated.[166]. The Basim grant of the Vākāṭaka king Vindhyaśakti II records as many as fourteen *parihāras.*[167] While all these may point to an increased burden of taxation, the incidence of all the taxes may not have fallen on every individual taxpayer.

166. *Sel. Ins.,* pp. 439-40 ; *EI,* XV, no. 11, l. 11.
167. *Ibid.,* pp. 408-9.

CHAPTER V

LEVY OF PROVISIONS AND FORCED LABOUR

The gradual disappearance of the Mauryan irrigation levy in our period and the non-mention of some of the Mauryan revenue terms in the Gupta sources should not be taken to be symptomatic of any fall in the burden of taxation. Apart from the king's normal grain share, most items of income in the shape of miscellaneous contributions from the agricultural class of earlier times continued throughout our period. We learn from Kauṭilya[1] that the superintendent of the slaughterhouse should take a sixth of the beasts of prey and about a tenth of birds, deer, fish and other animals captured, while a sixth of animals caught alive should be let off into the state forest. Megasthenes[2] also (according to Arrian) testifies to the class of herdsmen in the empire of the Mauryas as paying their tax in cattle. The law-books of our period do not refer to the different types of animals which find mention in the *Arthaśāstra ;* nor do they corroborate the statement of Megasthenes that only herdsmen were liable to contribute cattle to the state. Nevertheless, the law-books refer to what may be called a kind of tax on the cattlestock of the people Both Viṣṇu[3] and Manu[4] ordain that the king should take 1|50 of cattle. Patañjali refers to a flock of sheep as *avikaṭa,* and its owner, according to him, is stated to have paid a tribute or tax consisting of a ram to the king, which is called *avikaṭoraṇa.*[5] Bṛhaspati[6] also refers to the royal share in the cattlestock, though

1. *AŚ,* II. 26.
2. *HRS,* p. 39.
3. *Viṣṇu,* III, 25.
4. *Manu,* VII. 130-132.
5. *avikaṭa urano datàryavikaṭoraṇaḥ, Mahābhāṣya,* VI. 3.10
6. *Bṛhaspati, āpaddharma,* verse 6.

he prescribes the rate of 1|100 in this connection. While it may be inferred from the above that a lower rate of contribution in cattle was perhaps in vogue in post-Maurya times, there is nothing to show that only herdsmen were liable to such payments. It is not unlikely that the burden of cattle tax fell on the entire agricultural class and not on a particular section of the rural population.

No land grants of the imperial Guptas throw light on the cattle tax. The land charters of the Vākāṭakas and other Central Indian dynasties, however, give some indication of it. Most of the grants of Central India and the Deccan bear the expression *aparamparagobalivarddaḥ*.[7] Mirashi is of the opinion that "the use of the word *go* in addition to *balivardda* in the Vākāṭaka grants shows that the village was exempted from the obligation of giving to the state the first calf, male or female, of every cow in the village".[8] Ghoshal,[9] however, thinks that the term refers to the immunity from the obligation of furnishing cattle in relays for transport. His view is based on the interpretation of the term *aparamparabalivaddagahana*, which occurs in the Hirahadgalli grant of the Pallava prince Śivaskandavarman[10] and which has been construed by D. C. Sircar[11] to suggest that the expression refers to the immunity from supplying bullocks for the bullock carts used by royal officers when the latter went on tour. That the royal officers on tour may have been entitled to transport facilities is borne out by a grant of the Vākāṭaka Vindhyaśakti II,[12] which mentions the word *avaha*. The term *vaha* is often used to mean 'to carry',[13] and Sircar[14] takes *avaha* to stand for exemption of the villagers from carrying officer's load free of charge. Still another epigraph, dated A.D. 592, records exemption from

---

7. *CII*, III, no. 55, 1.27; no. 56, 1.28: *Sel. Ins.*, p. 409, 1.21; *EI*, XV, no. 4, 1.17 etc.
8. *EI*, XXVI, p. 155, n. 1.
9. *HRS*, p. 194.
10. *Sel. Ins.*, p. 439, 1.33.
11. Sircar, *The Successors of the Sātavāhanas*, p. 187.
12. *Sel. Ins.*, p. 409. 1.23.
13. Monier-Williams, *Sanskrit-English Dictionary*, *s. v. vaha.*
14. *Sel. Ins.*, p. 410, n. 1.

providing carts, presumably to the king's officers.[15] In view of these instances, Ghoshal's[16] contention that the villagers were made to supply draught cattle for the progress of royal officers appears convincing. Furthermore, in a grant of Prabhāvatīguptā[17] the word *aparampara* is followed by *apaśumedhyaḥ*, which, according to Sircar, refers to the custom of taking by the king animals such as goats, for sacrificial purposes. This may imply that cattle were provided not only for the transport of officials on tour but also for performing sacrifices. The purposes for which cattle are said to have been supplied to the state seem to imply that the contribution was perhaps occasional in the Gupta period, and not much in the nature of a regular tax as intended by the injunctions of the law-books.

The same appears true, as will be shown below, of many articles, which the legal literature includes in the regular body of king's income. Kauṭilya[18] makes a reference to contributions in raw materials and the like. With this may be compared the king's share of jungle products and the like mentioned in the *Smṛtis.* Viṣṇu[19] for instance, states that the king can take 1|6 of meat, honey, clarified butter, medicinal herbs, scents, flowers, roots, fruits, flavouring substances, wood, leaves and skin. Manu's[20] list includes grass as well. A passage of the *Viṣṇudharmottara*[21] may be cited to the same effect. Of the above-mentioned articles

---

15. The Charter of Viṣṇusena, *EI*, XXX, no. 30, 1.6.
16. *HRS*, p. 194.
17. *Sel. Ins.*, p. 414, 1.17. The practice of taking animals from the people for sacrifice is attested to by the *Mahāvastu*, which mentions king Surandarima as giving instructions to his people before a great sacrifice, in the following vein, "I shall offer a sacrifice with every kind of animal. So bring together all living things that live on land, those without feet, those with two, those with four and those with many." He is also stated to have issued orders to the fishermen asking them to supply all living things that lived in the water. (*Mahāvastu*, JJ. Jones (tr.) II, p. 92.)
18. *AŚ*, II. 35.
19. *Viṣṇu*, III. 25.
20. *Manu*, III. 130-132.
21. *Viṣṇudharmottara*, II, 61. 61-63.

meat, honey and fruits are obviously eatables; clarified butter may be taken to be some drink (*pāna*); wood and leaves may be fuel; and medicinal herbs, scents, flavouring substances, roots, flowers may have been necessary for different purposes in day-to-day life, while skins may have been used for preparing seats. In other words, most of the articles mentioned in the law-books constitute the main necessities of life; and Manu[22] ordains that the headman of the village should get all of what is daily payable by the villagers to the king in the shape of food (*anna*), drink (*pāna*), fuel and other things (*indhanādi*). It is not unlikely that the *rājapradeya* daily payable to the king or the village headman and the contribution of 1|6 of the above-mentioned articles indicated the same thing and not two different sets of payments. It would be not only extremely oppressive but also unrealistic to impose double impost on the same articles. Besides the rate of 1|6 is used probably in a conventional sense as in the case of basic land tax in the shape of the king's normal grain share.

The supply of provision by the villagers is further attested to by Gupta literary sources. We learn from the *Raghuvaṁśa* that when Aja started for his marriage, on the way he received cloth, grain and various other kinds of presents from the village people. Sometimes cowherds are described as visiting the king, when on tour, with gifts of newly made ghee.[23] Coming to the epigraphic material, though the land charters issued by the imperial Guptas do not refer to the supply of provisions, those of the Vākāṭakas bear the expression *apuṣpakṣīrasandohaḥ*.[24] This may be compared with a term in a Pallava grant of an earlier date which describes the gift-village as *adugdhadadhigahaṇa*, mening thereby that the village was rendered free from the obligation of supplying sweet and sour milk. A similar term for exemption (*parihāra*), *aharitakaśākapuphagahaṇa*, occurring in the same Pallava grant,

22. *Yāni rājapradeyāni pratyahaṁ grāmavāsibhiḥ* |
annapānendhanādīni grāmikastānyavāpnuyāt ||
—Manu, VII. 118.

23. *Raghu*, I. 45; V. 41.

24. *EI*, XV, no. 4, l. 17; XXII, no. 14, l 31; XXIV, no 10, l. 22; no. 37 (B), l. 20; XXVI, no. 21, l. 26; no. 16, l. 29; no. l. 19 etc.

signifies immunity from the supply of myrobalans, vegetables and flowers. When we compare the Vākāṭaka term *apuṣpakṣīrasandohaḥ* with the Pallava expression, it seems to refer to the immunity from the burden of supplying flowers and milk to the king's officers. Again, the Vākāṭaka inscriptions often record *acārāsanacarmāṅgārah*, which, according to Fleet,[26] means that the grant of land did not carry with it the right to pasturage, hides and charcoal. Ghoshal,[27] however, thinks that the term refers among other things to the immunity from the obligation of furnishing skins for seats to the wandering spies and charcoal for fuel. Certain inscriptions make very explicit reference to the supply of necessary things by the village people. The Basim plates of Vindhyaśakti II, for instance, record *akhaṭṭacollakaveṇesika*, which according to Mirashi, means immunity from providing cot, water-pots and servants, presumably to royal officers.[28] The Nagardhan plates of Svāmirāja dated A.D. 573 mention the term *jemakakara*,[29] which has been interpreted to mean a cess levied on the villagers for providing boarding to royal officers camping in the village; and most probably it belongs to this category of payments. Similarly, another epigraph referred to above[30] records an exemption according to which the inhabitants of an area are freed from the obligation of supplying beds or couches, seats and boiled rice to the king's officers when on tour. All these suggest the possibility that most of the above-mentioned articles listed in the legal literature as taxable may have been contributed in the form of provisions for the touring royal officers in the Gupta period.

Thus while the Smṛtis refer to such contributions in the sense of regular imposts payable at the rate of 1|6, the inscriptions

---

25. The Hirahadagalli Copper-plate inscription of Śivaskandavarman, *Sel. Ins.*, p. 437, l. 31. See also Sircar, *The Successors of the Sātavāhanas*, pp. 192-193.
26. *CII*, III, p. 242.
27. *HRS*. p. 195.
28. *EI*, XXVI, no. 20, l. 22.
29. *EI*, XXVII, no. 1, l. 19. For Mirashi's explanation see *Ibid*.
30. Charter of Viṣṇusena, *EI*, XXX, no. 30, 1. 6.

of the Gupta period mention them more or less as exactions realisable from the village folk at the time of the officer's visit. Besides, the contribution in meat, honey, clarified butter etc., which find mention in the *Smṛtis,* would comprise almost all the agricultural occupations of a simple village community,[31] and the lawgivers apparently seem to have in mind that no source of agricultural income should be left untaxed. But how far in practice these exactions were in the nature of taxes on various occupations in the countryside is largely a matter of speculation. No less conjectural is the view that the rate of 1|6 was rigidly observed in post-Maurya and Gupta times; after all, the mention of the rate of 1|6 for such contributions may have been only traditional and figurative. In any case, at least in the Gupta age, provisions seem to have been occasionally supplied to royal officers on tour. This may imply that what the law-books apparently include in the body of king's regular receipts was only periodically levied in the Gupta period.

Some of our sources—especially the land grants of Northern India—do not, however, enumerate the above-mentioned dues paid by the villages; instead they use the fiscal expression *bhoga.* The inscriptions other than those of the Pallavas and the Vākāṭakas record *bhāgabhogakara,*[32] which Ghoshal takes as one compound word. But this does not seem to be convincing. In a passage of the *Arthaśāstra*[33] persons taking fields and embanked reservoirs (*setu*) on lease from private owners on condition of rendering *bhāgabhoga* are distinguished from those who hold the same on condition of *avakraya* (annual rent), *prakraya* (stipulated price), *adhi* (mortgage) and so forth. Here *bhāgabhoga* is, according to Ghoshal, a specific share of the resulting product; and on this basis he interprets *bhāgabhogakara* as a definite portion of the agricultural produce payable to the king.[34] This would imply that the king's normal grain share was often indicated by the term

31. *HRS,* p. 63.
32. *HRS,* p. 214.
33. *AŚ,* III, 9.
34. *HRS,* p. 214.

bhāga in the *Arthaśāstra* and *bali* in the *Smṛtis*. But this contention appears to be of doubtful validity in view of a passage of Manu,[35] who states that the king who takes his share in kind (*bali*), his taxes (*kara*), tolls and duties (*śulka*), daily presents and fines (*pratibhāga*) without giving protection soon sinks into hell. The word *pratibhāga* is interpreted by Medhātithi and Kullūka[36] as the daily presents of fruits, vegetables etc. Although Nārāyaṇa and Rāghavānanda[37] read it as *pratibhoga*, they do not suggest any change in its meaning. In our opinion the term *bhoga* of the Gupta inscriptions seems to be identical with the terms *pratibhāga* or *pratibhoga*; hence Ghoshal's opinion that *bhoga* stands for the king's normal grain share known as *bhāga* or *bali* cannot be accepted.

The Gupta land grants record the expression *bhāgabhoga-kara*[38] which, as noted earlier, has been taken to be one comprehensive term. But in certain land charters we have the terms in a reversed order, viz., *bhogabhāga*.[39] If *bhoga* is a part of the composite expression *bhāgabhogakara*, as Ghoshal thinks it is, we do not know how to explain the occurrence of the terms of the compound in a reversed order. Moreover, *bhāga* is often separately used to denote the normal royal share of the agricultural produce.[40] In all likelihood, therefore, *bhoga* of the inscriptions is a fiscal expression meaning something different from *bhāga*, the main item of land revenue.

On the basis of the Rāṣṭrakūṭa records Altekar argues that since *bhoga* and *uparikara* do not occur in one and the same grant, both the terms may have been synonymous.[41] But this argument does not apply to our period. In the Khoh Copper-plate inscription of Sarvanātha (A.D. 513) *uparikara* is mentioned along with

35. *Manu*, VIII. 307.
36. Commentary on *Manu*, VIII. 307.
37. See Bühler, *The laws of Manu*, SBE, XXV, p. 307n.
38. See above.
39. The Mallar plates of Jayarāja, year 5 (*EI*, XXXIII, no. 29, l. 11).
40. *Supra.*
41. Altekar, *op. cit.*, pp. 216-217.

bhoga.[42] Again, in an inscription of the later period,[43] the two words are recorded together. Thus at least in our period, *bhoga* could not have been the same thing as *uparikara.* The nature of the dues comprehended by the term *bhoga,* however, can be determined from the above-mentioned commentaries on Manu VIII. 307, according to which it constitutes contributions in the form of vegetables, fruits, flowers, grain, etc. Elsewhere Manu[44] ordains that villagers should furnish food, drink and fuel etc., (*annapānendhanādi*) to the king, though he does not use the word *bhoga* or *pratibhoga* in this context. If, however, credence be given to the commentators' explanation of *pratibhāga,* it may be conjectured that contributions in the form of food, drink, fuel, etc., also came under the category of *bhoga.* In the light of what has been stated above, therefore, Sircar's[45] interpretation of *bhoga* as periodical supplies of fruits, firewood, flowers, etc., which the villagers had to furnish to the king, appears tenable. Moreover, the articles that are included in this category are obviously provisions, and it is reasonable to suppose that the *bhoga* may be the same as the right of enjoying a portion of flowers, milk, hide, charcoal etc., of the Vākāṭaka inscriptions.[46]

An important item of the king's income which may be discussed under the present head is his right to forced labour (*viṣṭi*). Kautilya[47] refers to forced labour (*viṣṭi*) as one of the branches of *vārtā.* He lays down that śūdra labourers (*karmakāras*) and artisans (*kārus*) and *dāsas* should do manual labour for the state instead of paying taxes. This labour was recruited by some supervisor (*viṣṭivandhaka*) and was paid. Although *viṣṭi* was a source of income to the state in the Mauryan period perhaps it was not imposed on the independent peasantry in the villages.

---

42. *CII,* III, no. 28, ll. 9, 17.
43. *Ibid.,* no. 39, ll. 67-68.
44. *Manu,* VII. 119.
45. *Sel. Ins.,* p. 372. n. 7.
46. *Supra.* It seems that such *parihāras as apuṣpakṣīrasandohaḥ, acarāsanacarmāṅgāraḥ* etc., mentioned in the Vākāṭaka inscriptions are concrete substitutes for the term *bhoga* which is not used in them.
47. *AŚ,* II. 4.

It seems that the practice continued in post-Maurya times, for Manu[48] ordains that śūdras, craftsmen and artisans discharge their dues by work. He[49] also states that they may be made to work one day each month for the king. A passage of Viṣṇu[50] may be cited to the same effect. There is, however, nothing in the legal texts to indicate that like the earlier period, *viṣṭi* was paid for in post-Mauryan times. It is probable that forced labour was unpaid in our period, so that it was referred to as oppressive both in the contemporary epigraphic and literary records. The Junagadh inscription of Rudradāman[52] states that the Sudarśana lake was constructed with resources from the king's own treasury without burdening the people, among other taxes, with forced labour (*viṣṭi*). Similarly, in *Mahāvaṁśa*,[53] which is assigned to about the fifth century A.D., a king is stated to have declined to make use of unpaid labour. In other words, *corvée* was considered to be a burden on the people by those kings who were broadmined and benevolent.

As noted earlier Manu and Viṣṇu lay down that śūdras, craftsmen and artisans should discharge their dues by work, which implies their exemption from taxes. But in course of time the non-taxpaying artisans were made to pay taxes in addition to free labour which naturally bore heavily on the people. The tendency to realise taxes from artisans is already shown by Manu according to whom weavers should pay 11 *palas*, and in the case of failure of payment in time 12 *palas*.[54] Moreover, the *Śānti Parva* lays down that artisans and traders should be taxed after taking into account the conditions and nature of their crafts.

48. *karmopakaraṇāḥ śūdrāḥ kāravaḥ śilpinastathā*, Manu, x. 120. Kullūka in his commentary states emphatically that even in bad times taxes should not be imposed on the śūdras.

49. *Manu*, VII. 138.

50. *Viṣṇu*, III. 32.

51. *Milinda.*, p. 147.

52. *EI*, VIII, no. 6, ll. 15-16.

53. *Mahāvaṁśa*, XXX.

54. Quoted from *Vyākhyāsaṁgraha, steyaprakaraṇa*, pp. 1727-8 in *Dharmakośa*, I. pt. 3, p. 1927.

Assessment may be made on the basis of the number of commodities produced and taxes may be collected in kind.[55] That artisans were taxed in the Gupta period is borne out by the charter of Viṣṇusena, palaeographically assignable to last decade of the sixth century A.D., which informs us that the *chimpakas; kolikas* and *padakāras*, who appear to have been followers of particular professions, possibly had to pay as tax half the money that would be the price of the things produced by them, according to the rate prevalent in that area.[56] Besides, a number of Gupta land grants refer to the tax-paying *kuṭumbins* and *kārus* (artisans.)[57] It is beyond doubt that the *kārus* were mostly śūdras,[58] who in earlier times seem to have been non-taxpayers. There is, however, nothing to show that the tax-paying artisans were exempted from the usual *corvée*. On the contrary, an inscription, referred to above,[59] states that smiths, chariot-makers (*rathakāras*), barbers (*nāpitas*) and potters (*kumbhakāras*) should be recruited for forced labour. Thus the nature of impressed labour underwent considerable change in our period. First, whereas in the Mauryan period it was paid for, in post-Maurya and Gupta times it tended to become unpaid. Second, unlike the earlier period, it seems to have been realised in addition to regular taxes. Due to these factors, *viṣṭi* became highly oppressive in course of time.

The occasion for the demand of unpaid labour was perhaps not fixed. A usual pretext might have been that of engaging free labourers on royal farms and state manufactures.[60] It is known from the *Arthaśāstra* that forced labour was employed in warfare where its functions are described as consisting in (a) cleansing the camp, the roads, the bridges, wells and landing stages, and (b) carrying machines, weapons, armour, instruments and provisions,

---

55. *ŚP*, 88. 11-12. Note on 12 in Cr. Ed., *Rājadharma*, pt. 2, Fas. 19, p. 668.
56. *EI*, XXX, no. 30, Law no. 72.
57. *CII*, III, no. 26, 1.6; no. 27, 1.16; 60, 1.13.
58. R. S. Sharma, *Śūdras in Ancient India*, p. 233.
59. *EI*, XXX, no. 30, Law no. 72.
60. *AŚ*, II. 7.

the wounded soldiers from the battle-fields.[61] If the practice continued it must have borne heavily on the people, because wars became more frequent in post-Maurya and Gupta times. It can be inferred from a post-Maurya epigraph that *corvée* was demanded also for hydraulic constructions carried out by the state.[62] The *Mudrārākṣasa*[63] shows that forced labour was used also on such occasions as coronation. In any case there was perhaps no hard and fast rule as to when a king could exact forced labour and when he could not. This left scope for the abuse of the royal power.

The element of oppression may have been rendered stronger in the Gupta period, when the king's right to demand impressed labour was transferred to the donees who were the recipients of land grants. The use of the expression *sotpadyamānaviṣṭi* in many land grants means that the donee was entitled to the privilege of getting free labour as the occasion arose. The *Kāmasūtra*[64] of Vātsyāyana informs us that peasant women were compelled to perform unpaid work of various kinds, such as filling of the granaries of the village headman, taking things in and out of the house, cleaning the houses, working in the fields, purchasing of cotton, wood, flax, hem and thread, and the purchase, sale and exchange of various articles. This may not have been a direct source of income to the state, but may have been allowed to the village headman as a part of his remuneration. It seems that forced labour included all conceivable kinds of work, for which any special occasion was not needed. In short, the practice of demanding forced labour tended to become oppressive in course of time and may have anticipated the medieval feudal tyranny.

61. *Ibid.*, X. 15.
62. *EI*, VIII, no. 6, ll. 15-16.
63. *Mudrārākṣasa*, Act II, Scene 2.
64. V. 5.5.

CHAPTER VI

COMMERCIAL TAXES

Apart from land revenue, taxes on saleable commodities seem to have been an important source of royal income; and our sources sometimes indicate principles which probably governed the assessment of such taxes. Thus Gautama,[1] who probably belongs to an earlier period, tells us that the king should take a duty of 1|20 of merchandise along with one article every month. Evidently, the levy of the duty at the rate of 1|20 of merchandise implies assessment in kind, while the king's getting one article every month is reminiscent of the custom of direct contribution from the merchants.[2] The rule of Baudhāyana[3] appears to be an improvement upon that of Gautama in that according to the former the king should charge upon goods imported by sea a duty of 10 *paṇas* in the hundred together with a choice article, and for other commodities duties varying according to their intrinsic value without oppressing the traders. According to Viṣṇu,[4] however, the king's portion of *śulka* should be 1|10 of the merchandise of his own country and 1|20 of the merchandise of foreign countries. Unlike Baudhāyana, here we have two distinct rates of duties, one (properly called tolls) being levied upon internal goods, and the other (strictly called customs duties) being realised on goods imported from foreign countries.[5] Again, whereas Baudhāyana prescribes one uniform rate of 10 *paṇas* in a hundred on imported goods together with *ad valorem* duties on other articles, Viṣṇu lays down two different rates for foreign and indigenous commodities. What is more important, while the

---

1. *Gautama*, X. 26, 35.
2. *HRS*, p. 81.
3. *Baudhāyana*, I, 10.18. 14-15.
4. *Viṣṇu*, III. 29-30.
5. *HRS*, p. 82

rate of 10 *paṇas* in a hundred laid down by Baudhāyana implies the duty to be assessed in cash evidently after appraisement by experts,[6] the injunction of Viṣṇu is symptomatic of assessment in kind. The *Periplus of the Erythraean Sea*[7] speaks of foreign merchants bringing very costly vessels of silver, singing boys, beautiful maidens for the harem, fine wines, thin clothing of the finest weaves and the choicest ointments for Indian kings. But it is difficult to say whether these offerings constituted any regular tax in the nature of duty or merely tributes to be paid by foreign traders as a mark of respect to the Indian kings. In any case, the practice of realising dues in kind from traders does not seem to be unknown in post-Maurya times.

The *Smṛtis*, however, imply assessment upon the money value of the commodity. Thus Manu[8] tells us that the king should realise 1|20 of that which persons having experience of toll-houses and skilled in estimating the value of all kinds of goods may fix as the value for each commodity. Similar is the view of Yājñavalkya,[9] according to whom the king may take a duty of 1|20 of the estimated value, whereas the *Bṛhaspatismṛti*[10] in its *āpaddharma* section states that the king is entitled to 1|20 of merchandise, meaning thereby that assessment was perhaps made in kind. Thus the lawgivers of our period, excepting Viṣṇu and Bṛhaspati, seem to recognise cash assessment as the usual practice.

The question whether the above mentioned duty was assessed on the value of the commodity or on the profits derived therefrom has been a matter of controversy among the commentators. Thus the passage of Manu[11] quoted above is taken by Medhātithi and Sarvajñanārāyaṇa to refer to 1|20 of the amount of merchandise, while Govindarāja, Kullūka and Rāghavānanda construe the passage to mean 1|20 of the profit derived from the same. Mitramiśra in his *Rājanītiprakāśa* states that although the

6. *Ibid.*
7. *The Periplus of the Erythraean Sea,* Paragraph no. 49.
8. *Maun,* VIII. 398.
9. *Yāj,* II. 261.
10. *paṇebhyo viṁśakaṁ datvā, Bṛhaspati, āpaddharma* section, verse 6.
11. *Manu,* VIII. 398.

text of Manu refers to 1|20 of the value of merchandise, it should be interpreted to refer to 1|20 of the excess on the principal ; for if the king were to take 1|20 of the principal, the merchant would be ruined.[12] The apprehension that assessment on the principal may lead to the financial ruin of the traders is disproved by another rule of Manu[13] that the king should fix the market rates of articles after considering, among other things, the probable profit and outlay. This implies that even if *śulka* was to be assessed on the estimated value of the commodities, the price was so fixed as to leave a margin of profit to traders. The fact that merchant's profit was not adversely affected is borne out by still another injunction of Manu,[14] according to whom the king should levy taxes (*karān*) upon merchants after carefully considering the affairs relating to purchase and sale, the distance travelled, the provisions consumed and the charges of securing the goods. This verse occurs practically in the same form in the *Śānti Parva.*[15] Ghoshal[16] thinks that "the particular tax here mentioned is an impost upon the net profits of the merchants". In our opinion, however, the use of *karān* (the plural form of *kara*) in the present context does not seem to indicate one tax but appears to imply all taxes imposed on the mercantile class. Although the passage shows an appreciation of the difficulties in assessing merchant's profits, it should not necessarily refer to an independent tax on the net profits.

The principle of assessment on the estimated value of the article is further corroborated by the above-cited passage of Yājñavalkya.[17] Vijñāneśvara takes it to mean that the king should take 1|20 of the price as fixed by himself ; and here the commentator has probably market price in mind and not the cost value. The assessment of *śulka* on the basis of market price, however, is disproved by the fact that our authorities recommend regulation

12. *Rājanītiprakāśa,* p. 164.
13. *Manu,* VIII. 401.
14. *Ibid.,* VII. 127.
15. *ŚP,* 88. 11.
16. *HRS,* p. 85.
17. *Yāj.,* II. 261.

of prices by the state in a separate context, but prescribe payment of *śulka* at the toll-house.[18] Moreover, in connection with price-fixation, Yājñavalkya states that the market rates should be so fixed as to be advantageous both to the buyer and the seller after adding to the (cost) value of the commodity, the expenses incurred (transport, hire etc.).[19] Vijñāneśvara holds that this rule applies to foreign commodities, and states that their rates are to be fixed so as to leave a profit of 10 per cent to the trader on the price of the article, which has to take account of transport charges, tolls, etc. In the present context, the market rate of a commodity evidently includes the expenses of journey, the amount paid as toll (*śulka*) and a profit of 10 per cent presumably on the total investment. Thus the basis of assessment could not possibly have been the market price but the cost value of the article.

Whatever be the principles and modes of assessing taxes and duties on merchants, our sources indicate that *śulka* was the most important item of royal income under the present head. Perhaps the earliest mention of *śulka* as a tax occurs in the *Atharva Veda*.[20] In the *Dharmasūtras*, such as Āpastamba,[21] Vasiṣṭha[22] and Gautama,[23] *śulka* is a familiar fiscal expression, though it is treated in the *Arthaśāstra* at some length. In the *Arthaśāstra*,[24] *śulka* heads the list of revenue items to be assessed on the *durga* (the fortified town), whereas *vaṇik, nadipāla, tara, vartani* and other items are included under the heading of *rāṣṭra* (the country part). In view of this Ghoshal[25] rightly suggests that *śulka* is specifically the tax levied on merchants inside the fortified town and is distinct from the ferry duties (*tara*) etc. that are stated to have been realised in the country parts. This view is supported by Kauṭilya, who lays down rules for the col-

18. *HRS*, p. 83.
19. *Yāj.*, II. 253.
20. *Atharva Veda*, III. 29.3
21. *Āpastamba*, II. 26.9.
22. *Vasiṣṭha*, XIX. 37.
23. *Gautama*, X. 25-26.
24. *ĀŚ*, II. 6.
25. *Indian Historiography*, p. 177.

lection of *śulka* by *sulkādhyakṣa* (collector of tolls and customs) at the toll house (*śulkaśālā*) situated near the main gate of the town.[26] But it is also stated in the *Arthaśāstra*[27] that the merchants should pay their share of *śulka* in accordance with the usage of the ports, which may mean that it could as well be collected at harbours. Moreover, according to Kauṭilya,[28] *śulka* should be imposed on all types of merchandise, either coming from the country parts (*bāhyam*) or manufactured inside the forts (*ābhyantaram*), or imported from foreign country (*ātithyam*). The fact that foreign as well as indigenous articles were subjected to this payment suggests that here *śulka* indicates both internal toll and customs duty. Again, elsewhere it is provided in the *Arthaśāstra* that even those ships that touch a port on their way should be made to pay *śulka,* which evidently shows some of sort of harbour toll and not any duty on merchandise. Therefore the meaning of *śulka* as used in the *Arthaśāstra* cannot be determined with precision.

The exact connotation of the term *śulka,* as occurring in the sources of our period, is equally difficult to ascertain. Though Patañjali[29] mentions *śulka* as a source of income to the state, it is not at all clear whether it was an octroi or customs duty or simply a general tax on mercantile products. The *Śānti Parva*[30] also refers to *śulka* but does not indicate anything more than the fact that *śulka* was probably a tax realised from merchants and traders in return for protection given to them by the king.

The Buddhist literature also testifies to the prevalence of *śulka.* Thus a *Jātaka* mentions a city officer as fixing the toll (*śulka*) for merchants.[31] In the *Divyāvadāna,* which repeatedly speaks of tolls and other duties paid by the merchants, a house-holder summons by the ringing of bell all persons wishing to accompany his son on a sea-voyage without payment of *śulka* among other

26. *AŚ,* II. 21
27. *Ibid.*, II. 28.
28. *Ibid.*, II. 22.
29. *Mahābhāṣya,* V. I. 47. p. 351, 1.21.
30. *ŚP,* 72.10.
31. *Jāt.*, IV. p. 132.

things.[32] In another story, contained in the same work, a merchant similarly invites all persons who wish to accompany him on a sea-voyage without payment of *śulka* and other charges.[33] Though in these instances, *śulka* is associated with sea-voyage, we do not know whether its payment was made on the ingress or egress of the merchandise. Similarly, the *Jātakamālā*[34] of Āryasūra, dated about 3rd century A.D., alludes to *śulka* being levied from traders and townsmen but does not indicate its exact nature.

The evidence of the law-books in this connection is equally inconclusive. Viṣṇu[35] takes *śulka* to denote a levy upon commodities of both indigenous and foreign origin. Manu[36] merely states the rate at which *śulka* should be realised and does not state whether it should be imposed on foreign or internal articles, or on both. Yājñavalkya[37] states that the king should take as duty (*śulka*) 1|20 of the estimated value but does not show whether it applies to all types of goods. Unlike the *Smṛtis,* the *Amarakośa,*[38] which probably belongs to the Gupta period, renders *śulka* as what is payable at the ferries etc. (*ghaṭṭādideya*). Commenting on it *Kṣīrasvāmin* states that *śulka* comprises the ferry duties, the tolls deposited at the military or police stations, and the transit duties paid by merchants. But there is no contemporary independent evidence to suggest such a wide connotation of *śulka.*

So far as the epigraphic evidence is concerned, the Junagadh inscription of Rudradāman[39] (c. A.D. 150) refers to *śulka* as a source of income to the state, but does not indicate its precise

32. *Div.,* p. 4.
33. *Ibid.,* p. 501.
34. *vicitra paṇyakrayavikrayasrayaṁ vaṇijānāṁ paurajanāṁ tathā nṛpaḥ | napati yaḥ śulkapathopakārināṁ virodhamayati sa kośasampadā ||* *Jātakamālā,* XXXII. 67.
35. *Supra.*
36. *Supra.*
37. *Supra.*
38. *Amar.,* II. 8.28.
39. *EI,* VIII, no. 6, 1.14.

nature. The Bihar Stone inscription of Skanda Gupta[40] mentions *śaulkika* as an officer. Reference to this officer is also found in an inscription[41] from the Central Indian region, belonging perhaps to the last quarter of the sixth century A.D. According to Fleet,[42] *śaulkika* was perhaps the collector of customs and tolls (*śulka*), which implies the prevalence of *śulka* in the Gupta period. But none of these references suggests the exact scope and content of this impost. So for lack of sufficient data the exact connotation of *śulka* cannot be ascertained; but it can be said with a considerable degree of certainty that it was a tax on commodities realised from traders and merchants, and that it may have included taxes on both foreign and indigenous articles. Moreover, epigraphic records suggest that *śulka* may have prevailed in Western, Central and Eastern India.

The inscription from the Gupta period onwards often records the expression *savātubhūtapratyāya*. The Maliya plate of Dharasena II[43] mentions this term. But it occurs in the Alina Copper plate of Śilāditya VII[44] in reverse order as *bhūtavāta*. Fleet[45] explains that *vāta* is derived either from *vā*, 'to blow', or from '*vai*', 'to become dried or withered', and *bhūta* is the past participle of *bhū*, which means 'to become'. But he does not elucidate the term any further. Dikshitar[46] points out that according to the Śrīmūla Commentary to the *Arthaśāstra* by T. Ganapati Sastri, *vāta* includes the fruit and flower gardens from which revenue went to the king's exchequer; and that *bhūta* may mean 'produced or obtained from'. Thus according to him *vātabhūta*, treated as a compound, may indicate a tax on fruit and flower gardens. But this view cannot be accepted, because no contemporary source refers to fruit and flower gardens as an independent source of

---

40. *CII*, III, no. 12, 1.29.
41. Charter of *Viṣṇusena*, EI, XXX, no. 30, 1.2.
42. *CII*, III, p. 52, no. 3.
43. *Ibid.*, no. 38, 1.25.
44. *Ibid.*, no. 39, 1.67.
45. *Ibid.*, p. 170, n. 9.
46. Dikshitar, *Hindu Administrative Institutions*, p. 178.

revenue. Ghoshal,[47] on the other hand, translates the term literally as "revenue derived from winds and elements". But it is difficult to imagine what such a mysterious income might have consisted of. Maity[48] suggests that the two terms *vāta* and *bhūta* should be taken separately as different kinds of cess for the maintenance of rites respectively for the winds (*vāta*) and for the spirits (*bhūta*). This view, however, is too conjectural to be acceptable, for no contemporary source refers to such a levy realised by the priestly class for the maintenance of rites.[49]

We can get some indication of the meaning of the term on the basis of the Rāṣṭrakūṭa inscriptions, which give several readings of the term, e.g., *saṁbhṛtopattapratyāya*[50] *bhūtapatapratyāya*[51] and *bhūtavātapratyāya,*[52] the last of which also occurs in the inscriptions of the Gupta period. Altekar explains the term *bhūtopattapratyāya* as a tax (*āya*) on (*prati*) 'what has been taken in' i.e., imported (*upatta*), and what has been produced (*bhūta*) in the village. He adds that the expression *saṁbhṛtopattapratyāya,* if not a mistake for *bhūtopattapratyāya,* would indicate a tax upon articles manufactured and stored (*saṁbhṛta*) and the goods imported. Further, Altekar takes *vāta* of *bhūtavātapratyāya,* which occurs in Gupta records as well as in those of later times, to refer to articles imported (*vā,* III conj., to wish to gain, to invite, to invoke) into the villages. Thus he thinks, perhaps rightly, that these expressions refer to general excise or customs duties,[53] which, as already noted, are denoted in earlier sources mostly as *śulka.* This is further supported by the fact that *śulka* never occurs together with *bhūtavātapratyāya.*[54]

Though both *śulka* and *vātabhūtapratyāya* or *bhūtapratyāya* probably refer to taxes on commodities, it is not possible to prepare

---

47. *HRS,* p. 291.
48. Maity, *op. cit.,* p. 63.
49. Cf. Altekar, *The Rāshṭrakūṭas and their Times,* p. 228, n. 48.
50. The Konnur inscription of Amoghavarṣa I, *EI,* VI, no. 4, 1.40.
51. The Baroda plates of Karkka, *IA,* XII, p. 161.
52. The Kavi plates, *IA,* VI, p. 145.
53. Altekar, *op. cit.,* p. 229.
54. *Ibid.*

an exhaustive list of articles which may have been subjected to the above payments. Kauṭilya[55] lays down a fairly long list of mercantile goods with a schedule of rates at which *śulka* should be severally charged upon them. Among the post-Maurya sources the lawgivers Viṣṇu and Manu refer specifically to certain commodities from which the king may have realised his own share, but in all likelihood they refer to them as miscellaneous contributions from the village people, discussed by us elsewhere.[56] In any case, it appears reasonable to presume that most of the articles of trade and commerce constituted a source of income to the state exchequer, though, for lack of evidence, it may not be possible to state with certainty the names of all of them.

The tax on liquor, however, deserves special mention in the present context. Kauṭilya[57] mentions liquor (*surā*) in a class of goods paying a duty 1|10 or 1|15, while intoxicants (*madya*) are included in another class paying a duty of 1|20 or 1|25. The term *surā* also occurs at one place in the *Arthaśāstra*[58] as an independent branch of revenue under the class 'fortified city' (*durga*) in the classified list of constituents of the king's income. The superintendent of liquors (*madyādhyakṣa*), according to Kauṭilya, should arrange for the manufacture of spirituous drink and leavening stuff as well as for their traffic within the city, the country part and the camp, while their sale should be concentrated at one place or carried on simultaneously at many places or arranged otherwise according to convenience. Kauṭilya adds that a duty (*śulka*) of five per cent should be charged upon such liquors as are not royal merchandise and a 'compensation-fee' (*vaidharaṇa*) as well as 'indemnity fee' (*vyājī*) should be realised from the same after the inspection of the daily sale.

It is, however, curious that the sources of our period are generally silent about any tax or duty to be charged upon liquors. Manu[59] mentions three kinds of liquors (*surā*), *viz.*, those distilled

55. *AŚ*, II. 22.
56. *Supra.*
57. *AŚ*, II. 22.
58. *Ibid.*, II. 6.
59. *Manu*, XI. 94.

from molasses (*gauḍi*), from ground rice (*paiṣṭi*) and from the *madhuka* flowers or from grapes or honey (*mādhvī*), but he does not mention any tax on any of them. On the contrary, some Buddhist works seem to betrary an anti-alcoholic sentiment. The *Mahāvastu*[60] explicitly states that abstention from drinking intoxicating liquors and spirits is *dharma*. Similarly, Āryasūra in his *Jātakamālā* condemns drinking to be an exceedingly bad action attended with many evils.[61] It is not possible to guess how far such discouragements were effective, but Fa-hsien, who visited India in the Gupta period, seems to suggest that the India of his time was completely dry. He reports that throughout the country the people did not kill any living creature nor drank intoxicating liquors. He adds that there were no butcher's shops or distilleries in market-places.[62] If this testimony could be relied on, Ghoshal[63] remarks, the revenue derived from the sale of liquors (which seems to be an important source of income in the Maurya period) was conspicuous by its absence in the Gupta period.

But the possibility of the wholesale prohibition pursued by the Gupta state and the consequent total abstention from drinking may be discounted in view of the evidence furnished by the contemporary and later indigenous sources. Kālidāsa refers to liquor shops in streets and other places of drinking.[64] Not only men but also women seem to have indulged in drinking. Kālidāsa perhaps reflects the popular feelings of the time when he remarks that intoxicating lends a special charm to women.[65] The popularity of wine among the womenfolk is further attested to by the Mandasor Stone inscription of Kumāra Gupta I and Bandhuvarman, dated A.D. 475-76,[66] which describes the sun as of "a dark-red colour, like the cheeks of intoxicated women". Perhaps this comparison is one from real life. Apart from these

60. J. J. Jones (Tr.), *Mahāvastu*, vol. II, p. 96.
61. *Jātakamālā*, XVII, p. 100.
62. Legge (Tr.) *Fa-hsien's Records of Buddhistic kingdoms*, p. 43.
63. *HRS*, p. 192.
64. *Śāk.*, p. 188 ; *Kumāra*, VI. 42.
65. *Kumāra.*, III. 38. cf. *Mālavikā*, p. 49.
66. *CII*, III, no. 18, 11. 2-3.

testimonies, Hsüan Tsang, the Chinese pilgrim who came to India in the time of Harṣavardhana, writes, "There are distinctions in the use of their wines and other beverages. The wines from the vine and the sugarcane are the drink of the kṣatriyas; the vaiśyas drink a strong distilled spirit; the Buddhist monks and the brahmins drink syrup of grapes and of sugar-cane; the low mixed castes are without any distinguishing drink".[67] Since all these imply widespread practice of drinking, the evidence of Fa hsien in favour of prohibition and the resultant loss of state revenue cannot be accepted without question.

Still more authentic information is supplied by the charter of Viṣṇusena, dated A.D. 592, which refers to some sort of tax on wine. It states that if one was caught while distilling liquor, the fine was three silver coins, and the fine was 1¼ silver coins if no bad motive could be substantiated.[68] The same record further mentions *kalvapāla,* who is understood by Sircar to have been the same as *kalyapāla* which occurs in the standard lexicons in the sense of 'a spirit-distiller'.[69] Thus it is unlikely that in our period the state may have adhered to the policy of prohibition; nor is there any reason to believe that the state lost its income from the manufacture and sale of liquor.

Although we have no positive proof to show that the state in post-Maurya and Gupta times pursued the policy of prohibition which might result in a considerable loss of revenue, there are reasons to believe that the kings may have had to incur a tangible financial loss due to the transfer of income from commercial taxes and levies to private individuals. That toll receipts, like any other revenue, might be transferred to a royal favourite is borne out by a *Jātaka* according to which the king might make a bequest of them to whoever pleased his fancy.[70] Though the legal and general literature of our period is silent on the point, a few inscriptions from the Gupta period onwards bear

---

67. Beal, *Buddhist Records of the Western World,* I, p. 89.
68. *EI,* XXX, no. 30, ll. 17-18.
69. *Ibid.,* l. 19.
70. *Jāt.,* VI, p. 347.

testimony to the bestowal of income from commercial levies upon the recipients of land grants. Thus the Siroda plates of Devarāja[71] from Goa, assignable to about 4th Century A.D., records the gift of toll etc. in the village to two brāhmaṇas named Govindasvāmin and Indrasvāmin. Land grants, as shown above, sometimes refer to exemption from *bhūtavāta* (alternatively *vātabhūta*), which means customs duties or tolls on commodities. This privilege may not have benefited the taxpayers as such ; on the contrary, the income derived from the item known as *vāta-bhūta* may have gone to the donee instead of the royal treasury. Later sources show a growing tendency to transfer such incomes to private individuals, usually to the brāhmaṇas, with the consequent decline in the total receipt of the king.

Mention may also be made under the present head of *klṛpta* and *upaklṛpta*[72] which occur in the list of exemptions recorded in several Vākāṭaka inscriptions and have been variously interpreted by different scholars. The *Ārtha-śāstra* is the only earlier source which mentions *klṛpta* as one of the sources of king's income.[73] Shamasastry explains the term as a 'fixed tax'[74] and Ghoshal[75] shares this view. What, however, may have been the precise nature of this 'fixed tax' is not indicated by them. But Sircar suggests another possibility. He points out that since *klṛptika* means 'purchased' *klṛpta* may mean sale tax.[76] But this contention is not supported by any independent evidence. Maity, on the other hand, suggests that whenever *klṛpta* and *upaklṛpta* occur they are either preceded or followed by the expression *sanidhisopanidhi*, which indicates the transfer of the king's right over the treasure troves and deposits to the donee. Therefore, in his opinion, the terms *klṛpta* and *upaklṛpta* may refer not to taxes but to some royal right over the land, the measure of which is not clear from inscriptions or other

71. *EI*, XXIV, no. 19, 11. 4-7.
72. *CII*, III, no. 55, 1. 29; no. 56, 1. 30 ; *JASB* (NS), XX, p. 52, etc.
73. *AŚ*, II. 6.
74. *Ibid.*, (tr. Shamasastry, Seventh Edition), p. 58.
75. *HRS*, p. 293.
76. *Sel. Ins.*, p. 414, n. 8.

sources.[77] Maity's view, however, is too conjectural. No less so in the view of Mirashi, according to whom the terms in question correspond to *bhāga* and *bhoga* as well as to *udraṅga* and *uparikara*. But we have already seen that *bhāgabhoga* occurs with *udraṅga* and *uparikara*, which may imply that these expressions may have indicated different types of taxes. Therefore, *klṛpta* and *upaklṛpta* cannot correspond at once to *bhāgabhoga* on the one hand, and *udraṅga* and *uparikara* on the other.

Still another interpretation of the term is offered by Saletore. He associates *klṛpta* with *klib*, meaning 'accomplishment'[78] and holds that it may have been a tax on finished products. He adds that since *upa* as a preposition or prefix to verbs and nouns means towards, near to, by the side of, together with, under, or down, the charge *upaklṛpta* must have been a tax either on goods akin to finished goods or on goods which were not finished.[79] We may here add that the *Arthaśāstra* in its chapter on *nāvādhyakṣa* states that villages situated on seashores or on the banks of rivers and lakes should pay a tax called *klṛpta*.[80] On this basis, it appears reasonable to guess that *klṛpta* and *upaklṛpta* were imposed on the finished or unfinished goods of those villages which had greater facilities of trade because of their situation on seashores or on the river banks.

An important source of king's income under the present head appears to have been road cess, ferry charges or boat-hire etc. The *Arthaśāstra*[81] mentions *vartani* in the sense of road toll on all goods entering the state, collected by the officer-in-charge of boundaries. This tax may have been levied because of the use made of the king's highway. With regard to the prevalence of road toll in South India in post-Maurya times, Pillai writes: "The principal thoroughfares in the interior of the country were guarded by the king's soldiers, and tolls were levied on

77. Maity *op. cit.*, p. 67.
78. Monier-Williams, *Sanskrit English Dictionary*, s.v. Klib.
79. *Life in the Gupta Age*, p. 353.
80. *AŚ*, II. 28.
81. AŚ, II. 21; cf. Bhaṭṭasvāmin's interpretation (*JBORS*, XII, pt. 1, p. 125).

those highways".[82] But as regards Northern India, the contemporary literary sources do not indicate the prevalence of road toll. Coming to the Gupta age, one of the Valabhi records, however, refers to the *vartamanapāla,* who has been taken to be in charge of a tax known as *vartam,* probably identical with *vartani* of the Arthaśāstra.[83] Thus although our sources do not mention any kind of road cess, it is not unlikely that such a payment was received by the state during our period.

Another kind of toll consisted of ferry charges, realised for the use of the government boats in crossing rivers and known as *tara* in the *Arthaśāstra.* Kauṭilya deals with this item of royal income in his chapter on the superintendent of ships (*nāvādhyakṣa*) where he introduces us to a schedule of rates for ferry charges which are as follows :[84]

1. Small animals and men carrying small loads — 1 *māṣa.*[85]
2. Loads carried on the head or shoulders, cattle and horses — 2 *māṣas.*
3. Camels and buffaloes — 4 *māṣas.*
4. Carts of small, medium and high speed — 5, 6, and 7 *māṣas* respectively.

Among the works of the post-Maurya and Gupta periods, however, only the *Manusmṛti* provides a schedule of rates for ferry charges. Manu prescribes ferry fees (*tarya* or *tarika*) according to the following scale :—

1. An empty cart — 1 *paṇa*
2. A man's load — ½ *paṇa*
3. An animal and a woman — ¼ *paṇa*
4. A man without load — ⅛ *paṇa*
5. Empty vessels and men without luggage — A trifle.

82. K. Pillai, *Tamils Enghteen Hundred Years Ago,* p. 109.
83. Virji, *A History of Saurāshṭra,* p. 245.
84. *AŚ,* II. 28.
85. It was a copper coin.

Manu further lays down that for long distances along the banks of rivers the fare (*tara*) should be proportioned to the distance and duration of the journey, while he does not mention any settled charge for journey on sea.[86] Although other law-books of our period do not refer to any rate of ferry toll, some of them directly or indirectly testify to its prevalence. Thus Viṣṇu mentions fares to be paid at ferries.[87] A verse of Nārada,[88] who exempts the brāhmaṇas from the ferry toll, may be taken to imply the general practice of paying tolls at ferries. Bṛhaspati also refers to ferry tolls (*taraśulka*[89]). As already noted, the *Amarakośa* renders *śulka* as a tax which is payable at ferries etc.[90]

That ferry toll was in vogue is also borne out by two, if not more, inscriptions. Thus a second century Cave inscription from Nasik[91] mentions Uṣavadāta as establishing free-ferries by boats. Another epigraph, the charter of Viṣṇusena, referred to above, records a scale of fixed rates of crossing-fares for different commodities. It states that the crossing-fare for a boatful of vessels (probably of metal) was to be 12 silver coins; but if they were meant for religious purposes the charge was only 1¼ silver coins.[92] For a boat, full of buffaloes and camels, the fare was 5¼ silver coins, and no reduction is envisaged even if these were meant for religious causes.[93] The amount realised for a boat, full of bulls, was 2 silver coins; but only ¼ silver coin was charged if they were intended for a religious rite.[94] The crossing-fare for a boat, loaded with asses, is stated to be 1¼ silver coins,[95] while paddy (or grain in general) is mentioned as taxed at half the amount prescribed for a boatful of vessels.[96] Besides these, the inscrip-

86. *Manu,* VIII. 404-406.
87. *Viṣṇu,* III. 16.
88. *Nārada,* XVIII. 38.
89. *Bṛhaspati,* XXIX. 12.
90. *Supra.*
91. *EI,* VIII, no. 8(10), 1. 2.
92. *Ibid,* XXX, no. 11. 21-22.
93. *Ibid.,* 1. 22.
94. *Ibid.*
95. *Ibid.,* 11. 22-23.
96. *Ibid.,* 11. 23-24.

tion records crossing-fares (*sulkātiyātrika*) for other things such as ginger sticks, bamboos, and wine.

However, certain classes of people were normally exempted from the payment of ferry toll. Manu[97] ordains that no ferry fee should be charged from a woman pregnant for two or more months, an ascetic, a forester and the brāhmaṇas who are students of the Veda. Viṣṇu[98] almost concurs with this view in so far as he prescribes a fine to be imposed upon a ferry man or an official who takes a fare or toll from a student, or a hermit (*vānaprastha*), or a religious mendicant (*bhikṣu*) or from a religious pilgrim. Nārada, however, grants the right to cross rivers without paying any fare only to the brāhmaṇas. Moreover, he not only concedes them the right of precedence over others in crossing a river but also lays down that the brāhmaṇas should not pay any ferry fees even when they engage in trading and use a ferry boat.[99] But none of the inscriptions of our period speaks of the above-mentioned privileges being granted to the brāhmaṇas. Although the Nasik Cave inscription of the second century, referred to above, mentions the establishment of free ferries, it does not suggest that the free use of ferry boats was a privilege of only the twice born people. Nevertheless, in view of their highest social status, it is not unlikely that the brāhmaṇas were normally exempt from the payment of any charge for the use of boats in crossing the rivers.

97. *Manu,* VIIII. 407.
98. *Viṣṇu,* V. 132.
99. *Supra.*

CHAPTER VII

FINES, HEIRLESS PROPERTY, TREASURE TROVE AND OTHER MISCELLANEOUS SOURCES OF ROYAL INCOME

Although we have dealt with a good number of the sources of state revenue, there still remain undiscussed several other items of royal income, e.g., fines, heirless property, gambling, etc. Early Indian sources show that monetary fines may have accounted for a considerable part of the total royal income. Kauṭilya recommends punishment in terms of wealth as a right of the king to raise money for the royal treasury.[1] In a passage of the *Śānti Parva* also, the imposition of fines is mentioned as a source of filling the treasury.[2] Elsewhere in the same work, reference is made to the pecuniary punishmest in terms of gold (*hiraṇya*) or wealth.[3] Manu also refers to fines as a source of the king's income.[4]

The *Arthaśāstra* mentions as many as 350 sources of monetary fines.[5] The law-books of our period do not refer to so many items of fine, for the scope of the activities of the state perhaps became restricted. Nevertheless, their number in the post-Maurya and Gupta periods is not negligible. Manu and Viṣṇu mention 64 and 96 offences respectively which may entail monetary fines. Nārada enumerates 60 such unlawful acts, while the number increases to 85 in the law-book of Bṛhaspati. Kātyāyana, however, mentions only 62 offences for which punishment is prescribed in terms of money. Although these figures do not reveal any regular pattern, the number of offences punishable with fines seems to have considerably decreased in the post-Maurya anl Gupta periods.

1. *AŚ*, IV. 9-10.
2. *ŚP*, 72.10.
3. *Ibid*.. 160. 68.
4. *Manu*, VIII. 307.
5. Gopal, *Mauryan Public Finance*, p. 132.

In view of the divergence of opinion among the jurists about the amount of fine to be imposed in respect of a particular offence, however, it is not possible to ascertain the rate at which fines were imposed in practice. Thus according to Manu[6] giving a blemished damsel to a suitor entailed a fine of 96 *paṇas*, whereas, according to Yājñavalkya,[7] the same offence was visited with the highest amercement. Again, according to Manu[8] vaiśyas and śūdras defaming kṣatriyas were to pay 25 and 12 *paṇas* respectively as fine, whereas, according to Bṛhaspati,[9] they were fined 100 and 500 *paṇas* respectively. Similarly in the case of sexual offences Manu[10] prescribed a fine of 500 *paṇas* if a brāhmaṇa committed adultery with a brāhmaṇī, but according to Viṣṇu,[11] the offender was required to pay the highest amercement. In certain offences the lawgivers evince a tendency to increase the amount of fine. Adulteration of commodities, for instance, involved according to Manu[12] a fine of 200 *paṇas*, and according to Viṣṇu[13] a fine of 1000 *paṇas* but, strangely enough, in the opinion of Yājñavalkya[14] it was only 16 *paṇas*. Thus in the light of these divergent juristic injunctions it is not possible to say how far they influenced the imposition of fines in practice. Nevertheless, considerable income may have accrued from judicial fines, even though there may have been a fall in the volume of receipts from this source during our period, as can be inferred from the fact that the items of monetary

---

6. *Manu,* VIII. 224.
7. *Yāj.,* I. 66. According to Manu (VIII. 138) 200 *paṇas* are declared to be the lowest amercement, 500 are considered to be the middlemost and 1,000 as the highest. In the opinion of Yājñavalkya (I. 366), however, 1080 *paṇas* constitute the highest punishment, half of which is the middlemost amercement ; and half of the latter is declared to be the lowest.
8. *Manu,* VIII. 268.
9. *Bṛhaspati,* XX. 6-11.
10. *Manu,* VIII. 378.
11. *Viṣṇu,* V. 40-43.
12. *Manu,* IX. 286.
13. *Viṣṇu,* V. 124.
14. *Yāj.,* II. 245-246.

fines mentioned in the contemporary law-books are far less than those stated in the *Arthaśāstra*.

That fines may have constituted a source of royal income is further suggested by contemporary epigraphic evidence. The land grants of Central India from the latter half of the 5th century A.D. often mention the clause *coravarjjam* or *cauravarjjam*.[15] Other terms of a similar nature found in the land grants are *corarājapatthyakārivarjjam*,[16] *coravarjjitaḥ*,[17] *coradaṇḍavarjjitaḥ*[18] and *coradrohakavarjjam*.[19] The elliptical expression, *coravarjjam*, lit. "with the exception of thieves," can be explained, according to Fleet,[20] by the fuller expression *coradaṇḍavarjjam* which means "with the exception of fines (imposed) on thieves." Vogel,[21] on the other hand, took the above expression of the grants to signify the exclusion of the donees from the special privilege of persecution of thieves such as was connoted by the term *cauroddharaṇa*. Ghoshal, however, disagrees with both the explanations. He opines that the context in which the term occurs in the land charters shows that it was an immunity granted in favour of the donee and not a right reserved for himself by the donor.[22] Secondly, in his opinion there is no evidence to prove that the transfer of the rights of jurisdiction was ever contemplated as possible in respect of the pious grants of land. Thirdly, Ghoshal connects the expression *coravarjjam* with a passage of the *Arthaśāstra*, which mentions *corarajju* in the list of the king's receipts probably in the sense of a police tax levied from the people for protection from thieves and robbers.[23] In other words, Ghoshal seeks to establish that

---

15. *CII*, III, no. 21, 1.13; no. 23, 1.10; no. 27, 1.14., etc.
16. The Surat plates of Vyāghrasena, dated A.D. 490, *EI*, XI, no. 21, 1.10.
17. The Karitalai Copper-plate inscription of Jayanātha, dated A.D. 493-94, *CII*, no. 26, 1.9.
18. The Sohawal Copper-plate inscription, dated A.D. 510, *EI*, XIX no. 21, 1.10.
19. The Khoh Copper-plate inscription of Saṁkṣobha, dated A.D. 528, *CII*, III, no. 25, 1. 15.
20. *Ibid.*, p. 98, n. 3.
21. Vogel, *Antiquities of Chamba State*, p. 129.
22. *HRS*, p. 211.
23. *Ibid.*, cf. Dikshitar, *Gupta Polity*, p. 173.

coravarjjam was a tax for the maintenance of village police and its mention in donative charters according to him may suggest that the income derived from it was assigned to the donee long with the land itself.

Ghoshal's explanation of the term *coravarjjam* is, however, untenable. He holds that the context in which this term occurs cannot mean the reservation of a right by the donor, but this is not convincing. In fact, there is nothing unusual if a land grant which records certain privileges for the beneficiary makes certain reservations in favour of the grantor. Moreover, the Gupta period furnishes at least half a dozen instances of grants of apparently settled villages made to the brāhmaṇas by the large feudatories in Central India, in which the residents, including the cultivators and artisans, were expressly asked by their respective rulers not only to pay the customary taxes to the donees but also to obey their commands.[24] These records thus give clear evidence of the surrender of the powers of administration. But some of them also bear the expressions *coravarjjitaḥ* or *coradaṇḍavarjjam,*[25] which may suggest that despite the transfer of the rights of administrative jurisdiction the rulers retained their right to punish thieves, which was one of the main bases of the state power. Further, the similarity between *corarajju* of the *Arthaśāstra* and *coravarjjam* of the inscriptions is too far-fetched to justify Ghoshal's identification of the one with the other. In our opinion the mention of *coravarjjam* in Gupta and later land grants may mean the exclusion of the donee from trying thieves and robbers, which in turn, perhaps meant that fines accruing from them belonged to the state and not to the donee.

From the beginning of the seventh century A.D. onwards, the land grants often mention the expression *sadaśāparādhah* or *sadaṇḍadaśāparādhaḥ* (with ten offences) in the list of privileges granted to the donees. Frequent reference to it is made in the Maitraka charters of the Valabhi region.[26] According to Fleet[27]

24. *CII,* III, no. 26, 1.10; no. 27, 1.12 etc.
25. *Ibid.*
26. *IA,* V, p. 212; VI pp. 12, 15; *JBBRAS,* I, pp. 27, 31, 34, 35; *JUB* (NS) III, pp. 82, 84, 87; XIX, p. 6 etc.
27. *CII,* III, p. 189n.

the *daśāparādha* indicated traditional ten offences, consisting of three specified sins of the body, three of the mind and four of the speech; and he takes the term *sadaśāparādhaḥ* of the inscriptions to mean the donee's right to the proceeds from fines for the commission of these offences. Beni Prasad,[28] however, rightly points out the improbability of offences of the mind being made the subject of legal punishment, though he prefers to take the phrase in the sense of judicial fines in general. On the other hand, Jolly[29] connects *daśāparādha* with the list of ten grave offences, which according to Nārada comprised transgression of royal commands, killing a female, mixtures of castes, adultery, robbery, pregnancy caused by another man than the husband, abuse, insulting language, assault and procuring abortion.[30]

Apart from differences of opinion about the list of specific offences referred to in the clause *sadaśāparādha,* it has been generally taken to involve the donee's right to the proceeds from the fines for the commission of ten offences by villagers, which presupposes his right of jurisdiction over the offences concerned.[31] Ghoshal, however, thinks that "there is no authority for the supposition that the grant of rights of jurisdiction was even contemplated in the case of holders of religious grants" and that the term *sadaśāparādha* refers to the right of the beneficiary to be exempted at least in part from the ordinary penalties for the commission of some traditional offences by the villagers.[32] This view cannot be accepted. We have already seen that the brāhmaṇas were often granted land with administrative power;[33] and in view of the growing

28. *The State in Ancient India,* p. 303.
29. Jolly, *Hindu Law and Custom,* p. 270.
30. *Nārada* (SBE), p. 234, verses 11-12.
31. B. C. Majumdar, *JBORS,* II, p. 33n.
32. *HRS,* p. 220.
33. *Supra.* Kane, however, does not think it possible to hold that a king authorised a private individual or individuals to exercise judicial power in such crimes as murder when the power of dealing with *sāhasa* was not conferred on *śreṇī* or *gaṇa* tribunals (*Hist. Dhram.,* III, p. 265).

tendency of administrative disintegration and decentralisation it is not improbable that the right to try some of the traditional offences may have been made over to the recipients of the land grants. Moreover, Ghoshal's contention that *sadaśāparādha* meant exemption from penalties for offences does not appear plausible. The sources of the period provide for certain privileges for the brāhmaṇas, but they nowhere state that the brāhmaṇas were exempt from punishment if they committed an offence. On the other hand, Manu[34] and Yājñavalkya[35] both emphasise that there is none who is exempt from punishment in the king's court whether the persons be the king's father or teacher or friend or mother or wife or son or family priest or brother or father-in-law or maternal uncle. It is therefore not possible to agree with Ghoshal's view that the donees were exempted from penalties for certain offences. Besides, on the basis of later records Altekar[36] points out that the expression *sadaśāparādha* occurs also in the grants made to temples; and in such grants the use of the term in the sense of exemption from punishments can hardly have any relevance. In our opinion, therefore, the expression probably stood for the donee's right to the proceeds from fines for the offences. This, in turn, implies that fines constituted a source of income to the state.

The escheat of heirless property to the state appears to have been another source of royal income. Gautama[37] declares that the learned brāhmaṇas are entitled to the property of a brāhmaṇa dying without heirs (*anapatya*) although the king is to seize the property of all others in such cases. Similarly according to Kauṭilya[38] the king is to acquire the property of persons dying without heirs, after leaving a sufficient amount for the maintenance of the widow and the funeral ceremony of the deceased. The only exception to this rule was that the property of learned brāhmaṇas devolved upon those versed in the three *Vedas*. Almost identical is the

34. *Manu,* VIII. 335.
35. *Jāj.,* I. 358.
36. Altekar, *Rāshtrakūṭas and their Times,* p. 236.
37. *Gautama,* XXVIII. 41-42.
38. *AŚ,* III. 5.

injunction of Vasiṣṭha,[39] who mentions a list of heirs ending with the spiritual preceptor and the pupil, and who ordains that on failure of these last the king shall take the property except that of a brāhmaṇa whose wealth shall be distributed among those at home in the *Vedas*.[40] The rule prescribed by Viṣṇu[41] and Manu[42] is almost the same. An interesting application of these rules is furnished by Nārada,[43] according to whom when a travelling merchant comes to his country and dies there, the king should guard his property till the heir comes forward; if the heir is not found, the king should make it over to his kinsmen and relatives failing whom the king should preserve the property strictly for three years after which he should appropriate it to himself. Nārada ,and Yājñavalkpa concur on the point. According to the latter[44] the wealth of a trader dying abroad shall be taken by his heirs *bāndhavas*, kinsmen or his copartners who may have accompanied him, and failing these by the king. Bṛhaspati[45] is of the opinion that if a kṣatriya, vaiśya or śudra dies without leaving a male issue or wife or brother, his property should be taken by the king. That Bṛhaspati makes no reference to the property of brāhmaṇas in the present context evidently implies that the general rule of the reversion of intestate property to the state was not applicable to them. According to Kātyāyana[46] heirless wealth goes to the king keeping aside as much as is sufficient to provide for the women, the servants and the expenses of the *śrāddhas* of the deceased; but

39. *Vasiṣṭha,* XVI. 83-87.
40. Vasiṣṭha also lays down that the property of impotent and insane persons should go to the king, who is, however, bound to maintain the dispossessed persons. (XIX, 35-36).
41. *Viṣṇu,* XVII. 13-14.
42. *Manu,* IX. 188-189.
43. *Nārada,* III. 16-18.
44. *Yāj.*, II. 264.
45. *Bṛhaspati,* XXVI, verse 119.
46. *Kātyāyana,* verse 931. Incidentally, it may be pointed out that the rule of Kātyāyana is reminiscent of the *Arthaśāstra* passage quoted above which provides for the maintenance of the widow and the performance of the funeral ceremony out of the wealth of the deceased.

in his opinion the wealth of a brāhmaṇa learned in the *Vedas* should be assigned to other learned brāhmaṇas. Thus an important fact that emerges from all these rules is that all heirless wealth may have escheated to the state, the only possible exception being that of the brāhmaṇas.

Reversion of heirless wealth to the king is illustrated by a few instances found in the Buddhist and Brāhmaṇical literature. The *Saṁyutta Nikāya,*[47] which belongs to an earlier period, refers to a sonless miserly house-holder of Śrāvastī, whose vast property is carried after his death to the royal palace by the king's order. The same reference is repeated in the stories contained in the *Jātaka* commentary[48] and *Dhammapada* commentary.[49] Moreover, the *Avadānaśataka* relates the story of an issueless merchant who laments that although he is very wealthy, he has neither son nor daughter, and that after his death all his property will escheat to the king.[50] The *Divyāvadāna* refers to the lamentations of an heirless king who apprehends that after his death all his wealth will go to another king.[51] An important illustration is provided by Kālidāsa's *Abhijñānaśākuntalam,*[52] where we come across a minister informing the king of a sea-faring trader who perishes from shipwreck and whose goods should lapse to the king in the absence of any issue. But Dusyanta, the pious king, having heard that one of the wives of the merchant is pregnant, orders that the property should revert to the foetus in the womb. It may be gathered from the examples cited above that while, on the one hand, the attitude of the lawgivers is characterised by some amount of moderation in so far as they prohibit the confiscation of property even if a distant kinsman could become a successor, the Buddhist and Brāhmaṇical literature, on the other hand, seems to prove that the moderate rule of the *Smṛtis* was perhaps stretched in practice to make the property of persons dying without a male

47. *Saṁyutta Nikāya,* pt. I, (PTS), p. 89.
48. *Jāt.,* III, p. 299.
49. *Dhammapada Comm.,* IV, p. 77.
50. *Avadānaśataka,* p. 13.
51. *Div.,* pp. 439-440.
52. *Śāk.,* Act VI.

issue liable to appropriation by the king.[53] This is further supported by the charter of Viṣṇusena, assignable perhaps to the last decade of the 6th Century A.D. This inscription records the expression *"aputrakaṁ na grāhyam."*[54] *Aputraka* means the property belonging to a person who dies without leaving a son. This seems to mean that such property should not be confiscated by royal officials disregarding the claim of any legal heir other than the son. Since the expression *"aputrakaṁ na grāhyam"* records a privilege granted to the merchants of a town, it may suggest that the claim of any successor other than the son may not have been normally recognised by the king. Thus the application of the rules of the *Smṛtis* was often limited to the benefit of the state.

Another source of the king's income comprised treasure trove(*nidhi*) and deposits (*upanidhi*). In the early Vedic texts we have no evidence to indicate that the king had a royal prerogative on treasure trove. This idea seems to have originated when the earliest law-books were compiled. Gautama is perhaps the first lawgiver who declares that the treasure trove belongs to the king except when it is found by a brāhmaṇa who duly performs his duties. He quotes in this connection the opinion of some according to whom the finder, not being a brāhmaṇa, shall get 1|6 of the treasure.[55] Similarly according to Vasiṣṭha the king is to take the treasure whose owner is not known and give 1|6 to the finder, though brāhmaṇas are exempted from the application of this rule.[56]

Although Kauṭilya recognises the king's right over a treasure and includes it in the list of royal receipts from some other source (*anyajāta*), there is nothing in the *Arthaśāstra* to show that a

---

53. *HRS*, p. 114.
54. *EI*, XXX, no. 30, 1.4. In one of the later inscriptions (*EI*, III, p. 263 ff.) the term *aputtrikādhana* occurs among other revenue terms. It literally means 'the property of one who has no appointed daughter to raise male issue for himself,' which being ownerless came into the possession of the king (*HRS*, p. 237).
55. *Gautama*, X. 43-45.
56. *Vasiṣṭha*, III. 13-14.

brāhmaṇa finder of a treasure enjoyed the same privileged position, as stated in the earlier law-books referred to above. According to Kauṭilya[57] when any person discovers mines, precious stones, or treasure trove, he should immediately inform the state authorities, who should give the finder a sixth part of the find (and only a twelfth if the finder be a state employee). Apparently by way of exception to this general rule, Kauṭilya states that the treasure trove valued beyond 10,00,000 (*paṇas*) was wholly the property of the state.[58] In other words, Kauṭilya allows the finder his share, but he restricts the application of this rule to the treasure of less value.[59] Notwithstanding the royal prerogative, Kauṭilya gives due consideration to the claim of the original owner. He states that such treasure troves as a man of pure and honest life can prove to be his ancestral property shall wholly be taken by the man himself, but taking possession of the same without establishing such claim, and in secret, shall be punished with fines of 500 and 1,000 *paṇas* respectively.[60]

Coming to the law-books of our period, although Manu ignores the finder's reward of 1|6, he accepts the original owner's claim to the treasure. According to him when a person claims the treasure trove and proves his title thereto, the king shall take from him 1|6 or 1|12, whereas any false claimant shall be fined eight times the value of the property in question.[61] When, however, a learned brāhmaṇa finds a treasure, Manu permits him to take the whole of it, for he is the lord of all.[62] In the same context he further ordains that when a king finds the treasure, he is to give 1|2

57. *AṢ*, IV, 1.
58. *Ibid* IV. 1.
59. *HRS*, p. 121.
60. *AṢ*, IV. 1.
61. *Manu*, VIII, 35-36. These verses perhaps refer to the case when the original hoarder is the person reporting the find himself. Some commentators such as Medhātithi, Kullūka and Rāghavānanda think that the option regarding the 'sixth' and 'twelfth' part is based "upon the character of the finder," while according to Nārāyaṇa the amount to be taken by the king depends "on the caste of the finder," who in the present case appears to be the original owner himself.
62. *Manu*, VIII. 37.

to the brāhmaṇas and send the other half to his own treasury.[63] This passage not only emphasises the privileged position of a brāhmaṇa even when he is not himself the finder, but also seeks to establish the royal right over the treasure. The king, Manu further states, is entitled to take 1|12 of the ancient hoards and metals found underground by virtue of his ensuring protection and being the lord of the soil.[64] Since taxation as noted earlier, was often considered as fee for protection, the king could easily be understood to have the right to all treasure trove or at least a part thereof.

Like Manu, Viṣṇu also is of the opinion that when a king finds the treasure, he is to make over 1|2 to the brāhmaṇas and take the other half himself,[65] and like most of the lawgivers Viṣṇu thinks that a brāhmaṇa who finds a treasure should retain the whole of it.[66] Viṣṇu, however, introduces an element of caste consideration. Thus according to him when a kṣatriya finds a treasure he shall make over 1|4 to the king and a brāhmaṇa each and retain the remaining half; a vaiśya shall give 1|4 to the king, 1|2 to the brāhmaṇa, and retain 1|4 for himself; a śūdra shall divide the find into twelve parts, give five parts each to the king and the brāhmaṇa, and shall retain the remaining two for himself.[67] It is obvious that Viṣṇu not only allows a brāhmaṇa, finding a treasure, to keep the whole of it, but also provides for the payment of a stipulated portion to him even when members of other castes come across the same.[68]

63. *Ibid.*, 38.
64. *Ibid.*, 39. "In place of 1|2 in the above, Medhātithi has 'share' or 'part' in general, which he explains to mean 1|6 or 1|12 as mentioned in a preceding verse. But this forced interpretation is unnecessary, as the usual meaning of 1|2 fits in with the immediately preceding text" (*HRS*, p. 119, n. 1)
65. *Viṣṇu*, III. 56-57.
66. *Ibid.*, 58.
67. *Viṣṇu*, III. 59-61. Although the śūdra's share in the treasure trove is the smallest, it is double the share of the labour as provided by Kauṭilya.
68. The *Niśīthacurṇi* refers to a king who confiscated the treasure trove discovered by a merchant but honoured a brāhmaṇa who discovered a similar treasure trove. (*Niśīthacurṇi*, 20, p. 281. Quoted by Jain, *Life as depicted in Jaina Canons*, p. 62.)

Viṣṇu, however, does not seem to accept caste as a criterion for determining the royal share when a non-brāhmaṇa original hoarder claims the treasure; for he states that, of a treasure anciently hidden, members of all castes, excepting brāhmaṇas shall give a twelfth part to the king.[69]

While Yājñavalkya is silent about the right of the original owner of the treasure, he states that if the treasure is found by any one, barring a brāhmaṇa, the king is to take it after paying 1|6 to the finder.[70] This rule is mentioned, as has been seen above, in the works of Gautama, Vasiṣṭha and Kauṭilya, but not in those of Manu and Viṣṇu. Yājñavalkya, however, concurs with the two last-named jurists; he maintains that when the king finds a treasure he is to share it equally with the brāhmaṇas.[71] The privileged status of a brāhmaṇa finder as known from the other *Smṛtis* is, in fact, also upheld by Yājñavalkya, according to whom if a learned brāhmaṇa finds a treasure, he is to keep the whole of it, for he is the lord of all.[72]

The view of Nārada, however, is expressed in a cryptic language. In his opinion, when a person discovers a treasure deposited by others, he is to present it to the king, for all treasures

69. *Viṣṇu*, III. 63.

70. *Yāj.*, II. 35. On the basis of the interpretation of Vijñāneśvara this verse may be translated as follows: "The king should give a sixth part of treasure trove found by any other person. In case when information is not given by the finder, he (the finder) must be made to pay a fine (in addition to the king's share)." The plain meaning, however, could be that the king was to take 1|6 of the treasure found. The latter meaning may have led Jolly to think that the later law-books with regard to treasure trove show a departure from the original theory, inasmuch as the king is less thought of in later examples. In reality, however, the tendency to restrict the king's rights to treasure trove is not seen before the famous commentator Mitramiśra who takes a passage of *Manu* (VIII. 39) to mean that the king should keep the other half of the treasure in his treasury so as to restore it to the rightful owner when he appears. (*HRS*, p. 122).

71. *Yāj.*, II. 34.

72. *Ibid.*, II. 34

other than those found by the brāhmaṇas go to the latter.[73] Again, when a brāhmaṇa finds the treasure, he is also to announce it to the king, and he may take it after it has been given by the latter.[74] While the announcement of the discovery of a treasure by a brāhmaṇa to the king gives top priority to the latter's right over the same, the injunctions of Nārada are silent about the reward of 1|6 to the finder[75] and the person who may claim the treasure and prove his ownership over it.

The king's right over treasure troves and deposits is further corroborated by a number of land grants of the Vākāṭaka-Gupta period. The land charters of the Vākāṭakas, for instance, mention *sanidhi* and *sopanidhi* in the list of privileges granted to the beneficiaries.[76] These terms as occurring in numerous epigraphic records of the period have been taken to denote treasure troves and deposits, and their mention along with other privileges may mean that the donees were perhaps given the right over all treasures found in the land that was donated. This in turn indicates that treasure troves and buried wealth were perhaps normally thought to belong to the king.

Gambling also appears to have been a source of royal income. The *Arthaśāstra* includes gambling (*dyūta*) in the list of the various constituents of state income under the head 'fortified city.' While treating the law of gambling and betting Kauṭilya introduces us to the superintendent of gambling (*dyūtādhyakṣa*), who is required

73. *Nārada*, VII. 6.
74. *Ibid.*, VII. 7.
75. It has been shown above that some authorities often mention 1|6 of the treasure as the share of the finder whereas others state 1|6 or 1|12 as being taken by the king when the treasure is claimed by its original owner. The usual tax rate claimed by the king was also perhaps 1|6, though the rate of 1|12 was also not unknown (see Manu quoted above). On this basis one may suggest some kind of relationship between the theories of treasure trove and those of taxation. For want of evidence, however, nothing can be said with certainty. (Cf. *JNSI*, XXIII, Golden Jubilee Number, p. 136, n. 2).
76. Most of the Vākāṭaka charters bear these expressions. The Rāṣṭrakūṭa records use the expression *nidhinikṣepasametaḥ* in this connection (cf. *IA*, II, p. 301 ; XIX, p. 346 etc.).

to confine the play to one place and levy a fine of 12 *paṇas* from those playing elsewhere.[77] The superintendent is, further, instructed to take from the winner a tax of 5 per cent on the stakes won, together with the fees for supplying water, accommodation, dice and other accessories of play.[78] Although the *Arthaśāstra* recognises gambling as a source of royal income, it also points out its evils. According to Kauṭilya lack of recognition of wealth properly acquired, açquisition of ill-gotten wealth, loss of wealth without enjoyment, staying away from answering the calls of nature, and contracting diseases from not taking timely meals are the evils of gambling.[79] Kauṭilya adds that it is especially due to gambling that assemblies and royal confederacies possessing characteristics of assemblies are split into factions and are consequently destroyed.[80] Notwithstanding these evils, Kauṭilya allows gambling perhaps on account of the income derived from it as well as for political purposes, viz., to find out spies, spendthrifts and thieves.[81]

Like the *Arthaśāstra,* the law-books of our period maintain a twofold attitude towards gambling; while some of them place it under a ban on moral grounds, others sanction it in the interest of the king's treasury. Manu,[82] for instance, ordains that the king should punish gamblers because they afflict the good subjects. At another place Manu[83] includes gamblers in a class of thorns by the side of the king's subjects. The same attitude is also shown in the *Śānti Parva,*[84] which states that liquor-shops, pimps and prostitutes, gamblers and keepers of gaming houses and such other persons as are sources of disorder to the state should all be checked. A passage from Nārada,[85] however, may be cited to the effect that

77. *AŚ,* III. 20.
78. *Ibid.* Dice were supplied at the rate of one *kākaṇi* per pair.
79. *Ibid.,* VIII. 3.
80. *Ibid.*
81. *Ibid.,* III. 19.
82. *Manu,* IX. 224-228.
83. *Ibid.,* IX. 258.
84. *ŚP,* 89. 13-14.
85. *Nārada,* XVII. 8.

if a gambler pays to the king the share due to him and plays in public, he should not be considered as committing any wrong. Similarly, Yājñavalkya[86] allows gambling under state supervision on the ground that it leads to the detection of thieves, though, according to him, those who carry on gambling secretly should be branded and banished. Kātyāyana[87] pleads for total prohibition of gambling, but he lays down that if it has to continue it should be allowed to be done openly with an arch erected near the door of the gaming hall so that respectable men may not be mistaken about its real nature and that the king should make it yield revenue.[88] He adds that a gambler, after giving to the king his share, may carry on gambling openly without being guilty of any fault.[89] Thus it can be seen that whereas Manu prohibits gambling, other lawgivers permit it provided it is practised openly by paying a tax to the state.

Kauṭilya[90] lays down that a gambler should pay to the state at the rate of 5 per cent of the stakes won. Nārada[91] is of the opinion that the master of the gaming-house (*sabhika*) should arrange the game and pay the stakes which have been won, his own profit for conducting the game amounting to 10 per cent. Yājñavalkya,[92] however, prescribes two distinct rates for such payments to the person in charge of gaming-houses. He states that the keeper of a gambling house shall take from a gambler 5 per cent where the wager is 100 *paṇas* or more, and 10 per cent when the stake is less than 100 *paṇas*. Aparārka[93] explains that the *sabhika* was to receive 5 per cent from the victorious gambler and 10 per cent from the losing gambler. Further, according to Yājñavalkya the *sabhika* (master of the gaming house) should,

86. *Yāj.*, II, 202-203.
87. *Kātyāyana*, verse 934.
88. *Ibid.*, verse 935.
89. *Ibid.*, verse 939.
90. *Supra.*
91. *Nārada*, XVII. 2.
92. *Yāj.*, II. 199.
93. Quoted in *Hist. Dharm.*, p. 539.

beside conducting the play in the hall, pay to the king a fixed portion.[94] Kātyāyana lays down that the keeper of the gaming house should himself pay to the king the latter's dues after taking from the defeated party 10 per cent as his profit.[95] It appears that despite the divergence of opinion, the rate of 10 per cent may have received a general recognition. It may be further noted that the law-books do not prescribe any additional charge for the supply of dice and other auxiliaries of play as the *Arthaśāstra* does. It is, therefore, not unlikely that the rate of 10 per cent laid down in the *Smṛtis* may have included not only the king's share but also the fee payable probably to the *sabhika,* who is stated to have supplied the necessary things for gambling.

Apart from the above-mentioned items of taxation, the hitherto unknown tendency to impose taxes or levies on some religious or domestic rites seems to have begun crystallising from the Gupta period onwards. Thus the charter of Viṣṇusena records a privilege in favour of the local merchants in the following manner: *vivāhayajñotsavasīmantonnayaneṣu ca śulkaṁ na pradāpayet.*[97] This is interpreted by Sircar[98] to mean that ceremonies such as marriage were not to be taxed. But Kosambi[99] takes the above-stated clause to imply that there was no (frontier) tax to be charged on (people crossing to attend) a marriage, *yajña,* sacrifice, pilgrimage-festival, or a lying-in ceremony. In either case, it is clear that some sort of income was derived from those who performed certain domestic and religious rites and sacraments. This is further borne out by the same charter, for it records the caluse: *varayātrāyāṁ śulkādi(ti)yātrike rūpakāḥ dvādaśa; paṭṭakadhārmike rūpakaḥ sopādaḥ ru*1¼.[100] This clause, according to Sircar,[101] means that if the procession of a bride groom had to cross

94. *Yāj.*, II. 200.
95. *Kātyāyana,* verse 936.
97. *EI,* XXX, no. 30, 1.25.
98. *Ibid.,* p. 177.
99. *JESHO,* II, p. 289.
100. *EI,* XXX, no. 30, ll. 25-26.
101. *Ibid,.* p. 178. Cf. Kosambi, "Indian Feudal Trade Charters", *JESHO,* II, p. 289.

the boundary of the kingdom or district to reach the house of the bride, it had to pay the crossing fee of 12 silver coins; but if it was legalised by means of a *paṭṭaka,* a passport, the fare was only 1¼ silver coins. Thus not only the performance of marriage was taxed but the marriage party had also to pay something.

That the practice of taxing certain domestic rites and ceremonies continued in later times can be inferred from the fact that the undated Rajim plate of Tīvaradeva, who seems to have flourished in Central India some time after the eighth century A.D., mentions the term *dāradraṇaka* (marriage cess?).[102] The dictionaries give the meaning of *dāra,* to be cleft, gap, hole, ploughed field, a wife, but do not mention either the word *draṇaka* or the root by which it could be explained. Fleet is of opinion that *dāradraṇaka* may refer either to some agricultural cess or to a marriage tax.[103] It has been further argued that since the term is recorded in connection with the granting of a village, it is likely that the fiscal term denotes agricultural tax and not a tax on marriage.[104] Even if *dāradraṇaka* cannot be taken to mean a marriage-cess, later inscriptions conclusively prove that ceremonies such as marriage, *upanayana* and even attainment of puberty were subjected to taxation.[105]

Apart from the items of royal income discussed in the foregoing pages, notice may be taken of the group of sources of revenue which are essentially irregular in their character. We may begin by mentioning the rule relating to the fleecing of various classes of persons regarded as unrighteous and impious. An important instance of this kind occurs in a section of the *Śānti Parva,*[106] where the brāhmaṇas are divided into four grades, viz., those that are equivalent to the gods, the śūdras, the kṣatriyas and the vaiśyas respectively. With regard to the second grade of brāhmaṇas, it is stated in the *Śānti Parva* that the righteous ruler

102. *CII,* III, no. 81, 21-22.
103. *Ibid.,* p. 299n.
104. Saletore, *Life in the Gupta Age,* p. 353.
105. Altekar, *Rāṣṭrakūṭas and their Times,* p. 232; Cf. the receipts of the office called *gṛhakṛtya* in the *Rājataraṅgiṇī,* V, 157; VII. 42.
106. *ŚP,* 77. 2-6.

may realise from them compulsory labour (*viṣṭi*) as well as an agricultural tax (*bali*).[107] With regard to the third and fourth, we are told that the king with a depleted treasury should impose on them the agricultural tax.[108] In support of this striking provision the *Śānti Parva* quotes a Vedic maxim to prove that the king is the master of the wealth of all persons who are not brāhmaṇas, as well as of those brāhmaṇas who are not devoted to their religious duties.[109] According to this theory the kṣatriya should take the wealth of all such persons as never perform religious rites and sacrifices,[110] and with such wealth he should maintain the army and celebrate sacrifices.[111] But the *Śānti Parva* also permits confiscation to defray the expenses of the state. Thus if the sacrifice begun by anybody, especially by a brāhmaṇa, cannot be completed for want of only a fourth part of the estimated expenses, the king may take away from his kinsmen the wealth of a vaiśya who is possessed of a large flock of cattle but is averse to sacrifice and abstains from quaffing Soma.[112] The rule is applicable to the śūdras as well.[113] Manu makes similar injunction in the present context.[114] No other source of our period, however, mentions confiscation of the property of an unrighteous person as a means of swelling the treasury. The royal prerogative of taking away an impious person's wealth is not mentioned in most of the law-books, apparently because of its dangerous implications for the brāhmaṇas.

Although there is no other evidence to prove that the impious and undutiful brāhmaṇas were liable to a special levy, there are reasons to believe that from the last quarter of the sixth century A.D. or from the early years of the seventh, non-brāhmaṇas were sometimes made to pay some kind of tithe for the exclusive benefit of the priestly class. Several inscriptions of the Maitrakas

107. *Ibid.*, 77.7.
108. *Ibid.*, 77. 8-9.
109. *Ibid.*, 10. Cf. *Ibid.*, 78. 2.
110. *Ibid.*, 134. 2.
111. *Ibid.*, 4.
112. *Ibid.*, 159. 7.
113. *Ibid.*, 8.
114. *Manu*, XI. 11-13.

of Valabhī mention that the land is granted to the donee with the exception of the "endowments previously given in favour of the temples and brāhmaṇas, and the brāhmaṇa's twentieth" (*purvvapradattadevabrahmadeyabrāhmaṇaviṁśatirahitaḥ*).[115] The term *brāhmaṇāviṁśati* has been taken by Bühler[116] to mean a tithe imposed upon the villages for the brāhmaṇas. Ghoshal follows this explanation, in support of which he refers to the conditions prevailing in certain states in Rajputana where in later times the brāhmaṇas were entitled to realise a petty tithe from the agriculturists at the rate of 1|40 of the summer harvest.[117] The type of due indicated by *brāhmaṇaviṁśati*, however, was paid at the rate of one twentieth as the expression itself suggests. Evidently this tithe was perhaps payable only by the non-brāhmaṇas. In view of this later practice it may be guessed that the idea of taxing the impious brāhmaṇas and śūdras referred to in the above-quoted passage of the *Śānti Parva*, if at all followed in practice, may have been limited to the non-brāhmaṇas. Besides, the exaggerated claim of the brāhmaṇas to fiscal exemptions and privileges makes it doubtful whether the impious among them were even made to pay any special tax.[118]

Another class of king's receipts of an essentially irregular nature is concerned with what may be called an organised or unorganised plunder of foreign states. The *Arthaśāstra*[119] mentions seven different classes of troops, of whom two are required to be maintained by means of raw material (*kupya*) or by the plunder of foreign states (*vilopa*). This evidently points to a system of organised plunder of foreign territories somewhat resembling the *chauth* and *sardeśmukhī* of the Maratha states.[120] Although the law-books of our period do not provide any exact parallel they furnish some instances of licensed plundering of

115. *IA*. VII, pp. 75, 79, 85 ; XV, p. 340 ; *EI*, VIII, no. 20(A), 1. 45 ; no. 20(B), 1.48.
116. *IA*, XV, p. 337.
117. *HRS*, p. 221 and n. 2.
118. For the exemptions of the brāhmaṇas from taxation see chapter X
119. *AŚ*, IX. 2.
120. *HRS*, p. 124.

foreign states by private individuals, who perhaps paid a certain share of the profit to the king. Thus according to Bṛhaspati when anything is brought from a hostile country by freebooters, with the permission of their lord, they should give a sixth part to the king[121] and share the remainder among themselves in due proportion. Kātyāyana lays down that the booty which is brought by a pillaging party at the command of their king from an enemy country shall be divided by them after setting a tenth part for their king.[122] Bṛhaspati lays down the rate of 1|6, Kātyāyana prescribes that of 1|10. The *Smṛticandrikā* explains that Bṛhaspati's verse applies to a very powerful enemy, while that of Kātyāyana to a weak one.[123] On the other hand, Caṇḍeśvara in his *Vivādaratnākara*[124] states that 1|6 or 1|10 depends upon the proximity or otherwise of the country. Whichever of the two explanations be correct, there is little doubt that plundering of enemy territories by private individuals under some sort of license may have fetched a considerable income to the state.

Tributes from the vanquished chieftains and rulers or tribes may have contributed to the king's coffers. In a passage of Manu income from war is stated to have been a legitimate source of the livelihood of kings.[125] In the *Mahābhārata*,[126] Arjuna is described as taking tributes from the conquered chieftains. Even in times of peace they were perhaps obliged to submit to an extraordinary demand. Thus when Duryodhana expressed his desire to perform the *rajasūya* sacrifice, the *purohita* spoke to him : "All these rulers of the earth who have, O king, become tributary to thee will pay the tributes in gold, both pure and impure."[127] The works of Kālidāsa also refer to tributes that the defeated kings generally paid to their conquerors. He describes a con-

121. *Bṛhaspati*, XIII. 38.
122. *Kātyāyana*, verse 633.
123. *Ibid.*, p. 249n.
124. *Ibid.*
125. *Manu*, VII. 98.
126. *Mbh.*, II, 27. 28 ; II, 30. 28 ; II, 28. 6.
127. *Ibid.* III, 255, 16-17.

queror as overrunning the country and realising horses,[128] elephants,[129] heaps of gold,[130] and other precious presents.[131] Presents, technically known as *upāyana*,[132] which is also mentioned in the Allahabad Pillar inscription of Samudra Gupta,[133] seem to have come also from foreign powers and foiled adversaries who paid tributes in money. It may be a reasonable guess that the income from such presents and tributes during the time of the imperial Guptas may have been really enormous, because of the expansionist policy which they pursued with remarkable success. Moreover, the farflung nature of the empire perhaps made it difficult to realise taxes directly from the people; and it is not improbable that the Gupta emperors, to a certain extent, remained content with tributes from defeated kings.

128. *Raghu*, IV. 70.
129. *Ibid.*, 83.
130. *Ibid.*, 70.
131. *Ibid.*, 84.
132. *Ibid.*, 79, 84; XVI. 32.
133. *CII*, III, no. 1, 1.24.

CHAPTER VIII

EMERGENCY REVENUE

A notable feature of the revenue system embodied in the literature of law and polity is that it not only contains a scheme of taxation for normal times but also seeks to provide for the exceptional needs of the king or the state.[1] Thus according to Kauṭilya, an important measure to replenish a depleted treasury is to levy benevolences (*praṇaya*) from the people, which, however, should not be resorted to more than once.[2] The dealers in gold, silver, diamonds, precious stones, pearls, coral, horses and elephants should pay as much as 50 per cent, those in cloth and lower metals 40 per cent, grain traders and wagon train organisers 30 per cent, and so on.[3] The way which Kauṭilya suggests to raise money amounts, in our opinion, to oppression. The entire property of a goldsmith is to be confiscated; the richest travelling merchants are to be quietly murdered as if by a robber or an enemy.[4] A brāhmaṇa that Kauṭilya is, it is strange that he recommends confiscation of temple treasures, setting up of new cults, putting up sudden miracles—all to collect money from the credulous for the king.[5] It seems that such measures were actually adopted by the Mauryas, for Patañjali reports that they had established cults for the sake of money.[6]

The levy of *praṇaya* did not disappear in post-Maurya and Gupta times. In the Junagadh Rock inscription,[7] Rudradāman

1. *HRS*, p. 125.
2. *AŚ*, V. 2.
3. *Ibid.*
4. *Ibid.*
5. *Ibid.*
6. *Mauryairhiraṇyārthibhir arcāḥ prakalpitāḥ*, Patañjali on Pāṇini, 5 3. 99.
7. *EI*, VIII, no. 6, 11. 15-16.

almost takes pride in having built the Sudarśana dam without oppressing his people with the imposition of *praṇaya* and other taxes. This may be taken to mean that the levy of *praṇaya* was considered to be undesirable and was avoided whenever possible. The Basim plate of Vindhyaśakti II[8], assignable to the fourth century A.D., also testifies to the prevalence of demanding *praṇaya*, which is not mentioned in any other contemporary inscription.

Nor is the levy of *praṇaya* mentioned in the law-books of our period. It is likely that it fell in comparative desuetude in post-Maurya and Gupta periods, during which certain inflationary measures seem to have been taken to meet the exigencies of time as can be inferred from the study of the metrology of the contemporary coinage. In the later period of the Kuṣāṇa rule, the real values of various denominations in the monetary system seem to have decreased, and as one would expect, the gold coinage was increasingly debased and the copper denominations were progressively reduced in weight.[9] It is not unlikely that recourse to such inflationary expedients was taken to face the economic crisis which may have resulted from the political instability of the Scythian period. Similarly with regard to the reign of Skanda Gupta, the grandson of Candra Gupta II, Smith mentions a specific financial expedient illustrating the fiscal policy of the Guptas during an extraordinary crisis. He writes, "The gold coins of his (Skanda Gupta's) early and prosperous days agree in both weight and finesse with those of his ancestors, but the later issues which increased in gross weight so as to suit the ancient Hindu *suvarṇa* exhibit a decline in the amount of pure gold in each piece from 108 to 73 grains".[10] The Hūṇas were a source of great trouble to the Empire, and to financially back his efforts to drive them out Skanda Gupta may have deliberately caused some inflation in the economy. But there is some difficulty in accepting this view, as it has been suggested[11] that the

8. *Sel. Ins.*, p. 409, l. 21.
9. *JNSI*, XXII, p. 63.
10. Smith, *Early History of India*, 4th edn., p. 328.
11. Allan, *Catalogue of Coins of the Gupta Dynasties and of Śaśāṅka, king of Gauḍa*, Introduction, pp. XCVIII-XCV.

debased gold coins belonged to the most easterly Gupta dominions which were not affected by the Hūṇa invasion. In any case, it appears significant that inflation, which was unknown in earlier times, was sometimes caused deliberately during our period.

Again, though the Kauṭilyan trickiness is not reflected in later literature, the views embodied in the *Śānti Parva,* which treats the question of emergency finance in a very perfunctory manner, leaves enough scope for financial oppression. In a chapter of the *rājadharma* section of the *Śānti Parva,* Bhīṣma, asked to suggest the course the king should pursue when his friends are declining and foes increasing, when his treasury is exhausted and army non-existent, replies unenigmatically that the king should seize the wealth of all persons except ascetics and brāhmaṇas.[12] Almost a similar doctrine is inculcated in the *āpaddharma* section of the *Śānti Parva* where an old verse is cited to the effect that the king is entitled to confiscate the wealth of robbers and of those who do not perform religious acts.[13] Seizure of property, irrespective of any consideration except religious, can by no means be justified; in fact, it betrays a lack of political acumen on the part of those who recommend it.

A more reasonable emergency measure suggested in some of the works, however, is that of public borrowing. Some sort of public loan is implied in a statement of Kauṭilya. According to him when the king thinks that by taking a repayable income or loan (*pratyādeya*), he may cause his enemy's treasury, army, and other defensive resources to dwindle and may thoroughly explicit the mines, timber and elephant forests, irrigational works and roads of traffic of the enemy, he may take a *pratyādeya,* re-payable income or loan. Kauṭilya explains *ādeya* as that which is easily acquired and secured without the necessary of its being returned to others, and *pratyādeya* as that which is to be returned to others and is difficult to get; it is not considered to be destructive in effect. This tradition is also recorded in the *Śānti Parva,* wherein a king states the following: "To meet this calamity and

12. *ŚP,* 128. 20-21.
13. *Supra,*

dreadful danger I seek your wealth for concerted measures for your protection. When the danger passes away, I will repay you what I now take".[14] A similar approach is reflected in the *Avadānaśataka*, a Buddhist work of post-Maurya times, which records the tradition of a merchant advancing a loan of gold coins (*suvarṇas*) to Prasenajit, king of Kosala, to help him in war with the king of Magadha.[15]

The legal literature of our period, however, reveals a departure from all that has been said above. Unlike Kauṭilya, Manu is not only laconic on emergency taxation but also reticent about the levy of *praṇaya*. According to him[16] a king can take even 1|4 of the crop in times of distress without incurring any sin. This passage is usually interpreted by the commentators to mean that the king is justified in realising one-fourth of the produce during financial embarrassments, instead of the usual one-sixth. Further, in the same context it is laid down that the kṣatriya who protects the vaiśyas by his weapons may collect from them 1|8 as tax on grain and 1|20 as *śulka* with the minimum of one *kārṣāpaṇa*.[17] According to Sarvajñanārāyaṇa and Nandan, however, the tax on grain is here stated to be 1|4 in the case of śūdras and 1|8 in the case of vaiśyas. How far differential rates of revenue were observed in practice is difficult to say. Among the lawgivers the solitary instance is that of Bṛhaspati who lays down the rate of 1|20 in normal times[18] for brāhmaṇas as against the rates of 1|6, 1|9 and 1|10 for other castes. As regards increase in *śulka*, Nārāyaṇa and Nandana construe the passage to suggest a minimum rate of 1|20. Nārāyaṇa, however, adds that some people read *triṁśatkārṣāpaṇavaram*, 'at least one *kārṣāpaṇa*

---

14. *ŚP*, 87. 29-32.
15. *Avadānaśataka*, p. 56.
16. *Manu*, X. 118.
17. *dhānye aṣṭamaṁ viśaṁ śulkaṁ visaṁ kārṣāpaṇavaram |*
karmopakaraṇāḥ śūdrāḥ kāravaḥ śilpinastathā ||
—*Manu*, X. 120.

The interpretation here is based on the authority of Medhātithi, Govinda, Kullūka and Rāghavānanda.
18. *Bṛhaspati*, XIII, verse 16.

out of thirty', instead of *viṁśaṁkārṣāpaṇavaram ;* and this reading is not convincing in view of another passage of the *Manusmṛti* where the normal rate of *śulka* is stated to be 1|20, and which therefore cannot reasonably be the emergency rate.[19] So far as taxes on śūdras, craftsmen and artisans are concerned, Manu ordains that they discharge their dues by doing service to the king.[20] Nārāyaṇa holds that in times of emergency no increase in the quota of work to be done by them is indicated, whereas Medhātithi thinks that they may be made to work more than they do normally. In any case, Manu suggests nothing more than a rise in the normal rates of revenue in times of crisis.

The injunctions of Bṛhaspati are characterised by a greater degree of leniency than is shown by Manu. According to him even in times of emergency the king is entitled only to 1|6 of the produce, which has been generally recognised by the jurists to be the normal rate of land tax. Similarly, Bṛhaspati[21] prescribes the rate of 1|20 for vendible commodities and 1|100 for cash and gold. The rate of one-twentieth is, however, prescribed by Manu for normal times; while Bṛhaspati's mention of 1|100 as the rate of levy on cash and gold is less than the rate of 1|50 prescribed by Manu.

It appears from the above that although unlike the *Arthaśāstra* and the *Śānti Parva,* the attitude to the problem of emergency finance reflected in the *Smṛtis* is not oppressive, there is a striking unanimity among the lawgivers. Besides, it is difficult to ascertain how far a king, when in narrow financial straits, observed the rules laid down in the *Smṛtis.* On the other hand, if the exemption of brāhmaṇas from taxation was observed

---

19. If credence is given to Govinda, Kullūka and Rāghavānanda, who on the basis of *Manu,* V. 130, take 1|50 as the usual rate of *śulka,* even the rate of 1|20 would appear plausible in times of emergency. But the crucial passage refers to tax on gold and cattle, and not to *śulka* as such. According to *Manu,* VIII. 398, *śulka* should be realised at the rate of 1|20 in normal times.

20. *Manu,* X. 120.

21. *Bṛhaspati,* (*āpaddharmakāṇḍam*), verse 7.

22. *Manu,* VIII. 398.

even in times of emergency, as is prescribed in the law-books,[23] the king may have gained enough latitude to tyrannise over the people of the lower *varṇas* by throwing on them the maximum weight of financial extortion, which in turn may have, to a certain extent, led to some kind of polarisation of social classes.

---

23 *Manu*, VII. 133 ; *Bṛhaspati*, *āpaddharmakāṇḍam*, verse 20.

CHAPTER IX

CROWN LANDS, FORESTS, MINES, ETC.

Apart from the revenues from lands cultivated and occupied by private individuals, the king's landed property constituted an important source of his income. The *Arthaśāstra* provides for the office of the superintendent of agriculture (*sītādhyakṣa*) who should employ a band of trained assistants, labourers, slaves and prisoners to cultivate crown lands. He is further required to supply them with agricultural implements and appliances as well as the human and animal labour needed for cultivation.[1] In the same context Kauṭilya tells us that fields that are left unsown (*vāpātirikta*)[2] may be worked up by those who cultivate the fields in return for half of the harvest (*ardhasītika*) or else by those who live by their own labour and receive 1|4 or 1|5 of the harvest. The mention of the expression *svabhūmi* in the present context implies that the passage refers to the cultivation of crown lands either by slaves and hired labourers employed by the state officers or by the tenants under their supervision. The contrary view, Ghoshal rightly suggests,[3] is disproved by the fact that a special revenue term, *sītā*, is used for the whole produce from this source instead of the more usual *bhāga*, which represents the king's grain share levied on the ordinary revenue-paying lands. Further, the minute rules laid down in the present context regarding the sowing and reaping of crops, the payment of agricultural labourers and the like would be quite out of place if the superintendent of agriculture were to be any other than the steward of the royal farm.

---

1. *AŚ*, II. 24.
2. *HRS*, p. 30, n. 1.
3. *Ibid.*, pp. 30-31.

Though the literature of our period does not make any direct reference to crown lands, it mentions sharecroppers who seem to have cultivated the king's land. Viṣṇu[4] states that the food offered by an *ārdhika* may be taken. The commentator Nandapaṇḍita defines an *ārdhika* as one who yields half the produce of his fields to the king.[5] Manu also refers to *ārdhika*; and Yājñavalkya[7] uses the word *ardhasīrin* in the same sense. Strangely enough, while the sharecropper in the *Arthaśāstra* receives land from the state, in Manu and Yājñavalkya, he receives it from the individual.[8] There is, however, a Pallava land grant of the third century A.D. which informs us that four sharecroppers remained attached to the land even when it was given away to brāhmaṇas.[9] Here it would mean that before the land in question was granted, the king got it cultivated by sharecroppers (*ārdhikas*). But probably the practice did not obtain on any considerable scale in North India.

The epigraphs further show that a certain portion of cultivable land was directly owned and probably cultivated by the state in the Deccan. Gautamīputra Śātakarṇi grants what he describes as "our fields" (*amhakheta*) in the Nasik region.[10] In the same locality the same king donates 100 *nivartanas* of land out of 'the fields belonging to us' (*rājakamkheta amhasatakam*).[11] A Pallava inscription also records the grant of a piece of land which formed part of the king's domain of 800 *paṭṭikas*.[12] Apparently these plots of land were cultivated by the agents of the king and constituted a source of income to him. In the Gupta period, a grant

---

4. *Viṣṇu*, LVII. 16.
5. Nandapandita on *Viṣṇu*, LVII. 16.
6. *Manu*, IV. 253.
7. *Yāj.*, I. 166.
8. R. S. Sharma, *Śūdras in Ancient India*, p. 217, n. 4.
9. *EI*, I, no. 1, 1.39. A grant of Vijaydevavarman of the thirteenth regnal year from Ellore in Godavari district (*EI*, IX, no. 8, 1.11) records an endowment of land to a brāhmaṇa together with a house-site for men who receive half the crop (*addhiya manussāṇam*).
10. *EI*, VIII, no. 8 (4), 1.3.
11. *Ibid.*, no. 8(5), 1.9.
12. *Ibid.*, no. 23, 1.16.

(A.D. 525) of Dhruvasena I belonging to the Amreli District in the Bombay region records the grant of 100 *pādāvartas* of *sītā* land.[13] Evidently here *sītā* is reminiscent of crown lands which is described in the *Arthaśāstra* as being supervised by the *sītādhyakṣa*.

In North India no land grant directly refers to crown lands, but some information may be gleaned from the eleven extant Bengal charters, which record land sale transactions.[14] At least eight out of these eleven refer to the state as selling land for religious purposes. Out of those eight, no less than four inscriptions record the sale of cultivable plots of land. Therefore, it is reasonable to suppose that lands, owned, enjoyed and cultivated by the king, continued to exist throughout our period, though due to the increasing number of grants of land, some of which may have been out of king's lands, the state may have sustained a considerable loss in its income.

Forests (*vana*) may have been an important source of royal income as it is mentioned in the *Arthaśāstra* as one of the constituents of *āyaśarīra* (body of income).[15] Forest as a source of king's wealth is defined by Kauṭilya as comprising productive forests including elephant forests, and game forests (*paśumṛgavana*).[16] The first kind of forests is stated in the *Arthaśāstra* to have been under the supervision of a department with a large staff and a superintendent of forest produce (*kupyādhyakṣa*),[17] which may suggest that such forests were under the king's control and occupation. The king's lordship over forest is borne out by the fact that the superintendent of forest produce (*kupyādhyakṣa*) is instructed to impose fines upon those who felled trees in the forest[18] and those who stole game and useful products from the forests concerned.[19] He is further required in the *Arthaśāstra*

---

13. *Ibid.*, XXXI, no. 39(A), 1.13.
14. Maity, *op. cit.*, Appendix II.
15. *AŚ*, II. 3.
16. *Ibid.*
17. *Ibid.*, II. 17.
18. *Ibid.*
19. *AŚ*, IV. 10.

to collect important products such as timber, skins, bones, horns, metals, charcoal and fodder, and to arrange for them to be turned into commodities, such manufactures being designed both for means of livelihood and for defence of the capital city.[20] Elsewhere Kauṭilya[21] makes a direct reference to this point mentioning the royal merchandise of internal origin derived from the forests. Evidently the *Arthaśāstra* gives the impression that the king perhaps held a monopoly over forests, but in practice this may not have been the case. A *Jātaka* story refers to a forester (*vanacarako*) who collects wares in forest (*araññe upajjanaka-bhaṇḍam ādāya*) and disposes them in the city.[22] This may imply that fowlers and hunters, who probably had no land to cultivate and no arts to pursue, made forest as the source of their living. Besides, the forest is often referred to in the *Jātakas* as infested with and sometimes dominated by robber-bands. No wonder if royal monopoly over forest products may not have been always possible.

The law-books of our period do not clearly show whether the state derived any income from forest products. Viṣṇu[23] is the only lawgiver to state that the king should appoint able officials to look after forests having elephants (*nāgavana*). Yājñavalkya[24] lays down that the king should build his fort in a place surrounded among other things by forests, but he does not say whether such forests were owned by the king. Kāmandaka[25] considers at some length the question of setting up game forests for the recreation of the king, but does not tell us anything about royal monopoly over productive forests. It may be, however, inferred from Kālidāsa that the wild extensively growing forests produced, besides building timber and fuel, the sacred skin of the

20. *Ibid.*, II, 17.
21. *Ibid.*, II. 35.
22. *Jat.*, III, p. 150.
23. *ākaraśulka'aranāgavaneṣu āptān niyuñjīta, Viṣṇu*, III. 16.
24. *Yāj.*, I. 321.
25. *Kāmand.*, XIV. 28-41.

ruru[26] and *kṛṣṇasāra*,[27] deer and of other animals,[28] musk (*mṛganābhi*)[29] obtained from the navel of the roaming deer, lac[30] and the yak tail (*camarī*)[31] commonly used as a symbol of royalty and serving as a flywhisk. But he does not refer to the king's monopoly over forests, though he refers to the king's exclusive right over elephants.[32] There is, however, a reference to forest officers (*araṇyādhikṛta*) in a Pallava grant.[33] This suggests that some forests were exploited exclusively to the king's benefit. Thus although the sources of our period are completely reticent about reserved forests mentioned in the *Arthaśāstra*, it would be wrong to think that such forests altogether disappeared in post-Maurya and Gupta times.

We have already noted that besides the raw materials mentioned by Kauṭilya and Kālidāsa in the list of forest products, the forests also provided elephants, which were a valuable asset in ancient Indian warfare.[34] We learn from Megasthenes[35] that in the Maurya period no private person was allowed to keep either a horse or an elephant, for these animals were held to be the special property of the king. Quoting from Megasthenes Strabo[36] states that royal stables were provided for horses and elephants and a royal magazine for arms, because the soldier had to return his elephants to the stables. The number of horses and elephants possessed by the king may have been considerable. Kauṭilya provides for the offices of superintendents of horses and

---

26. *Raghu.*, III. 31.
27. *Ibid.*, IV. 13.
28. *Ṛtu.*, VI. 13.
29. *Ibid.*, VI. 13.
30. *Kumāra.*, I. 13.
31. *Raghu.*, XVI. 2.
32. *Infra.*
33. *EI*, I, no. 6, l. 5.
34. After death too elephants may have been a source of income because of their tusks which are a costly material.
35. Strabo, XV. 14-43; McCrindle, *Ancient India as described by Megasthenes and Arrian*, p. 90.
36. Strabo, XV. 52; McCrindle, *Ancient India as described in Classical Literature*, p. 55.

of elephants.[37] As noted earlier, Viṣṇu also makes a similar provision in regard to elephants. A passage from the *Śānti Parva*[38] may be cited to the same effect. The tradition of elephants being the exclusive possession of the king is recorded in the *Raghuvaṁśa*,[39] in which, among other things, elephants from forests are said to constitute the wages of the king for protecting the earth. But perhaps from the post-Maurya period the position had begun to change. According to the *Milindapañho*[40] the best of elephants and horses belonged to the king, which may mean that royal possession was limited only to the elephants and horses of the best quality. This monopoly seems to have been further undermined in the Gupta period. Nārada[41] ordains that owners of elephants and horses should not pay any fine for mischief caused by these animals, for they are looked upon as protectors of the king's subjects. This may imply that horses and elephants were owned by private individuals, although superintendents of those animals are mentioned as important functionaries by Bṛhaspati[42]. In any case, it appears that the royal monopoly over elephants and horses was undermined in the Gupta period. Similarly, in view of the reticence of the law-givers about royal monopoly over forests, it is not improbable that the king's right over forests and income therefrom may have been affected adversely in North India during post-Maurya and Gupta times, presumably because of the feudalisation of state apparatus.[43]

Early Indian sources often refer to mines as an item of royal income under the present head. According to Kauṭilya, treasury has its origin in mines, and accordingly the *Arthaśāstra* devotes

37. *AŚ*, II. 30-32.
38. *ŚP*, 69. 28.
39. *Raghu*, XVII. 66; Kāmandaka (IV. 52) makes only a passing reference to elephant forests but does not say about king's monopoly over elephants.
40. *Milinda*, p. 192.
41. *Nārada*, XI. 32; cf. 30.
42. *Bṛhaspati, Saṁskārakāṇḍam*, verse 505.
43. For feudal elements in the Gupta period see R. S. Sharma, *Indian Feudalism*, Calcutta, 1965, Chapter, I.

one full chapter to mining operations under the supervision of the superintendent of mines (*ākarādhyakṣa*).[44] It is laid down that any person who steals mineral products or carries on mining operations without licence shall be bound with chains and caused to work as prisoner.[45] This obviously implies that mines were a state monopoly, and no private person could work them without a licence from the state.[46] From those who worked the mines on a lease, the Mauryan state seems to have received also a premium (*vyājī*) because of its share of the minerals being taken in royal weights, which were 5 per cent heavier than the market standards.[47] It can be further inferred from an *Arthaśāstra* passage that the state directly worked those mines which did not require much outlay, but others, which needed large investments or which yielded minerals used in the manufactories of vessels, were leased out for royalty.[48] Thus although the mines were regarded beyond doubt a state monopoly, the policy of the *Arthaśāstra* tended to confine the state management only to those that were easy to work.[49]

There is, however, lack of consolidated evidence about state monopoly of mines in post-Maurya and Gupta periods, though some inference may be drawn from the stray references available in contemporary literature. Viṣṇu[50] expressly declares that the king should appropriate the whole output of mines and lays down that he should appoint able officials for looking after them.[51] A passage from the *Śānti Parva* too enjoins that the king should employ officers for mines among other things, which may indicate the king's control over mines.[52] Similarly Manu mentions the mines as a source of revenue for which trusted officials are to be

44. *AŚ*. II. 12.
45. *Ibid.*, II. 1.
46. *Ibid.*, II. 12.
47. *Ibid.*
48. *Ibid.*
49. *HRS*, p. 107.
50. *Viṣṇu*, III. 55.
51. *Ibid.*, III. 16.
52. *ŚP*, 69.29.

employed by the king.[53] All this shows that the state continued to derive income from mining in post-Maurya times.

References to mining operations under the aegis of the state in the law-books of the Gupta period are vague. Yājñavalkya[54] states at one place that a thing especially ordered to be reserved by or worthy of a king (*rājayogyam*) shall, if sold to a stranger, belong to the king. The expression *rājayogyam* is explained by Vijñāneśvara as precious stones, pearls etc. (*maṇimāṇikya*), but we do not know whether the term included mines. Kātyāyana[54] enjoins the king to personally look after what is paid at the pits (*garta*). Though the expression *garta* may refer to mines,[56] it does not seem to indicate the king's monopoly over them. The *Amarakośa*[57] mentions *khaṇi* and *ākara* for mines, but no clue is available about their ownership. Kāmandaka,[58] however, points out that working of mines and quarries was a source of revenue to the state, though he does not indicate the extent of royal rights over them. Of the literary sources of the Gupta period, the *Raghuvaṁśa*[59] is the only work which states clearly that, among other things, mines constitute the wages (*vetana*) of the king, which is corroborated by a number of contemporary land grants from Central India.

The Basim plate of the Vākāṭaka Vindhyaśakti II records the expression *alavaṇakeṇṇakkhāṇaka*,[60] which has been translated by Mirashi[61] as "except from the purchase and digging of salt." The Poona plates of Prabhāvatīguptā,[62] however, bears *kliṇvakreṇi-khānakaḥ*, interpreted as the purchase of fermenting drugs and mines.[63] Fleet reads the term in the Chammak and Siwani

53. *Manu*, VII. 62.
54. *Yāj*., II, 261.
55. *Kātyāyana*, verses 947-948.
56. *Ibid*., p. 333n.
57. *Amar*., II. 3.7
58. *Khanyākaradhanādānam, Kāmandaka*, V. 78.
59. *Raghu*., XVII. 66.
60. *EI*, XXVI, no. 20, 1.20.
61. *Ibid*., p. 154.
62. *Sel. Ins*., p. 414, 1.17.
63. *EI*, XV, p. 43.

Copper-plates of Pravarasena II[64] as *khanakaḥ*, but Diksit and Pathak in the Poona plate of Prabhāvatīguptā[65] read it as *khānakaḥ*, which is the nearest approximation to the Sanskrit word, meaning a mine. The word *khānaka* means a miner, but in the present context it seems to indicate the mine and not the miner.[66] It may be pointed out that the term *alavaṇakeṇṇakkhānaka* appears in almost all the land grants of the Vākāṭaka rulers which means that mines were given to the donees together with the piece of land. Besides, the Vākāṭaka records also refer to the transfer of the right of enjoying the hidden treasures and deposits together with land,[67] which may perhaps mean the transfer of ownership of mines, which otherwise were under the direct control of the state.

An important fact in this connection is that salt is included in the category of mines. Kauṭilya defines mines as consisting, among other things, of salt. According to him the superintendent of salt (*lavaṇādhyakṣa*) should collect out of the prepared salt the king's share (*lavaṇabhāga*) and rent (*prakraya*) ; he is also to collect out of the sale of salt the price (*mūlya*), the *rūpa* (a charge upon mines and imported salt) and the *vyājī*[68] (compensation fee). The first apparently refers to the manufacture of salt by private persons under a state licence, and the second to private sales of salt under similar conditions.[69]

It is strange that although the law-books of the period under study refer to mines as a source of royal income, they do not make any specific mention of salt mines or income therefrom. Among the post-Maurya works, only the *Śānti Parva*[70] touches the point and enjoins that the king should set honest and trustworthy men for supervision over salt. The *Amarakośa*[71] men

64. *CII*, III, no. 55, 1.28 ; no. 56, 1.29.
65. *EI*, XV, no. 4, 1.17.
66. Maity, *op. cit.*, p. 99, n. 2.
67. See below.
68. *AŚ*, II. 12.
69. *HRS*, p. 106.
70. *ŚP*, 69. 29.
71. *Amar.*, VI. 104-106.

tions two types of salt, one from sea water and the other from rock; but this work does not tell us how far salt was a source of income to the state.

The inscriptions of the period, however, yield some information on the point. The Nasik Cave inscription of the Sātavāhana king Gautamīputra Śātakarṇi (dated A.D. 124)[72] bears the expression *aloṇakhādakam*, which also occurs in his other epigraph dated A.D. 130 from the same place. Though the land grants of the imperial Guptas are silent on the point, several Vākāṭaka land charters, as noted earlier, use the expression *alavaṇakeṇṇakkhānakaḥ* or its variant. The mention of the word *lavaṇa* followed by *khānakaḥ* may mean that the kings transferred their right over mines to the recipients of donations of land.[73] This, in turn, may imply that generally salt mines may have been owned by the state, and their transfer accompanied by a gift of land, was one of the privileges granted to the donees.[74] It is, however, curious that none of the inscriptions from Northern India, which was directly ruled by the Guptas, refers to the transfer of salt mines or other mines to the brāhmaṇas. This may be because of the fact that mines existed mainly in Central India and not in Northern India where there was very little to transfer. Thus it appears that crown land, forests, animals etc. continued to remain a source of the king's income. But on account of the increasing number of land grants together with the economic advantages derivable from the donated land, the royal treasury must have incurred considerable financial loss.

---

72. *Sel. Ins.*, p. 192, 1.4.
73. *Ibid.*, p. 194, 1.5. The Pallava grants mention similar terms, e.g., Mayidavolu inscription of Śivaskandavarman (*ibid.*, p. 435, 1. 13).
74. The Hirahadagalli Copper-plate inscription of Śivaskandavarman (*ibid.*, p. 440, 11. 34-35) mentions eighteen privileges granted to the donees though it does not enumerate all of them. Cf. the Basim inscription of the Vākāṭaka Vindhyaśakti II (*ibid.*, p. 407, 1.24) which bears the expression "*savvajātiparihāra-parihitañca*" but does not refer to 18 *parihāras*.

CHAPTER X

FISCAL IMMUNITIES

The state in ancient India perhaps suffered a considerable loss in its total revenue receipts on account of certain classes of people being exempted from the payment of taxes. Apart from the brāhmaṇas, whose fiscal privileges will be discussed below, the law-books often exempt miscellaneous group of persons from taxation. According to Āpastamba[1] women of all classes, boys before attaining menhood, those who live with preceptors for study, the virtuous ascetics, the śūdras who live by washing the feet of other classes, the blind, the dumb, the deaf and the diseased, and those who are forbidden to acquire property are not to pay taxes. With this may be compared the list of exempted people furnished by Vasistha, according to whom, in addition to brāhmaṇas, the king's men, the helpless, one who has renounced the world, the infant and the old, the young man who is a student, the newly confined women, widows returning to their former families and maidens and wives of servants are exempted from paying taxes.[2] Vasiṣṭha further quotes a passage from Manu to the effect that the infant, the messenger and one who has renounced the world are immune from the payment of *śulka*.[3] It is clear that both the lists have more or less in common certain classes of women, the infant, the student and the ascetic, though the scope of Āpastamba's rule with regard to the first is more comprehensive than the injunction of Vasiṣṭha. But Vasistha has, besides, the class of king's servants, whereas Āpastamba, who is assignable to a period earlier than that of the former, adds that of the śūdras and those who are prohibited from acquiring property.

---

1. *Āpastamba,* II, 10, 26 ; 10. 17.
2. *Vasiṣṭha,* VIII, 37.
3. Ghoshal thinks that here *sulka* must evidently be understood in the general sense of taxes (*HRS,* p. 136, n. 3.)

Similar provisions are made in the law-books of Manu and Viṣṇu. Accordng to the former, the blind, the idiot, the cripple and the man of seventy years of age are exempted from the payment of all taxes.[4] Ghoshal rightly points out that these evidently correspond to the blind, the diseased and the aged persons of the earlier lists.[5] Manu also lays down that besides the brāhmaṇas and the students of the *Vedas*, women carrying two months or more, ascetics and the hermits should not pay tolls at any ferry.[6] Manu's injunctions are identical with the rule of Viṣṇu who prescribes a fine of ten *paṇas* for the realisation of *śulka* from the Vedic student, the hermit in the forest (*vānaprastha*), the ascetic, the pregnant woman and the mendicant monks (*tīrthāṇusārin*).[7] It appears plausible that the different classes of persons were exempted from the payment of a tax because of the humanitarian consideration for their incapacity to work and earn their living, but the śūdras were entitled to this privilege perhaps because they were not the property-owning class.

Among those exempted from taxation, by far the most important were the brāhmaṇas, especially the learned ones (*śrotriyas*). Certain passages of the *Śatapatha Brāhmaṇa* indicate that even in the earlier period the brāhmaṇas were not taxed.[8] The idea crystallised further in the law-books. Thus Āpastamba[9] ordains that learned brāhmanas (*śrotriyas*) are not to pay taxes. The rules of the *Arthaśāstra* also indicate the fiscal immunity of the brāhmaṇas. The king, who is to settle a new or re-settle an old territory, is contemplated by Kauṭilya[10] as making tax-free grants of land (*brahmadeya*) to certain classes of brāhmaṇas, such as the sacrificial priest, the spiritual preceptor, the chaplain (*purohita*) and the learned brāhmaṇa. This evidently implies that the lands

---

4. *Manu*, VIII. 394.
5. *HRS*, p. 140.
6. *Manu*, VIII. 407.
7. *Viṣṇu*, V. 132.
8. *Śat. Br.*, XIII. 6.2.18, quoted Kane, *Hist. Dharm.*, II, pt. I, p. 143, n. 321.
9. *akaraḥ śrotriyaḥ*, *Āpastamba*, II, 10.26.10.
10. *AŚ*, II. 1.

of the brāhmaṇas granted by the king were normally exempted from taxation. Again, in connection with emergency measures for replenishing or filling the treasury, Kauṭilya expressly states that the property of a learned brāhmaṇa should be exempted from benevolences and other irregular exactions.[11] Similarly, Manu ordains that, even though dying, the king should not levy a tax from the *śrotriya*.[12] The exemption of the learned brāhmaṇas is borne out indirectly by a passage of the *Śānti Parva,* which states that a religious king should make those who are not *śrotriyas* and who do not kindle the sacred fire render taxes and forced labour (*viṣṭi*).[13] Nārada is also of opinion that a wise man should abstain from imposing a toll on a *śrotriya's* property which belongs to his household, though the property used for trading purposes is not declared exempt from taxes. The fact that the lawgivers confine the fiscal exemptions to the class of learned brāhmaṇas should not, however, be taken too far. In fact, the jurists themselves sometimes extend this privilege to all brāhmaṇas. Vasiṣṭha, who has been quoted above to show that only *śrotriyas* were tax-free, states that a king, who rules in accordance with the sacred law, may take a sixth of the wealth of his subjects except from brāhmaṇas.[14] The reason assigned was the general belief that the king shared in the religious merit accumulated by the brāhmaṇas. Thus in justifying the brāhmaṇa's claim for immunity Vasiṣṭha quotes three Vedic texts to the effect that the king shares 1|6 of the brāhmaṇa's spiritual merit acquired by the performance of sacrifices and charitable works, that the brāhmaṇa is not to be devoured because he enriches the *Vedas* and secures immunity from danger, and lastly that Soma is the king of the brāmaṇas.[15] Viṣṇu advises that the king should not realise any tax from the brāhmaṇas, because they pay taxes to him in the

11. *Ibid.,* V. 2.
12. *Manu,* VII. 133.
13. *ŚP,* 76. 5.
14. *Vasiṣṭha,* I. 42-43.
15. *Ibid.,* I. 44-46.

shape of pious acts.[16] According to Nārada[17] all brāhmaṇas are free from the payment of fare or toll at a ferry. He adds that the alms received by brāhmaṇas should not be liable to taxation. The exemption of the brāhmaṇas from the payment of toll at a ferry is also indicated in a passage of the *Viṣṇudharmottara Purāṇa*.[18] The position that emerges is contradictory; on the one hand the lawgivers exempt only the learned brāhmaṇas from taxation, and on the other they seem to extend the privilege to all brāhmaṇas.

As noted earlier, the law-books explain the Brāhmaṇical privilege of exemption by the idea of exchange. In other words, the gift of religious merits accumulated by the brāhmaṇas through the discharge of their recognised duties such as performance of sacrificial rites, learning and preaching the *Vedas*, writing and other cultural activities, was perhaps supposed to take the place of taxes. Strictly followed, this principle would confine the idea of tax-exemption to the learned brāhmaṇas instead of extending it to the entire class of the brāhmaṇas many of whom may have followed other means of livelihood such as agriculture etc.[19] Besides, it has been suggested that only a few brāhmaṇas may have been unacquainted with the Vedic literature and hence the fiscal privileges might benefit the whole brāhmaṇa class.[20] Although it is difficult to agree to the view that most of the brāhmaṇas knew the *Vedas*, it is significant to note that according to Manu the brāhmaṇa, learned or unlearned, is a great divi-

---

16. *Viṣṇu*, III. 26-27. A similar idea is embodied in the *Raghuvaṁśa* (XVII. 65) of Kālidāsa who states that by protecting asceticism from obstacles and wealth from robbers the king was made the enjoyer of one-sixth of the spiritual earnings of the *āśramas* and the different castes according to their respective capacities.
17. *Nārada*, XVIII. 36.
18. *Viṣṇudharmottara*, II. 61.58.
19. The law-books of the period provide that brāhmaṇas might legitimately take to cultivation in certain cases. (See *Manu*, X. 81-82; Yāj., III. 35; *Nārada*, I. 56-60.)
20. R. S. Sharma, *Economic Aspects of Caste System*, (Patna, 1952) p. 6.

nity, just as consecrated or unconsecrated fire is a great divinity.[21] In view of this passage, it appears reasonable to guess that the distinction between learned or unlearned brāhmaṇas in matters of fiscal exemption did not perhaps count much.

The highly privileged position of the brāhmaṇas is further indicated by the practice of giving away land to them, which is emphatically recommended in the contemporary legal writings. Āpastamba,[22] who belongs to an earlier period, enjoins the king to make gifts of land and money to the brāhmaṇas without detriment to his own men. The *Dīgha Nikāya*[23] also mentions several instances of *brahmadeya* (lands given to the brāhmaṇas). Such grants, however, do not seem to have been tax-free in pre-Maurya times, because neither the word *akara* nor any other expression indicating immunity of taxes is found in the string of adjectives qualifying the land granted.[24] It is, therefore, likely that during the earlier period the practice of granting land with fiscal exemption did not exist. For the first time, however, Kauṭilya,[25] in connection with the arrangements for settling new and old territories (*bhūtapūrvamabhūtapūrvamvā*) states that the king should make grants of *brahmadeya* lands, exempted from taxes and fines (*adaṇḍakarāṇi*), to the sacrificial priest (*ṛtvik*), the spiritual preceptor (*ācārya*), the priest (*purohita*) and those learned in the *Vedas* (*śrotriyas*). The *brahmadeya* of the *Arthaśāstra* differs from that of the *Dīgha-Nikāya* inasmuch as according to the former it is to be free from taxes.

In post-Maurya times, unlike the *Arthaśāstra*, the law-books do not refer to revenue-free grants of land, but they eulogise the practice of giving land to the brāhmaṇas as the most meritorious of all gifts. Vasiṣṭha quotes a verse according to which whatever sin a man may commit in straightened circumstances is removed

---

21. *Manu*, IX. 317.
22. *Āpastamba*, II, 10.26.1; cf. *Gautama*, X. 9.
23. *Dīgha Nikāya*, I, 87 ; III. 114, 131, 224.
24. R. S. Sharma, *Political Ideas and Institutions*, p. 137.
25. *AŚ*, II. 1-2.

by making a gift of only as much land as is equal to *gocarma*.[26] According to Viṣṇu[27] the king should donate land and money to the brāhmaṇas; and the *Anuśāsana Parva* of the *Mahābhārata* devotes a whole chapter to the praise of making gifts of land (*bhūmidāna-praśaṁsā*). Manu[28] and Yājñavalkya[29] declare that objects of enjoyment and various kinds of riches given by the king to the brāhmaṇas are imperishable treasure, and the latter even lays down the procedure for making gifts of land. But none of these sources speaks of revenue-free grants as Kauṭilya does. In the law-books generally the idea of brāhmaṇas' exemption from taxes and the practice of bestowing land upon them are mentioned separately in different contexts. Bṛhaspati, who probably flourished in the Gupta period, is the only jurist who associates the idea of fiscal exemption with land gifts to the brāhmaṇas and thus refers to revenue-free grants of land. He states that the ruler should bestow upon the brāhmaṇas, houses and landed property, exempt from taxation, declaring in a written grant, that the revenue is remitted.[30] This is, however, not to suggest that the practice of creating revenue-free land holdings in favour of the brāhmaṇas was unknown before the Gupta period, because as we have already seen, Kauṭilya also refers to the grant of such land. But while the recommendation of Kauṭilya applies to new settlements, that of Bṛhaspati seems to have been of a general nature. Probably Bṛhaspati legalises a practice which had become widespread.

It is, hovever, curious that we do not come across any inscription recording grant of land with fiscal exemptions in North India before the Gupta period. The earliest epigraphic record, a Sātavāhana inscription of the first century B.C., which refers to the grant of a village as a gift in the *aśvamedha* sacrifice, be-

26. *Vasiṣṭha*, 29. 16. For the definition of *gocarma* see *Hist. Dharm*, II, pt. 2, p. 859n.
27. *Viṣṇu*, III. 81, 84. 84.
28. *Manu*, VII. 82.
29. *Yāj.*, I. 315.
30. *Bṛhaspati*, XVII. 3-4.

longs to Nanaghat in Western India.[31] Similarly, two cave inscriptions of Uṣavadāta, which mention gifts of sixteen villages to the brāhmaṇas and the gods, belong to the Nasik region.[32] But these inscriptions do not indicate the abandonment of any administrative and fiscal rights by the donor. Suprisingly, administrative and fiscal rights were perhaps given up for the first time in the grants to the Buddhist monks by the Sātavāhana ruler Gautamīputra Śātakarṇi.[33] These land grants bear the expression *alavaṇakhatakam,* meaning the transfer of the king's control over salt, which implies that the king retained certain other sources of revenue. In any case, according to the inscriptions the Sātavāhanas seem to have been the first to introduce the practice of creating revenue-free holdings, though the donees may not have been granted total exemption from taxes.

Land grants with fiscal immunities seem to have become frequent in Central and North India from the 5th Century A.D. onwards as can be inferred from a fairly good number of contemporary Vākāṭaka charters. Unlike the earlier grants, those of the Vākāṭakas indicate that the ruler gave up his control over all the sources of revenue. The immunities recorded in the Vākāṭaka inscriptions are specified in the more complete examples as consisting of (1) *akaradāyī* (not to pay taxes), (2) *abhaṭacchatraprāveśyaḥ* (not to be entered by regular or irregular soldiers), (3) *aparamparagovalivarddaḥ* (not to supply cattle for the transport of touring officials), (4) *apuṣpakṣīrasandohaḥ* (not to supply milk etc. to officers), (5) *acārāsanacarmāṅgāraḥ* (not to provide hide and charcoal), (6) *alavaṇaklinnakreṇikhanakaḥ* (free from the purchase and digging of salt), (7) *apaśumedhyaḥ* (not to supply animals for sacrificial purposes) (8) *sanidhiḥ* (with the right to treasures), (9) *sopanidhiḥ* (with the right to deposits), and (10) *saklṛptopaklṛptaḥ* (with *klṛpta* and *upaklṛpta*). The Basim plates of Vindhyaśakti II[34] provide a still bigger list of

31. *Sel. Ins.,* pp. 186f.
32. *EI,* no. 8(10), 8(14a).
33. *Sel. Ins.,* pp. 192-194.
34. *EI,* XXVI, no. 20, l. 19-26.

fiscal concessions. This record reads "......we grant the following exemptions from restrictions for it (which are) incident to a village belonging to brāhmaṇas proficient in the four *Vedas*, as approved by the former kings, viz. (1) it is to be exempt from (the entrance of) the district police (*araṭṭhasamvinayika*) ; (2) it is to be exempt from the purchase and digging of salt (*alavaṇakeṇṇakkhanaka*) ; (3) it is to be exempt from the presents of gold and grain (*ahiraṇṇadhāṇṇappaṇayadeya*) ; (4) it does not entitle (the state) to (the royalties on) flowers and milk (*apuṣphakkīraggahaṇa*), and (5) to the cows and bullocks for transport (*aparamparagobalivardda*); (6) it does not provide pasture, hides and charcoal (*acārasiddhikācammaṅgālika*); (7) it is not to be entered by soldiers (*abhaḍḍappāvesa*) ; (8) it is not to provide cots, water-pots and servants (*akhaṭṭacollakaveṇesika*) ; (9) it is exempt from taxes (*akarada*) ; (10) it is not to provide horses (*avaha*) ; (11) it carries with it the right to treasures and deposits (*sanidhi sopanidhi*), (12) and to the fields on the borders with *kuśa* grass (*sakutuppanta*), (13) to platform and important documents (*samañcamahākaraṇa*) ; (14) it is to be exempted with immunities of all kinds (*savvajātiparihāraparihitāñca*)."[35] Besides stating that the grant is accompanied by all immunities, the record enumerates, as can be seen above, as many as fourteen exemptions. We may add that a few earlier Pallava inscriptions mention eighteen exemptions though only eight of them are specified.[36] Thus if we take the Sātavāhana ard Pallava inscriptions into account, it would appear that fiscal exemptions in land grants to brāhmaṇas first began in South India and then spread to Central and Northern India.

35. The Basim plates of Vindhyaśakti II, *EI*, XXVI, no. 20, 11. 19-26. The translation of the text by Mirashi has been followed. The fiscal terms referred to in the present context have been discussed in connection with miscellaneous contributions by the villagers.

36. The Hirahadagalli plate of Śivaskandavarman, *Sel. Ins.*, pp. 439-440. Ll. 34-35. The Ongudu plates of Vijayaskandavarman II (*EI*, XV. no. II (A). L. 12) also states the number of exemptions to be eighteen.

Exemption was also practised in the region of modern Bundelkhand and Baghelkhand, where two dynasties ruled almost contemporaneously during the Gupta period. The dates of the Parivrājaka Mahārājas of Dabhāla, who were the feudatories of the Gupta Empire, range from A.D. 475-76 to A.D. 528-29, and those of the Mahārājas of Ucchakalpa from A.D. 493-94 to A.D. 533-34. The land grants of the Parivrājaka rulers, like those of the Vākātakas, are made mostly in favour of the brāhmaṇas, who are granted the right to *udraṅga* and *uparikara* and freed from the interference of regular and irregular soldiers (*acāṭabhaṭaprāveśyḥ*), though the right to punish thieves and robbers and to the fines accruing from them is retained by the ruler. The inscriptions of the Mahārājas of Ucchakalpa mostly record donations by persons of various of classes (including writers, merchants and worshippers of the *Bhāgavata* sect) for the purpose of repair and worship of temples, though grants to individual brāhmaṇas were not altogether unknown.[37] Usually they transfer land to donees with *udraṅga* and *uparikara*, with the exemption from the entrance of *cāṭas* and *bhaṭas*, and, in two cases, with *halikākara* (tax on plough[38] ?). Further, the inhabitants are ordered to pay to the donee the customary tax called *bhāgabhogakara, hiraṇya* and other revenues. It would thus appear that the list of exemptions in the Vākāṭaka land grants is more comprehensive, though certain immunities mentioned in the grants of Parivrājakas and the chiefs of Ucchakalpa do not occur in it.

Since the land grants ascribed to Samudra Gupta are dismissed as spurious, we do not have as much evidence of such grants by the Gupta emperors in the regions directly ruled by them as by their feudatories in Central India. Although the extent of the grant cannot be determined, the Bihar Stone inscription of Skanda Gupta,[39] dated A.D. 489, gives the impression that whole villages were granted by the Gupta emperors on the same terms

37. *CII*, III, no. 26.
38. *Ibid.*, no. 30, 1. 13; *EI*, XIX, no. 21, 1. 10.
39. *CII*, III, no. 12.

as their feudatories.[40] The Gupta rulers also gave their willing consent to the grants made by individuals as can be inferred from seven copper-plate inscriptions of North Bengal and four charters of a similar character from the Faridpur district of Eastern Bengal. These grants involved sale and purchase of fields of different sizes, and such transactions could be effected only with the approval of the local council and the local officials of the central government. Although exemption from different taxes is not recorded in these grants, it is apparent that the state was willing to forego its share of the produce in favour of brāhmaṇas or temples in consideration of one-sixth of spiritual merit that was supposed to accrue to it on account of land gifts made by private individuals.[41]

The above-mentioned grants perhaps caused considerable loss to the state income, more so because in most cases cultivated lands seem to have been donated. The use of the terms *khila*[42] and *aprahata*[43] in the Bengal charters of the Guptas has been interpreted to mean that waste and uncultivated lands were given to the brāhmaṇas,[44] which would imply but little loss of revenue. But on close examination it appears that the terms *khila* and *aprahata* do not mean waste and untilled land in all cases. In the Baigram Copper-plate of A.D. 448,[45] *khila-kṣetra* is accompanied by some homestead land (*vāstu*) for a class of persons serving the temples (*talavāṭaka*),[46] which suggests that it was not entirely waste land. Similarly, in the Damodarpur Copper-plate inscription of A.D. 543, the phrases *aprahata* and *khila* seem to have been used in a conventional sense, for in this case land is

---

40. R. S. Sharma, "A Survey of Land System in India (*c.* 200 B.C.-A.D. 650)", *JBRS,* XLIV, p. 229.
41. The Nandapur Copper-plates of the Gupta year 169, *EI,* XXIII, no. 8, l. 11 ; The Paharpur Copper-plates of the Gupta year, 159, *EI,* XX, no. 5, l. 16.
42. *EI,* XV, no. 7(1), ll. 7-8.
43. *Ibid.,* l. 7.
44. *EI,* XV, p. 131, no. 9. *HRS,* p. 198 ; Maity, *op. cit.,* p. 23-24
45. *Sel. Ins.,* p. 343. ll. 5-9.
46. *Ibid.,* p. 343, l. 9 and n. 9.

so scarce that 5 *kulyavāpas* of land have to be purchased at four different places.[47] Besides, here also untilled (*aprahata*) and fallow (*khila*) land is accompanied by building land (*vāstu*),[48] which makes it doubtful whether the land was waste. And finally, the land in question is not always described as *aprahata*, for at one place the whole area of five *kulyavāpas* is defined as *khila*.[49] Similarly, it may be inferred from another Damodarpur Copper-plate inscription of the last quarter of the 5th Century A.D.[50] that four *kulyavāpas* of land meant for a gift to a god called Kokāmukhasvāmin and seven *kulyavāpas* to Śvetavarāhasvāmin, both purchased by a merchant, were cultivated areas beyond any doubt.[51]

Also in the eastern parts of modern Madhya Pradesh ruled by the Parivrājaka feudatories of the Guptas, where village grants seem to have been more frequent than donations of plots of land, the use of terms denoting uncultivated land appears to have been more or less conventional. Although several grants in Central India were made "according to the maxim of fallow land" (*bhūmicchidranyāya*), there is perhaps nothing else to suggest that villages were not cultivated and settled. Thus in the Khoh Copper-plate inscription of Sarvanātha (A.D. 513), the villages of Vyāghrapallikā and Kācarapallikā, which were granted according to this maxim, were obviously settled villages.[52] They were inhabited by brāhmāṇas and others, to whom the order regarding the grant was conveyed.[53] The communication of such information to the brāhmaṇas and other inhabitants is also recorded in several other contemporary inscriptions of Central India. All this shows that often cultivated and settled land was bestowed upon the donees; and this perhaps resulted in an enormous loss of income and revenue.

---

47. *EI*, XV, no. 1(5), ll. 15-18.
48. Ibid.
49. *Ibid.*, ll. 17-18.
50. *EI*, XV, no. 7(4), ll. 10-11.
51. R. S. Sharma, *Political Ideas and Institutions*, p. 218.
52. *CII*, III, no. 31.
53. *Ibid.*, l. 7.

The type of land tenure indicated by the epigraphs of our period further shows that each grant of land meant a permanent loss of revenue that could otherwise be derived from it by the state. The term *bhūmicchidrayāya,* which occurs in several grants from Central India has been taken by Ghoshal to mean the gift of the full right of ownership such as is acquired by a person making barren land cultivable for the first time.[54] Barnett, who follows the rendering of Yādavaprakāśa and Kauṭilya, believes that *bhūmicchidranyaya* would mean the same condition as that under which tenants hold land in wilderness, forests, i.e. *precario* with reservation of the king's right to eject them at will.[55] While Ghoshal's view needs further explanation, that of Barnett cannot be accepted. The records reveal that according to the *bhūmicchidranyāya* land was granted in perpetuity not only to the donee but also to his posterity. It is stated in the Khoh Copper-plate inscription of Sarvanātha that the villages of Vyāghrapallikā and Kācarapallikā were given away according to the *bhūmicchidranyāya* to be enjoyed by the sons and sons' sons of the donee.[56] Similarly the Maliya Copper-plate inscription (A.D. 571-72) of Dharasena II informs us that the village Antarātra was bestowed upon the brāhmaṇa Rudrabhūti "to endure for the same time with the moon, the sun, the ocean, the rivers and the earth; (and) to be enjoyed by the succession of (his) sons and sons' sons".[57] These clauses evidently suggest that land was donated in perpetuity.

Perpetual grants of land can also be inferred from the Bengal charters, which record donations of land according to the *nīvi-*

54. *HRS,* p. 195; *IHQ,* V, p. 385. For the discussion of different views see Maity *op. cit,* pp. 30-32.

55. *JARS,* 1931, p. 165. In the chapter on the *bhūmicchidravidhānam* in the *Arthaśāstra* (II. 2) Kauṭilya seems to differentiate the *bhūmicchidra* land from the settled parts (*grāma* or *nagara*) including cultivable areas, which he treats in a separate chapter (*janapadaniveśa*). Yādavaprakāśa in his *Vaijayantī* (quoted, Maity, *op. cit.,* p. 31) suggests that the term *bhūmicchidra* means land unfit for cultivation (*bhūmicchidraṇakṛṣyayogya*).

56. *CII,* III, no. 31. 1. 10.

57. *Ibid.,* III, no. 38, 1. 38

dharma,[58] the *aksayanīvidharma*[59] or the *akṣayanīvi*,[60] *apradādharma*[61] and *apradākṣaya-nīvi* or the *apradākṣayanīvimaryādā*.[62] The word *nīvi* of the inscription is to be explained as the fixed capital out of the interest on which a particular expense is to be met[63] for ever. However, to make a gift of land according to the *nīvidharma* is to give it on condition that the endowment is to be maintained as perpetual. The donee can only spend the interest for specified purposes. This interpretation is also supported by the Damodarpur Copper-plate,[64] which states that the land should be enjoyed as long as the moon, the sun and the stars exist. In other words, the *nīvidharma* means a grant in perpetuity without the right of alienation. A similar meaning is ascribed to the term *akṣayanīvidharma*, in which the word *akṣaya* is perhaps added to give more emphasis to the permanence of the endowment.[65] Like the *nīvidharma*, *akṣayanīvidharma* is also accompanied by the expression "*sāśvatacandrārkkatāraka*", as in the Paharpur[66] and the Baigram[67] Copper-plates. These records thus indicate that the endowment was perpetual and could be held eternally. As regards *apradādharma* Maity[68] points out that *apradā* literally means *napradā*, i.e., either that which cannot be alienated or that which does not yield anything. Thus, in his opinion, the grant of land according to the *apradādharma* perhaps means that the donee has all the rights to enjoy such property but has no right to dispose of it. So such grants were also perpetual, which is further supported by the Damodarpur Copper-

58. *EI*, XV, no. 7(1), 1. 9.
59. *Ibid*, XX, no. 5, 1. 19.
60. *Sel. Ins.*, p. 345, 11. 19-20.
61. *EI*, XV, no. 7(5), 1. 18.
62. *Ibid.*, no. 7(2), 11. 6-7.
63. *Ibid.*, VIII, p. 82 ; p. XV. p. 131 ; XVIII, p. 347.
64. *Ibid.*, XV, no. 7(1), 1. 8.
65. Maity, *op. cit.*, p. 27.
66. *EI*, XX. no. 5, 1. 20
67. *Sel. Ins.*, p. 344, 1. 11.
68. Maity, *op. cit.*, p. 29.

plate of A.D. 433-34 where it is stated that one Amṛtadeva endowed five *kulyavāpas* of *khila* land with *vāstu* according to *apradādharma* to Bhagavān Śvetavarāhasvāmin (i.e., the god Viṣṇu) for use for ever (*sāśvatkālabhogya*).[69] The record requires the administrative agents to respect the grant.[70] In other words, the *apradādharma*, like the *nīvidharma*, implies that the original endowment must not be diminished or destroyed, but must be preserved intact in perpetuity.[71] It follows from all this that land grants were mostly perpetual, though in certain cases the donee was deprived of the right to freely dispose of the land.

It may, however, be suggested that resumption of a gift of land or village was not altogether unknown. The grant of the Vākāṭaka ruler Pravarasena II[72] clearly lays down that the thousand brāhmaṇas to whom a village is granted can hold it only on condition that they commit no treason against the kingdom, do not slay brāhmaṇas, do not commit theft and adultery, do not poison kings, do not wage wars, and do no wrong to other villagers. In contrast to other contemporary land charters, this inscription shows that sometimes land grant was executed in favour of the brāhmaṇas not only to acquire religious merit but also to prevent them from acting in opposition;[73] and that their land was liable to confiscation if they behaved in a manner not conducive to the interest of the state. Such cases of resumption of gifted land or village may have been exceptional and do not contradict the general practice of making perpetual grants, which were safeguarded from even remote chances of confiscation by means of curses and denunciations, sometimes, expressed in very strong words in the epigraphs. The Sanchi Stone inscription of Candra Gupta II, records that "whosoever shall interfere with this arrangement (of the grant)—he shall become invested with (the guilt of) the slaughter of a cow or of a brāhmaṇa and with

69. *EI*, XV, no. 7(5), 1. 18.
70. *Ibid.*, 1. 19.
71. Maity, *op. cit.*, p. 29 cf, *Sel. Ins.*, p. 284, n. 10.
72. *CII*, III, no. 55, 11. 41-43.
73. Cf. R. S. Sharma, *Political Ideas and Institutions*, p. 204.

the five sins that entail immediate retribution."[74] This is repeated in the Gadhwa inscription.[75] Similar clauses appear in the Vākāṭaka and other contemporary land grants.

Fiscal exemptions were granted not only to the brāhmaṇas but also to the temples. We learn of two grants of land to a temple of the goddess Piṣṭapurī in Central India, during the first half of the sixth century A.D.[76] In the second half of the same century a settled village in the Gaya district, "possessed of great wealth and enjoyment", was granted to the goddess Bhavānī by the Maukhari chieftain Anantavarman.[77] In Bengal, during the 5th and 6th centuries A.D. plots of land were given to the temples of Govindasvāmin,[78] Svetavarāhasvāmin[79] and Kokāmukhasvāmin.[80] Although some grants of land were made to the gods and goddesses leading to the rise of land owning temples, most recipients of land endowments were the brāhmaṇas. An analysis of the grants dated in the Kalacuri-Cedi era, from the middle of the 3rd century A.D. to about A.D. 750, shows that of thirty-one grants, two were made to the Buddhist monasteries, three to Hindu temples, and the remaining 26 to brāhmaṇas.[81]

While, on the one hand, land grants with fiscal exemptions involved loss of revenue to the state, on the other, they tended to increase the burden on peasants and thus served to accelerate the process of social polarisation. Brāhmaṇas may have done useful work by providing education and catering to the religious needs of the people, but they do not seem to have been directly associated much with the productive activities which were carried on by the lower *varṇas*. The brāhmaṇas were liberally rewarded for their work, but at the cost of the lower *varṇas* who worked as peasants in the villages. The creation of tax-free holdings for

74. *CII*, no. 5, 11. 10.
75. *Ibid.*, no. 7, 11. 16-17.
76. *Ibid.*, no. 25, 11. 14-15 ; *Ibid.*, no. 31, 11. 7-11.
77. *Ibid.*, no. 50, 1. 10.
78. *Sel. Ins.*, p. 343, 1. 4.
79. *Ibid.*, p. 388-9.
80. *EI*, XV, no. 7(4), 11. 5-7.
81. *CII*, IV, Introduction, p. CXLIX.

the brāhmaṇas added to the high social and economic status which they already enjoyed, thus sharpening the difference between various classes. This social cleavage may have been further widened by the fact that the donees were given also the right to govern the inhabitants of the villages granted to them.[82] This is corroborated by Buddhaghoṣa, who explains the term *brahmadeyya* in early Pāli texts as carrying with it judicial and administrative rights.[83] What is striking, sometimes the right to govern was free from any interference by the king and his officers. Realisation of dues in the donated villages, therefore, may have been governed by the whims and caprices of the individual beneficiaries, who could conveniently choose to oppress the people to their own benefit. The epigraphs instruct the donees not to realise such taxes from the people as are not due to the king,[84] but in view of the fact that the donees wielded considerable economic and political power and did not apprehend royal interference, it is not possible that they always acted according to the ideals set forth in the charters.

82. In several Central Indian land grants of the Gupta period the inhabitants of gift-villages are repeatedly exhorted to obey the commands of the donee (*CII*, no. 26, 1. 10; no. 27, 1. 12; no. 29, 1. 18; no. 29, 11. 14-15 etc.). Similarly, the charters of the Maitraka rulers describe the gift-villages as *rājakīyānāmahastaprakṣepanīya* (*JUB*, (NS) I, pp. 18, 27, 31, 34, 56 etc.), which means non-interference by royal officers in the affairs of a donated area of land or village.

83. PTS, *Pali-English Dictionary, s. v. brahmadeyya.*

84. *CII*, III, no. 26, 11. 11-12; no. 27, 1. 13; no. 28, 1. 20 etc.

CHAPTER XI

FISCAL UNITS

The variety of taxes discussed in the foregoing pages presupposes an elaborate and efficient system of revenue administration. For general administrative convenience the kingdom was divided into a number of units which, in their turn, were sub-divided into smaller ones. There is nothing in the post-Maurya and Gupta sources to indicate the prevalence of separate units for revenue assessment and collection. Nor should we expect that in ancient times, when there was very little differentiation of functions, there could be so much separation between fiscal and the general administration as to lead to the establishment of exclusively fiscal units. In the land grants from the Gupta period a certain piece of donated land or village is almost invariably described as being situated within certain units of the empire. More important is the fact that such grants of land are mostly accompanied by fiscal immunities and privileges. The mention of fiscal exemption and territorial divisions in one and the same inscription indicates that the latter served as fiscal units as well.

The antiquity of village as the lowest unit of fiscal administration can be traced back to pre-Maurya times. The word *grāma* occurs even in the *Ṛgveda*, though its administrative importance is not clear from the Vedic references.[1] In any case, village came to be recognised as a unit of administration in pre-Maurya times when perhaps collectors were appointed over groups of villages.[2] In Maurya times, as the head of one village or several villages, the *gopa* had to perform several administrative functions.

---

1. *Hist. Dharm.*, III, p. 153.

The post-Maurya sources indicate that village emerged as an important administrative division. Manu's reference to *grāmika* shows that village was a unit of administration.[3] A passage of the *Mahābhāṣya*. also suggests the same.[4] The *Milindapañho* mentions *gāmasāmika* in the sense of the lord of a village.[5] The *Gāthāsaptaśatī* refers to *gramaṇū* in a similar sense.[6] The *Jātakas* too mention the *gāmanī*[7] and the *gāmabhojaka*.[8] In the Gupta period, the village headman is known to Vātsyāyana who refers to him in his *Kāmasūtra*.[9] Again, the *Mahāvaṁśa* relates the story of the householder Rohana, who was headman in the village of Kitti near the Koṭṭa mountain.[10]

That village was an administrative unit in post-Maurya and Gupta times is amply corroborated by several epigraphic records. A *grāmika* is expressly mentioned in the Mathura Jain inscription of the time of Vāsudeva.[11] Another Jain votive epigraph from the same place, probably assignable to the Kuṣāṇa period, mentions two generations of an apparently local *grāmika*.[12] Contemporary South Indian records use the term *grāma* to describe such places as Rasopadra,[13] Pisājipadakam[14] and Sālmalipada.[15] An inscription on a relic casket from Charsadda in the Peshawar region refers to a *grāmasvāmī* named Avakhajdasa[16] but does not give any indication of a village being a unit of administration.

In the Gupta period, mention is made of Revatīgrāma in

2. Basham, *The Wonder that was India*, p. 105.
3. *Manu*, VII. 115-116.
4. *Mahābhāṣya*, V. 2 19. p. 340, 1. 8.
5. *Milinda.*, p. 147.
6. *Gāthāsaptaśatī*, VII. 28, 31.
7. *Jāt.*, IV, p. 310.
8. *Ibid.*, I, pp. 199, 354, 483 ; II, pp. 136, 300.
9. *Kāmasūtra*, V, 5. 5.
10. *Mahāvaṁsa*, XXIII. 55.
11. *Lüders' List*, no. 69(a).
12. *Ibid.*, no. 48.
13. *Ibid.*, no. 963.
14. *EI*, VIII, no. 8(2), 1. 11.
15. *Ibid.*, no. 8(3), 1. 13.
16. *Ibid.*, XXIV, no. 2(i), 1. 10.

the spurious Gaya grant of Samudra Gupta.[17] The Bihar Stone-pillar inscription of Skanda Gupta calls a village field as the *grāmakṣetram*.[18] The undated Bhitari pillar inscription of the same ruler clearly refers to *grāma* in the words : *grāmaṁ enaṁ sa vidadhe pituḥ puṇyābhivṛddhaye*.[19] The Kahaum epigraph of Skanda Gupta points to the *grāma*,[20] which occurs also in the records of the Parivrājaka Mahārājas.[21] Reference to *grāma* in these land grants may indicate that village was a unit of administration.

Pran Nath, principally relying on a commentator of the Jain work called *prājñāpanopaṅga*, interprets *grāma* as "an estate or survey village which can pay 18 kinds of taxes."[22] This would rule out the possibility of the village being a political unit. The view of Pran Nath, however, is untenable for the passage on which the explanation of *grāma* as an estate is based is misunderstood by him.[23] Nor does his interpretation of the text of Yājñavalkya, whom he quotes to support his theory, appear acceptable. Yājñavalkya[24] states that the disputes about the boundary of a field should be settled by *sāmantas* (neighbours), and *samagrāmāḥ* which has been taken by Pran Nath to mean "persons possessing equal estates."[25] The translation of *grāma* as estate, however, does not suit all the contexts in which it is used. Therefore, in our opinion, normally *grāma* stood for village, which was evidently the smallest territorial unit for administrative purposes.

The next larger division of administration was *āhāra*, which was originally a fiscal unit. This was already prevalent under the Mauryas as can be inferred from the Sarnath edict, which

---

17. *CII*, III, no. 60, l. 7.
18. *Ibid.*, no. 12, l. 26.
19. *Ibid.*, no. 13, l. 18.
20. *Ibid*, III, no. 15, l. 5.
21. *Ibid.*, no. 21, l. 10.
22. *Economic Condition of Ancient India*, p. 26.
23. *JORM*, IV, pp. 211 ff ; cf. *Hist. Dharm.*, III, p. 140, n. 182.
24. *Yāj.*, II. 152.
25. *Op. cit.*, p. 212.

refers to *āhāla* (Sans. *āhāra*).[26] This term is also mentioned in post-Maurya epigraphs. The Sanchi stūpa, and the Nasik and Kanheri inscriptions refer to Ujeni *āhāra*,[27] Govardhana *āhāra*,[28] Māmala *āhāra*,[29] Sopāraka *āhāra*[30] and Kapura *āhāra*.[31] These inscriptions, however, belong to Central and Western India and may not reflect the conditions prevailing in Eastern India;[32] and there is nothing to prove the prevalence of *āhāra* units in the eastern region during post-Maurya times.

The term *āhāra* occurs also in the Gupta inscriptions, but the unit was mainly confined to Central and Western India. Thus the Poona plate of Prabhāvatīgupta of the 13th regnal year refers to a gift of land in Supratiṣṭha *āhāra* to the east of the village Velavaṇaka.[33] The Supratiṣṭha *āhāra* is also known from the Wadgaon and Kothuraka grants of the Vākāṭaka ruler Pravarasena II.[34] Apart from these Vākāṭaka records, *āhāra* finds frequent mention in the land grants of the Maitraka kings, who ruled in Saurāṣṭra. In some of their documents, however, there occurs *āharaṇī* instead of *āhāra*. Thus in the Ganesgad plates of Dhruvasena I, dated A.D. 526-27, mention is made of the village of Hariyāṇaka, which is described as belonging to Akṣasahaprāpa of the Hastavapra *āharaṇī*.[35] The Palitana plates of the same ruler mention the Jyeṣṭhaka *grāma* belonging to the Akṣasaraka *prāveśya* in the Hastavapra *āharaṇī*.[36] Still another

---

26. *Sel. Ins.*, p. 76, 1. 9.
27. *Lüders' List*, no. 268.
28. *Ibid.*, no. 1124.
29. *Ibid.*, no. 1105.
30. *Ibid.*, no. 988.
31. *Ibid.*, no. 1133.
32. The existence of *āhāra* in Gujarat-Kathiawad region can be further inferred from its prevalence in Aparānta (modern Konkan), the Deccan, Karnataka and the South under the Āndhras, Cuṭu-Śatakarṇīs, Kadambas and the early Pallavas from the 2nd to the 5th centuries A.D. (Sankalia, *The Archeology of Gujarat*, p. 193).
33. *EI*, XV, no. 4, 1. 10.
34. *Ibid.*, XXVII, no. 16, 1. 17; XXVI, no. 21, 1. 17.
35. *Ibid.*, III, no. 46, 1. 12.
36. *Ibid.*, XVII, no. 7, 1. 12.

grant of the same ruler from the same place of the year 206 records the bestowal of several plots of land in the villages Madhakaṇā, Tapasīya and Tiniśaka, all in the Hastavapra *āharaṇī*, on Kumār-aśarman and Jarābhajin of the Śāṇḍilya *gotra.*[37] It seem that *āhāra* and *āharaṇī* were used interchangeably in the administrative nomen-clature of the Maitrakas of Valabhī. Again, in a grant of Dharasena II of the year 270, the expression *Kheṭakāhāraviṣaya* is recorded.[38] This may be taken to imply that the term *āhāra* and *viṣaya* were sometimes used synonymously.[39]

It has been suggested by Saletore that there is "an apparent connection between the *āhāra*, a territorial unit, and *agrahāra*, a village granted to a brāhmaṇa.[40] Dikshitar adds that if there was any close relationship between the two, it is possible that *āhāra*, like the *agrahāra*, was one for the use of which the reason was partly religious, for the formation and grant of an *agrahāra* was considered to be an act of religious duty and charity.[41] This view, however, is highly conjectural. The word *āhāra* is derived from *ā+hṛ*, meaning to offer, in the present context, some form of food, the produce of land, later other taxes.[42] The connotation of the term, thus, appears to be more fiscal than religious. Hence in our opinion, *āhāra* was a unit of administration—both fiscal and political, having little to do with *agrahāra* which was a technical expression denoting a gift-village bestowed upon a brāhmaṇa.

Viṣaya, which has been generally accepted to mean a district, was another administrative unit in certain parts of the country during our period. The antiquity of the term goes back to the third century B.C., for the Sarnath Pillar Edict of Aśoka refers to the Koṭa *viṣaya* (*Koṭṭa viṣaya*).[43] The term *viṣaya* does not occur

---

37. *Ibid.*, XI, no. 9(i), 11. 16-19.
38. *IA*, VII, p. 70.
39. Virji, *Ancient History of Saurāshtra*, p. 235 ; *CII*, III, p. 173 n.
40. *Life in the Gupta Age*, p. 314.
41. *Gupta Polity*, p. 238.
42. Sankalia, *Studies in the Historical and Cultural Geography and Ethnology of Gujarat*, p. 22 ; cf. Monier-Williams, *Sanskrit-English Dictionary*, s.v. *āhāra*.
43. *Sel. Ins.*, p. 76, 1.10

in the post-Maurya epigraphs, but the possibility of its being known during the post-Maurya period cannot altogether be discounted. The Allahabad Pillar inscription of Samudra Gupta[44] mentions the existence of *viṣaya* and *bhukti* in the dominions of the Kuṣāṇas. The prevalence of *viṣaya* units in pre-Gupta times is corroborated by the *Suvarṇaprabhāsottamasūtra*, a Buddhist Mahayānist text of the third century A.D., which, while defining a *devaputra*, refers to kings ruling in *viṣayas*.[45] But in any case, there is nothing to prove that *viṣaya* was known in Western India in post-Maurya times, for they do not find mention in the Śātavāhana records.

The word *viṣaya* occurs frequently in the Gupta inscriptions. Four out of the five Damodarpur charters, ranging from A.D. 443 to A.D. 533, refer to Koṭivarṣa *viṣaya*, situated in the Puṇḍravardhana *bhukti;* and the latest among them describes it as being administered by the *viṣayapati* Svāyambhūdeva.[46] Similarly, in the Dhanaidaha Copper-plate inscription of Kumāra Gupta I, assignable to A.D. 432-33, we come across the *viṣaya* of Khada-(ṭa)pāra, which, like Koṭivarṣa, formed part of Puṇḍravardhana *bhukti*.[47] Again, in the undated Bihar Stone inscription of Skanda Gupta, the town of Ajapura is said to have been situated in an unnamed *viṣaya*.[48]

The Gupta records further imply the existence of this unit in Central India as well. We gather from the Indore grant of Skanda Gupta, dated A.D. 465-66, that the officer in charge of a *viṣaya*, the *viṣayapati* Sarvanāga, governed Antarvedi[49] or the country lying between the Ganges and the Jamuna. *Viṣaya* as a political division was perhaps also adopted by the Hūṇa rulers

44. *CII*, III, no. 1, 11.23-24.
45. *yad iha* [*var. idaṁ*] *lokapālebhir etarhi mama pṛcchitaḥ* |
sarvasattvahitārthāya vaksye'haṁ śāstraṁ uttamam ||
narāṇāṁ sambhavaṁ vakṣye yuktvāham manujālaye |
hetunā yena rājāno bhavanti viṣayeṣu ca || —*JA*, 1934, p. 3.
46. *EI*, XV, no. 7(1), 1.3; no. 7(2), ,1.3; no. 7(4) 1.3; no. 7(5) 11. 3-4.
47. *Ibid.*, XVIII, no. 23, 1.7.
48. *CII*, III, no. 12, 1.25.
49. *Ibid.*, no. 16, 1.4.

of Central India, for the Eran Boar inscription of Toramāṇa, who achieved political prominence shortly after Budha Gupta, informs us that Dhānyaviṣṇu built a stone temple "in his own *viṣaya* of Arikiṇa."[50]

The *viṣaya* unit was also current in Saurāṣṭra, which was ruled by the Maitraka kings of Valabhī, the feudatories of the imperial Guptas. In a grant of Dharasena IV, dated A.D. 650, there occurs the expression : *"Śivabhāgapura viṣaye ghṛtālaya-bhūmau phaṅgulapallikāgrāmaḥ,"*[51] according to which the *grāma, bhūmi* and *viṣaya* formed three successive units of administration.

Although from the provenance of the inscriptions referred to above, it appears that *viṣaya* was perhaps an important unit of administration in most parts of the country, the actual expanse of the territory covered by the term is difficult to ascertain. As noted earlier, Puṇḍravardhana *bhukti* included Koṭivarṣa *viṣaya* and Khada(ṭa)pāraka *viṣaya ;* and this would mean that *viṣaya* was a smaller unit than *bhukti.* This is also borne out by the Deo-Barnarka inscription of Jīvitagupta.[52] In the Mandasor Stone inscription (A.D. 473-74) of Kumāra Gupta I and Bandhuvarman, however, the whole of Lāṭa is called a *viṣaya.*[53] Sircar points out that Lāṭa was a country to the west of west Mālava and Navasārikā (modern Nausari) was one of its chief cities.[54] From this, it may be guessed that in some parts of Central India, *viṣaya* covered a fairly big area, though we do not know its position in relation to *bhukti.* So far as the Maitraka kingdom is concerned, Virji opines that, as the Hastavapra *āhāra,* the Kauṇḍinyapura *viṣaya* and the Vardhamāna *bhukti* formed the main divisions of Saurāṣṭra, the unit *āhāra* seems to be synonymous with *viṣaya* and *bhukti.*[55] Since none of the Maitraka inscriptions mentions any unit bigger

50. *Ibid.,* no. 36, 1.7.
51. *I.A.,* VII, p. 79.
52. *CII,* III, p. 218, n. 5.
53. *Ibid.,* no. 18, 1.3.
54. *Sel. Ins.,* p. 290, n. 1.
55. Virji, *op. cit.,* p. 235.

than *āhāra, bhukti* and *viṣaya,* all of which were synonymous, it appears that these were the largest units of administration, though the area covered by each may have been different.

Bhukti, which means enjoyment, is often referred to in the inscriptions as a unit of administration. The Allahabad panegyric of Samudra Gupta indicates that the dominions of the Kuṣāṇas were divided into *bhuktis* and *viṣayas.*[56] The prevalence of *bhukti* in pre-Gupta times, however, is not corroborated by any source, and hence may have been a projection of Gupta administrative divisions into Kuṣāṇa times. In any case, *bhukti* was an important unit of administration from the Gupta period onwards. The Damodarpur Copper-plate grant of Kumāra Gupta, ascribed to the fifth century, mentions an *uparika* in the province (*bhukti*) of Puṇḍravardhana and the *Kumārāmātya* Vetravarman appointed by him in the *viṣaya* of Koṭivarṣa.[57] Another epigraph of the same ruler from the same place dated A.D. 447 refers to Koṭivarṣa *viṣaya* situated in the Puṇḍravardhana *bhukti.*[58] A similar reference is available in still another inscription from Damodarpur of the reign of Budha Gupta.[59] The Mallasarul plate of Vijayasena[60] refers to Vardhamāna *bhukti.* From the above-mentioned epigraphs it appears that in Eastern India, *bhukti* was a bigger unit than a *viṣaya.* This division continued even during the days of Harṣa as is indicated by his Madhuban plates which refer to Somakuṇḍaka *grāma* belonging to the Kuṇḍadhanī *viṣaya* in the Śrāvastī *bhukti.*[61]

Bhukti, however, does not seem to have been very popular in Central India and Northern Deccan ruled by the Vākāṭakas

56. *CII,* III, no. 1, 23-24.
57. *EI,* XV, no. 7(1), 11. 2-4.
58. *Ibid.,* no. 7(2), 11. 2-3.
59. *Ibid.,* no. 7(4), 11. 2-3.
60. *Ibid.,* XXIII, no. 24, 1.3 Apart from these *bhuktis,* we have reference in inscriptions of the Gupta and early post-Gupta age to Tīra *bhukti* (North Bihar), Nagara *bhukti* (South Bihar), and Ahicchatra *bhukti,* all situated in the Ganges Valley (Raychaudhuri, *Political History of Ancient India,* p. 560.)
61. *EI,* VII, no. 22, 1.8

whose inscriptions rarely mention it. But this unit was not altogether unknown in the Vākāṭaka dominions, for an epigraph of Pravarasena II from the Wardha district records a grant of land in Mahallalāṭa *grāma*, which is described as being situated in the Asi *bhukti*.[62] This inscription, however, does not refer to any unit between the *grāma* and the *bhukti*, which may suggest that in the kingdom of the Vākāṭakas *bhukti* was constituted by villages and not by the *viṣayas* as in Eastern India, which was ruled directly by the imperial Guptas. In other words, *bhukti* in the Central Indian region covered perhaps a smaller area than in those parts of the country which were under the direct sway of the Gupta emperors.[63]

With regard to the Gujarat-Kathiawad region Sankalia writes, "It is doubtful if any part of Kathiawad or Gujarat was named a *bhukti* as in Bihar and Bengal.[64]" The Nagowa plates of Dhruvasena II,[65] of course, speak of Mālavaka *bhukti*, but the record is dated A.D. 639-40 and thus should not necessarily reflect the condition prevailing prior to the middle of the 6th century A.D. Besides, Mālavaka *bhukti* is also known as Mālavaka *viṣaya* and thus, if at all *bhukti* was known in the Maitraka kingdom, it was perhaps a synonym of *viṣaya*.

The term *bhukti* has been compared with *bhoga*, a term of similar import, which occurs in the Bhumara Pillar inscription of Hastin, dated A.D. 508.[66] The principal sentence of this record has been translated by Fleet as follows : "In [the boundary of] the kingdom of the *Mahārāja* Hastin who meditates on the feet of (the god) Mahādeva ; at [the village of] Āmblodā; [and] in [the boundary of] the *bhoga* of the *Mahārāja* Sarvanātha ; [this

62. *Ibid.*, XXIV, no. 37(A & B), 1.13.

63. It has been suggested by Raychaudhuri that *bhukti* of South India may be comparable to modern to *tāluk* or *tahsil*. Vide Yazdani (ed.), *Early History of Deccan,* I, p. 49.

64. Sankalia, *Archaeology of Gujarat,* p. 194.

65. *EI, VIII,* no. 20, 11. 41-42.

66. *CII,* III, no. 24. 11. 1-7.

boundary-pillar] has been set up."[67] According to Fleet, "*bhoga*, literally enjoyment, possession, government is a technical territorial term, probably of much the same purport as the *bhukti* of other inscriptios."[68] It is true that, like *bhukti*, 'a province,' the word *bhoga* is often used to indicate a district of a kingdom. In several copper-plate grants, the gift-village is stated to have been situated in a particular territorial unit styled *bhoga*.[69] But none of these inscriptions belongs to our period. There is, of course, a reference to the Paṭṭana *bhoga* in the Siripuram plates of Anantavarman, assignable to the early sixth century A.D.[70] Since this epigraph belongs to the Vizagapatam district in the eastern Deccan, and there is no North Indian epigraphic evidence to prove the use of *bhoga* in the sense of an administrative unit, it is difficult to state with certainty that *bhoga*, wherever it occurs, indicates a territorial division. In any case, at least in the Bhumara Pillar inscription of Hastin, cited above, *bhoga* does not appear to be a territorial term. If this meaning be assigned to the term, Sircar rightly points out,[71] we can hardly escape the conclusion that *Mahārāja Sarvanāthabhoga* was a small district of the kingdom of Hastin, even though its name was associated with that of Mahārāja Sarvanātha, apparently the contemporary Ucchakalpa king of that name. This does not appear to support the suggestion that the pillar in question was set up in order to demarcate the boundary between the kingdoms of Hastin and Sarvanātha. In the present context, therefore, the phrase *mahārājasarvanāthabhoga* clearly means the territory enjoyed by Mahārāja Sarvanātha and not any administrative unit.

Another territorial division mentioned in a few Gupta land-sale charters from Eastern India is the *vīthī*. The Mallasarul Copper-plate of Vijayasena records a grant of eight *kulyavāpas* of

67. *Ibid.*, pp. 111-112.

68. *Ibid.*, p. 112, n. 1

69. *EI*, VI, no. 29, 11. 19-20 ; XIX, no. 8, 11. 25-27 ; XXIII, no. 10, 1. 16 etc.

70. *Ibid.*, XXIV, no. 9, 1. 15.

71. *Ibid.*, XXXIII, p. 169.

land in the village of Vettragarta within the Vakattaka *vīthī* of the Vardhamana *bhukti*.[72] The relevant passage in this grant refers to no other territorial unit between a *vīthī* and a *bhukti* and thus implies that the latter included the former. But often *vīthī* is mentioned as forming a part of the *viṣaya*, which was a smaller unit than the *bhukti*. The Kalaikuri Copper-plate inscription of the Gupta year 120 (A.D. 430), assignable to the reign of Kumāra Gupta, mentions the Śṛṅgavera *vīthī* with its headquarters Pūrṇakauśika, situated most probably in the Puṇḍravardhana *viṣaya*.[73] The Nandapur inscription of the year 169 refers to Nanda *vīthī* as lying under the jurisdiction of Ambila *grāma-agrahāra*, where the headquarters of *vīṣayapati* Chatramaha were probably situated.[74] That the *vīthī* was under the jurisdiction of the *viṣaya* is also attested by a later inscription which mentions Kumudasūtra *vīthī* in the Gayā *viṣaya*.[75] From the above, it appears that the *vīthi* divisions generally formed part of the *viṣaya*, though they could as well be under the jurisdiction of a *bhukti*.

Most of the *vīthīs* that we know from the epigraphs were perhaps situated on the banks of rivers. The Vakattaka *vīthī* of the Mallasarul plates of Vijayasena included a strip of the country along the north bank of the Damodar river. The Nanda *vīthī* identical with Nandapur, the findspot of the grant, was situated on the Ganges.[76] Similar references are also available from later Bengal records of the Pāla and Sena dynasties.[77] Thus it appears that the *vīthī* was a territorial division generally situated on river-banks.[78]

---

72. *Ibid.*, XXIII, no. 24, 1.5.
73. *IHQ*, XIX, p. 24.
74. *EI*, XXIII, no. 8, 11. 1-3.
75. *Ibid.*, XVII, no. 17, 1.27.
76. *Ibid.*, XXIII, p. 53.
77. For reference see *EI*, XXIII, pp. 158-159.
78. Cf. Dikshitar, *op. cit.*, p. 233. The *Amarakośa* uses the word *vīthī* in the sense of a row, range (II. 4.4) or a road (III. 3.87). Kālidāsa also uses the expression *rājavīthī* in the sense of a road (*Raghu*, XVIII. 39). But this meaning does not suit the context in which *vīthī* is mentioned in the epigraphs.

Towns and even large cities went by the name of *pura*. In the Mandasor inscription of Kumāra Gupta and Bandhuvarman, dated A.D. 473-74, mention is made of Daśa*pura*, now known as Dasor.[79] A city called Sarabha*pura* is said to have been the place wherefrom the Arang plates of Mahājayarāja were issued.[80] It appears that Daśa*pura* and Sarabha*pura*, from where the above—mentioned grants were issued, were administrative headquarters. But strangely enough, no contemporary inscription from Eastern India refers to *pura* as being an administrative division. Nevertheless, it is not improbable that towns constituted separate units as distinguished from village units.

Nor do the inscriptions of Saurāṣṭra mention *pura* as a fiscal unit, though they indicate the prevalence of towns as units of administration. An inscription of Dhruvasena I of the Maitraka dynasty mentions *drāṅgika*, which has been translated by Bühler as "the head of the town."[81] A Valabhī grant (A.D. 556) of the Maitraka Guhasena records the grant of a village in Maṇḍalī *draṅga* and communicates the order to the *drāṅgika*, among others.[82] During the reign of his son Dharasena II, this unit must have been in use, and an officer, probably in charge of such a territorial division, may have been known as a *drāṅgika*.[83] Since *draṅga* means a town,[84] *drāṅgika* may therefore denote an officer looking after its administration. In short, it appears that town formed a unit of administration.

The Maitraka inscriptions of Saurāṣṭra from the Gupta period onwards also mention *sthalī* as a territorial division, but it does not occur in earlier or contemporary records of other parts of the country. A grant of Dharasena I of Valabhī records the bestowal of two villages, Maheśvaradāsenaka, in the Hastavapra *āharaṇī*, and Devabhadrapallikā in the *sthalī* of Dhārākeṭha, to

79. *CII*, III, no. 18, 1.4.

80. *Ibid.*, no. 40, 1.1 ; cf. *Ibid.*, no. 41, 1.1.

81. *IA*, IV, p. 105.

82. *Ibid.*, p. 175.

83. *CII*, III, no. 38, 1.20.

84. Monier-Williams, *Sanskrit-English Dictionary, s. v. draṅga*.

the beneficiaries.[85] Similarly the Jhar grant of Dharasena II mentions the name of the village of Vaṭa*grāma* in the Dīpaṇaka-*peṭha* and the Bilvakhāṭa *sthalī*.[86] Again, the Palitana plates of the same ruler, dated A.D. 571, record gift of pieces of land belonging to Bamvāvānaka *sthalī*, Nimbakūpa *sthalī* and Kadambapadra *sthalī*.[87] References to *sthalī* are found in several other Maitraka inscriptions.[88] In all, names of about eighteen *sthalīs* are found to have been recorded in Surāṣṭradeśa.[89]

The exact significance of the term *sthalī* in the contemporary administrative nomenclature is difficult to ascertain for lack of sufficient data. The above-cited inscription of Dharasena I, however, mentions the village of Devabhadrapallikā as being situated in the *sthalī* of Dhārākeṭha, which indicates that the *sthalī* was a larger unit than the *grāma*. Again, the Vala Copper-plate inscription of Śilāditya I records the grant of the village Puṇḍarakūpikā besides lands in three other villages, Uccapadra, Kakijja and Indrāṇipadraka; and all the four villages are stated to have been situated in the Puṣyānaka *sthalī*.[90] This shows that a *sthalī* consisted of several villages. The *sthalī*, however, does not appear to have been a big division. A Maitraka grant of A.D. 610 makes it clear that the three *sthalīs* mentioned in it were not far distant from one another.[91] The headquarters of Bilvakhāṭa, Jhari and Vaṭapallikā lay at a distance of about 40 miles from one another, thus covering an area of about 100 square miles.[92] In other words, *sthalī* perhaps comprised a comparatively smaller area than *āhāra*, *viṣaya* and *bhukti*.

It has been pointed out by Virji that since *sthalī* means a natural spot of ground, it was originally used to designate a natural

85. *IA*, VI, p. 12.
86. *Ibid.*, XV, p. 187.
87. *EI*, XI, no. 5, ll. 24-28.
88. *IA*, V, p. 212; VI, p. 12; XIV, p. 330; XV, p. 187, etc.
89. Virji, *op. cit.*, p. 239.
90. *IA*, XIV, p. 330.
91. *Ibid.*, XV, p. 187.
92. Virji, *op. cit.*, p. 239.

division.[93] Whatever be its origin, in our opinion, the frequent occurrence of the term in the inscriptions of Saurāṣṭra from the Gupta period onwards makes it likely that the *sthalī* became one of the usual administrative divisions, especially in the Maitraka kingdom.

A territorial division called the *paṭṭa,* of which the village formed a part, is mentioned in some epigraphs of Gupta times. The Khoh Copper-plate grant of the Parivrājaka king Hastin (A.D. 482-83), whose dominion extended over parts of Central India, refers to the *agrahāra* of Korparika in the northern *paṭṭa,*[94] which may suggest that some *agrahāras* or gift villages perhaps constituted a *paṭṭa.* The term occurs also in the Maitraka inscription which implies the prevalence of *paṭṭa* in Saurāṣṭra region. The Bantia grant refers to a village in Uttara *paṭṭa* (northern division) of the Kaundinyapura *viṣaya.*[95] Similarly the Valabhī grant of Dhruvasena III (A.D. 653-54) mentions the village of Paṭṭapa-draka in the Dakṣiṇa *paṭṭa* (southern division) of the Śivabhaga-pura *viṣaya.*[96] It appears from these instances that *paṭṭa* was a sub-division of *viṣaya.* Further, from the context of these grants it may be inferred that at least in Saurāṣṭra a *viṣaya* was divided into northern and southern parts, each comprising several villages.[97]

The word *paṭṭa,* according to Kittel,[98] means either a city, a town or a village. From this it would seem that *paṭṭa,* and *peṭha*[99] which means a market town, connote the same thing though this resemblance is not supported by any independent

---

93. *Ibid.*
94. *CII,* III, no. 22, 1.7.
95. *EI,* XXI, no. 30(a), 1.18.
96. *śivabhāgapura viṣaye dakṣiṇapaṭṭe paṭṭapadrakagrāmaḥ, Ibid.,* I, no. 13. 1.43.
97. *Paṭṭa* was a group of villages, the head of which was known as *paṭṭakila* in Western India in the Paramāra and Caulukya dominions; the later title *paṭel* is derived from it.
98. Kittel, *Kannaḍa-English Dictionary,* p. 926.
99. *Infra.*

evidence of our period: But the term *paṭṭa* seems to have close affinity with *paṭṭi* or *paṭṭika*, meaning a strip of land.[100] This word may also be connected with the term *pāṭaka*, which usually means a splitter or a divider, and thus may be interpreted to mean a sub-division of a *viṣaya*.

Peṭha, which obviously has some phonetic similarity with *paṭṭa*, sometimes occurs in the land grants of the Gupta age. The Khoh plates (A.D. 520-29) of Saṁkṣobha point to "half of the village of Opāṇi in the Maṇināga *peṭha*."[101] An inscription of *Mahārāja* Sarvanātha (A.D. 533-34), from the same locality, describes the villages of Vyāghrapallikā and Kācarapallikā as being in the Maṇināga *peṭha*.[102] All this shows that at least three villages, viz., Opāṇipallikā, Vyāghrapallikā and Kācarapallikā constituted Maṇināga *peṭha*, which possibly included more villages.

The term peṭha has so far been found occuring in only one Maitraka grant from Saurāṣṭra. This record refers to Vaṭa*grāma* in the Dipaṇaka *peṭha* in the Bilvakhāṭa *sthalī*,[103] which shows that *peṭha* was larger than a *grāma* but smaller than a *sthalī*.[104] But this may not apply to the region ruled by the Parivrājaka rulers, whose records do not allude to *sthalī*. On the other hand, the possibility that in Central India, *peṭha* denoted the same territorial division as was indicated by *sthalī* in the Maitraka kingdom of Saurāṣṭra, cannot altogether be discounted.

It has been suggested that *peṭha* may be traced to the root of Karnaṭaka influence, for even now in Kannada, the word means a market town, a place of sale, or a long street of shops in a town.[105] It is, however, surprising that a village should be said to be a part of a market town. Dikshitar suggests that probably the maket town was the centre or the nucleus of a group of adjoining villages for purposes of the administration of local

100. Virji, *op. cit.*, p. 239; Saletore, *op. cit.*, p. 309.

101. *ardhāñ ca maṇināgapeṭhe opāṇigrāma*, *CII*, III, no. 25, 1.14.

102. *Ibid.*, no. 31, 11. 6-7.

103. Jhar grant of Dharasena II (A.D. 571-72), *IA*, XV, p. 187.

104. Virji, *op. cit.*, p. 239.

105. Saletore, *op. cit.*, p. 314; cf. Kittel, *op. cit.*, p. 1015.

affairs.[106] Although this explanation appears quite plausible, it cannot be regarded as conclusive.

The term *pathaka*, denoting one of the territorial sub-divisions, is found in the epigraphic records of the Maitrakas of Valabhī. An inscription of Dharasena II records the grant of the village of Asilāpallikā in the Bandarijidri *pathaka* which was situated in the Kheṭakāhāra *viṣaya*.[107] It is stated in a grant of Dhruvasena II that Vasanta *grāma* was situated in the Kata *pathaka*, which later formed part of the Saurāṣṭra Country.[108] Although the latter inscription does not give any indication about its size in relation to other administrative divisions the former suggests that a village formed part of the *pathaka*, which was included in a *viṣaya*.

Moreover, in a charter of Dharasena IV, the village Desurkṣitijja in the Siṁhapallikā *pathaka* in Kheṭakāhāra is granted to the brāhmaṇa Nārāyaṇamitra.[109] Similarly, a later Maitraka land grant mentions the village Mahilābalīnama in the Uppalaheta *pathaka* in the Kheṭakāhāra.[110] From these two records, it appears that the Kheṭakāhāra included at least two *pathakas*, Siṁhapallikā and Uppalaheta, if not more. Two different references to [Bambu]vānaka in two grants[111] imply that a *sthalī* was perhaps included in a *pathaka*, for one refers to it as a *sthalī*, and the other mentions it simply as a village in the Katapaka *pathaka*.[112] This indicates that the *pathaka* cannot be connected with the *peṭha* which, as we have seen above, was a smaller unit than a *sthalī*.

106. Dikshitar, *Gupta Polity*, p. 238.

107. *Kheṭakāhāraviṣaye bandarijidripathakāntarggata asilāpallikagrāmaḥ*, *IA*, VII, p. 72; cf. *Ibid*., XV, p. 187.

108. *Ibid*., VI, p. 15. The Bhavnagar plates of Dharasena III of the year 304 records the endowment of a field in the village Dabhaka in the Kalapaka *pathaka* (*EI*, XXI, no. 30(b), 1.30).

109. *IA*, VII, p. 75.

110. *Ibid*., p. 85.

111. *EI*, XI, no. 5, 1.24; *JASB*, VII, p. 968.

112. Virji, *op. cit*., p. 235-36.

The word *prāveśya*, which occurs in some of the Maitraka documents, has been taken to be another administrative division. The Palitana grant (dated A.D. 527) of Dhruvasena I alludes to the Jyeṣṭhānaka *grāma* belonging to the Akṣasaraka *praveśya* in the Hastavapra *āharaṇī*.[113] The Ganesgad plates of the same ruler dated A.D. 526-27 mentions a gift of land in a village which is described as being in the Akṣasaraka *prāpa*, a sub-division of the Hastavapra *āharaṇī*.[114] Hultzsch interprets *prāpa* to mean a sub-division,[115] whereas Sten Konow takes *prāpīya* to be a synonym of *prāveśya* which also occurs in the Khariar plates of Mahāsudeva.[116] According to the latter it is not likely that *prāveśya* means anything else than what it does in the common phrase *acāṭabhaṭaprāveśya*. Accardingly, the phrase Akṣasaraka-*prāveśya* has been translated by Konow as "which is entered from Akṣasaraka." i.e., borders on Akṣasaraka.[117] Sukthankar, however, agrees with Hultzsch, who derives *prāpīya* from *prāpa* and interprets it to mean a territorial division smaller than *āhāra*.[118] Similarly the analogous term *prāveśya* should be looked upon, according to Sukthankar, as a *taddhita* of *praveśa*. In the Khariar plates of Mahāsudevarāja referred to above, a village is described as *kṣitimādāhārīya* and *navannakaetatprāveśya*. Sukthankar points out that the term *āhārīya* is derived from *āhāra* by the addition of the suffix *īya*, which, according to him, furnishes the clue to the explanation of the terms, *prāveśya* and *prāpīya*,

---

113. *EI*, XVIII, no. 7(A), 11. 12-13.
114. *Ibid.*, III, no. 46, 1.12.
115. *Ibid.*, p. 110.
116. *IA*, V, p. 20.
117. *EI*, XI, p. 110. The term Siviḍi *prāveśa* occurs in an inscription of Devendravarman (dated A.D. 893), hailing from Chidivalasa, a hamlet in the neighbourhood of Narasannapeta lying about 14 miles north of Chicacole (Srikākulam). According to Sircar, Siviḍi *prāveśa* means either "having access through Siviḍi" or "having its rent assessed with Siviḍi" (*JASB*, (Letters) XVIII, p. 78, n. 1). The latter explanation, however, does not appear to have any sound basis.
118. *EI*, III, p. 319.

these forms being derived by the addition of the secondary suffix *īya* to the strengthened forms of the roots *pra(a)viś* and *pra(a)p* (bring to, carry to). Therefore he rejects the argument of Konow in favour of that of Hultzsch and regards both *prāpa* and *prāveśya* as a territorial division.[119] This view, however, appears to be of doubtful validity. A grant of Dhruvasena refers to the village Pippalaruñkhari as lying on the western border of Ānumanjī,[120] whereas another charter,[121] that of Guhasena, mentions Sāmipadravāṭaka as Pippalaruñkhari *prāveśya* and describes Pippalaruñkhari as Ānumanjī *prāveśya*. From this Virji rightly infers that the term *prāveśya* does not denote an administrative division, but conveys the same sense as implied in the word 'ante', i.e., 'on the border of.' Similarly, Virji adds, the word *prāpīya* must also be construed to imply the ordinary sense "to be arrived at from," i.e., "lying in the vicinity of," as the roots '*viś*', with '*pra*' and '*ap*' with '*pra*' have only a minute difference in their meanings. Hence both the words must be taken to mean 'on the border of,' just as *samīpa* and *pratyāsanna* mean "in the vicinity of."[122] Thus in our opinion neither *prāveśya* nor *prāpa* indicates any territorial unit.

Apart from the political divisions discussed above, our sources sometimes speak of comparatively larger units such as *deśa, rāṣṭra, maṇḍala* and *khaṇḍa*. The antiquity of the word *deśa* goes back to the days of the *Vājasaneyi Saṁhitā* of the *Yajurveda*. But its occurrence in the early Vedic texts is very rare. It is more common in the Buddhist texts, where it is sometimes used as a synonym of *Janapada*. Thus the Majjhima *janapada*, 'the central region of India,' is also called Majjhima *deśa*.[123] In the Asokan inscription it appears singly as in

119. *Ibid.*, III, p. 323.
120. *IA*, IV, p. 105.
121. *Ibid.*, p. 174.
122. Virji, *op. cit.*, p. 243.
123. Yazdani (ed.), *Early History of Deccan*, I, p. 46.

the Fourteenth Rock Edict,[124] and as part of the expression *deśāyutika,* which occurs in the Second Separate Rock Edict.[125] In post-Maurya times, although the term is found in the Pallava records, those of the Sātavāhanas do not refer to it.

In the Gupta empire, however, *deśa* seems to have stood for the largest administrative division. The Sañchi Stone inscription (A.D. 412-13) of Candra Gupta II makes reference to the town of Nasti in the Sukuli *deśa.*[126] This means that in Central India the term *deśa* signified a unit larger certainly than town. The Kapalesvara grant of Mahābhava Gupta records the gift of a village of Daranḍa *grāma* belonging to Yodha *viṣaya* in the Kosala *deśa.*[127] It can be inferred from this that *deśa* was not only bigger than town but also bigger than a *viṣaya,* which was included in the former. We also learn that the village of Ariki *grāma* was situated in Tulumbakhanḍa in the Kosala *deśa,*[128] which may suggest that *deśa* was perhaps divided into *khanḍas,* though reference to the latter is too scanty and of too late a period to determine its relationship with other units of administration, and even this evidence is confined to the south-eastern part of the modern Madhya Pradesh.

Unlike the *deśa,* the *manḍala* unit does not seem to have been known to the epigraphs of the earlier period although the term occurs in the *Arthaśāstra* of Kauṭilya in the context of inter-state relations. It is first mentioned in the Nasik eulogy of Gautamīputra Śātakarṇi, who is described as one "whose feet were saluted by all provinces" (*savamanḍalābhivādita*).[129] Here the term *manḍala* does not perhaps denote an administrative unit. Besides, the territorial units actually named in the inscription of the dynasty, to which Gautamīputra Śātakarṇi belonged, are *āhāras* as noted earlier.

124. *Sel. Ins.,* p. 40, 1.5.
125. *Ibid.,* p. 47, 1. 12.
126. *CII,* III, no. 5, 1.4.
127. *IA,* V, p. 55.
128. *Ibid.,* XV, p. 112; *CII,* III, p. 32, n. 1.
129. *EI,* VIII, no. 8(2), 1.6.

The term in the sense of a territorial division, however, seems to have been current in the eastern parts of the Gupta empire. The Faridpur grant of Dharmāditya (A.D. 531) states that in Vāraka *maṇḍala*, which was granted to Sthānudatta through the former's favour, Jāyava, as lord of the district, was entrusted with its administration and direction.[130] Another grant of the same ruler, issued in the closing years of his reign and dated A.D. 567, also refers to Vāraka as a *maṇḍala*.[131] Still another inscription from Faridpur (A.D. 569) records that Vatsapāla[svāmī], who was appointed to supervise trade in Navyavakāśikā in Vāraka *maṇḍala*, apprised the district government of certain administrative matters.[132] On the basis of the above-mentioned records, it may be reasonable to hold that a *maṇḍala* comprised several *viṣayas*.[133] It is, however, curious that in contemporary records of Central and Western India, *maṇḍala* is conspicuously absent, though in later inscriptions from that region it finds frequent mention.[134]

None of the units discussed above, however, is mentioned in the law-books of our period. They recommend the adoption of the decimal system in forming the administrative division of the country, which is as old as Kauṭilya. According to him the kingdom should be divided into groups of 10 (*saṅgrahaṇa*), 200 (*kharvaṭika*), 400 (*droṇamukha*) and 800 (*sthānīya*) villages.[135] The administrative divisions accordnig to Manu slightly vary from those mentioned in the *Arthaśāstra*. He speaks of both smaller and larger groups. According to him the entire kingdom should be divided into the groups of 1, 10, 20, 100 and 1,000 villages. Between the units of 100 and 1000 villages he provides for three groups of 200, 300 and 500 villages known as *gulmas*.[136] Similarly it is stated in the *Śānti Parva* that the kingdom can be well

130. *IA*, XXXIX, p. 195.
131. *Ibid.*, p. 200.
132. *Ibid.*, p. 204. According to Hoernle and Pargiter the word Navyavakāsikā may not mean any town. (*Ibid.*, XXXIX, p. 210).
133. *Ibid.*, p. 211.
134. Yazdani, *op. cit.*, I, p. 47.
135. *AŚ*, II. 1.
136. *Manu*, VII. 114-117.

protected if it is divided into groups of 1, 10, 20, 100 and 1,000 villages.[137] Like Manu and the *Śānti Parva,* Viṣṇu mentions the divisions consisting of 1, 10 and 100 villages, and lastly adds *deśa* as an administrative unit.[138] Since he does not refer to the group of 1000 villages separately it is not improbable that it was denoted by the term *deśa.* It is equally probable that a separate group called *deśa* was brought into existence for the convenience of rural administration.[139]

Although the inscriptions of the Gupta period refer to *deśa,* they do not suggest whether the decimal system enunciated in the law-books and the *Śānti Parva* was adopted in practice. However, the inscriptions from the 8th Century A.D. onwards show the prevalence of the decimal or duodecimal arrangement (division into groups of 12 or multiples of 12).[140]It seems that the recommendations of the lawgivers in this connection did not find much favour with the rulers of post-Maurya and Gupta times, but it is difficult to state the reasons which led them to ignore the jurists on this subject.

---

137. *ŚP,* 87. 2-3.
138. *Viṣṇu,* III. 5.
139. Dikshitar, *Hindu Administrative Institutions,* p. 316.
140. For discussion see Yazdani, *op. cit.,* I, pp. 31-32 ; Pran Nath, *op. cit.,* pp. 51-52.

CHAPTER XII

REVENUE OFFICERS

The fiscal units discussed above presuppose the existence of a good number of officers for their administration. Village, which was the lowest administrative unit in ancient India, seems to have been under the control of a village-headman (*grāmaṇī*), whose office goes back to the later Vedic period.[1] The post became more important in post-Vedic times, for Bimbisāra is credited with the employment of 80,000 *grāmikas* in his kingdom.[2] It continued in Maurya times as is known from the *Arthaśāstra*.[3] During our period the village-headman is known by different names. Manu[4] refers to him as *grāmika*, but the *Gāthāsaptaśatī*[5] uses the term *gramaṇī* which also occurs in the *Mahābhāṣya*.[6] The *Milindapañho*[7] uses the word *grāmasāmika* in the sense of village-headman, and the *Jātakas*[8] call him *gāmabhojaka*.

The existence of the office of the village-headman is attested by a number of inscriptions of our period. In the votive epigraphs from the Mathura region of the Kuṣāṇa period,[9] we come across *grāmika*; and a Sātavāhana inscription refers to *gāmaṇī*.[10] A relic casket inscription from Charsadda, however, uses *grāmasvāmī* in

1. The *Śatapatha Brāhmaṇa* (v, 3.2) mentions the *grāmaṇī* as one of the eleven *ratnins* connected with *ratnināmhaviṃṣī* ceremony.
2. *Mahāvagga*, v. 1.3.
3. *AŚ*, II. 10.
4. *Manu*, VII. 116.
5. *Gāthāsaptaśatī*, I. 30 ; IV. 69 ; V. 10, 49, 69, etc.
6. *Mahābhāṣya*, V. 2.10. p. 340, 1.8
7. *Milinda.*, p. 147.
8. *Jāt.*, I, pp. 199, 483 ; II, p. 135 ; IV, p. 115, etc. The word *gāmabhojaka* occurs also in the Hirahadgalli plate of the Pallava King Śivaskandavarman (*Lüders' List*, no. 1200).
9. *Lüders' List*, nos. 48, 69(a).
10. *Ibid.*, no. 1333.

a similar sense. During the Gupta period in Eastern India, the village-headman is known as *grāmika* in the Damodarpur Copper-plate inscription;[11] and in the Maitraka charters of Saurāṣṭra he is mentioned as *grāmakūṭa*.[12] Thus it is clear that the office of the village-headman existed throughout our period in Northern and Western India, though it was known by different names in different areas.

How the headman was appointed in earlier times is not clear. A passage of Manu, however, shows that the *grāmika* was appointed by the king.[13] That the headman had a certain relationship with the king is attested by a *Jātaka* story, which describes him as being much concerned about the king's favour or disfavour.[14] In the *Kulāvaka Jātaka*[15] he is heavily chastised by the king for bringing false charges of treason against the whole body of villagers.

Some sources indicate the hereditary character of office of the headman. The *Gāthāsaptaśatī* alludes to a *grāmaṇī* advising his son to discharge his duties efficiently so that his name may remain untarnished even after death.[16] The hereditary nature of this office is also corroborated by epigraphic evidence of the Kuṣāna period. Thus a Jain votive inscription from Mathura of the time of Vāsudeva mentions two generations of an apparently local *grāmika*,[17] although Gupta inscriptions from Northern India do not testify to the hereditary nature of the village-headman. The Goa plates of the king Satyāśraya Dhruvarāja (A.D. 610) describe all the village officers including the village-headman as permanent residents of the place.[18] This may, to some extent, lend support to the hereditary nature of the headman's office, but how far this record may reflect the conditions prevailing in the North India is a matter of speculation. The Supia Pillar inscription of the time of Skanda Gupta (A.D. 460-61) shows that

11. *EI*, XV, no. 7(3), l. 3.
12. Valabhī forged plates of Dharasena II, *IA*, X, p. 28.
13. *Manu*, VII. 115.
14. *Jāt.*, IV, p. 310.
15. *Ibid.*, IV, p. 115.
16. *Gāthāsaptaśatī*, VII, 32.
17. *Lüders' List*, no. 48.
18. *JBBRAS*, XVI, p. 365.

the post was not hereditary. It mentions Śrīdatta, Varga and Chandaka as the three sons of the banker Hari-śreṣṭhin, whose father was Kaivarti-śreṣṭhin.[19] It is significant that Śrīdatta, who was probably the eldest among all the three brothers mentioned in the epigraph, is described as a *kuṭumbika* or husbandman;[20] and the second brother is called a *grāmika*.[21] Evidently their father Hari-śreṣṭhin and grandfather Kaivarti-śreṣṭhin were bankers, but of the three sons of the former the first was a husbandman (*kuṭumbika*) and the second a *grāmika*. This means that the office of the *grāmika* was not always hereditary.

No less important are the duties and functions of the headman. In the Vedic literature the *grāmaṇī* is portrayed as leading the village in times of war and presiding over its religious rites in times of peace,[22] but there is no indication of his revenue functions. Kauṭilya, does not mention his duties. It is merely stated in the *Arthaśāstra* that when he goes out on some business concerning the whole locality, villagers are to accompany him by turns, failing which they are to pay a fine of one or a half *paṇa*.[23] Reference to this officer in the *Arthaśāstra* is so meagre as to suggest that the headman was not very important in the sphere of local administration.

Some functions of the headman may be gleaned from the post-Maurya sources. The *Gāthāsaptaśatī* speaks of a *grāmaṇī* leading an expedition against the Vindhya free-booters who were probably threatening the peace of the village.[24] Manu, however, does not indicate that the headman was entrusted with the defence of the village. He ordains that in the midst of two, three, five or a hundred villages the king should appoint as administrator of state supplied with a picket of guards (*gulma*).[25] The fact that such police outposts were stationed in the groups of villages

19. *EI*, XXXIII, p. 307.
20. *Ibid.*, no. 56 (2), 1.10.
21. *Ibid.*, 1.15.
22. Altekar, *Village Communities in Western India*, Introduction, p. x.
23. *AŚ*, III. 10.
24. *Gāthāsaptaśatī*, VII 31.
25. *Manu*, VII. 114.

may suggest that maintenance of local peace and tranquility was now the responsibility of the police outpost and not of the village headman.

The headman is associated with the fiscal administration as well. Manu entrusts him with the task of collecting royal dues in the form of grain, drink, fuel, etc.[26] The revenue function of this officer is also attested by the *Milindapañho*, which refers to a village-headman who summoned all the village householders through his messenger to the front of his house for the purpose of levying taxes from them on the king's behalf.[27] Fick, relying upon a solitary passage in the introductory episode of a *Jātaka* story,[28] opines that the *gāmabhojaka* was an official appointed to collect the revenue of a village. The *Jātakas*, however, mention about half a dozen officers as *tuṇḍiyas, akāsiyas, niggāhakas, balisādhakas, rājakammikas* and *rajjugāhakas*, who are associated with different aspects of tax assessment and collection. The *tuṇḍiyas* were not regular tax-officers but a special class of collectors, employed to realise *bali* from the people by subjecting them to beating and binding.[29] The *akāsiyas*[30] were also oppressive tax-collectors who perhaps dispossessed the cultivators of their earnings. It appears that *tuṇḍiyas* and *akāsiyas* were special officers to receive taxes on behalf of the king in times of emergency or to collect additional taxes.[31] Unlike these two officers, the *balisādhakas*[32] and *niggāhakas*,[33] who are also mentioned in the commentary as *balisādhakas* seem to have been ordinary collectors who normally collected *bali* from the people. The *rājakammikas* were, however, regular tax-collectors who measured land and realised taxes.[34] Since in the *Jātakas*

26. *Manu*, VII. 118.
27. *Milinda.*, p. 147.
28. *Jāt.*, I, p. 354.
29. *Ibid.*, V, pp. 102-3, *gāthā* with commentary.
30. *Ibid.*, VI, p. 212. *Gāthā*.
31. Sharma, *Political Ideas and Institutions*, p. 135.
32. *Jāt.*, V, p. 106.
33. *Ibid.*, IV, p. 362.
34. *Ibid.*, IV, p. 169.

revenue collection seems to have been done largely by these officers, it is probable that the *gāmabhojaka* was not a collector himself; and, if at all he engaged in tax-collection, his function may have been mainly supervisory. In any case, on the basis of Manu and the *Milindapañho*, it may be suggested that realisation of royal revenue was one of the duties of the headman.

In the Gupta period, although the inscriptions refer to *grāmika* in the sense of headman, they do not enable us to form a clear idea of his functions. On the basis of Bhumara Pillar inscription of Hastin,[35] Saletore holds that one of the duties of the village-headman was to set up boundary pillars.[36] The inscription states that a boundary pillar was set up by one Śivadāsa, the grandson of Indana and the son of Vasu, who was a *grāmika*.[37] It is evident that Śivadāsa, who is credited with setting up the pillar, was not a *grāmika* himself although his father was. Therefore, the view of Saletore is untenable. The association of the village-headman with the rural administration, however, can be inferred from an undated epigraph, probably assignable to the reign of Budha Gupta. This inscription refers to one Nābhaka, a *gramika,* who applied to the authorities including the *grāmikas,* for permission to grant land to some brāhmaṇas.[38] This means that the *grāmika* played an important role in the land transactions effected in this area. Nothing more is known from the records of the Gupta period about the duties of the village headman. Moreover, in the absence of sufficient data it will be hazardous to conclude that he performed all the functions entrusted to him in earlier sources. The existence of the new officers, who came to be associated with village administration in the Gupta age and whom we shall discuss presently, suggests considerable change in the duties and functions of the *grāmika* during Gupta times.

---

35. *CII,* III, no. 24.
36. *Life in the Gupta Age,* p. 298.
37. *CII,* III, no. 24, ll. 4-6.
38. *EI,* XV, no. 7(3), ll. 3-4.

In addition to the village-headman, our sources often mention certain other officers connected with the fiscal administration. We have noted elsewhere that the *Arthaśāstra* provides for the office of *gopa*, who was in charge of 5 or 10 villages, and who was required to number the fields and mark them as cultivated and uncultivated, set their boundaries, note any remission of taxes regarding fields, and to keep an account of the exact number of cultivators, cowherds, merchants and artisans etc.[39] Although the sources of our period do not mention *gopa*, the epigraphs sometimes refer to an officer called *lekhaka*. A votive epigraph, belonging probably to the Kuṣāna period, mentions a *lekhaka* named Mūlagiri.[40] Two Kuda Cave inscriptions of post-Maurya times record the gifts of caves by one Śivabhukti, who was a *lekhaka* in the service of the *mahābhojaka* Māṇḍava Skandapālita.[41] The word *lekhaka* means a writer, and this officer may have been very much like a modern accountant, who was possibly connected with the maintenance of village registers, which constituted an essential feature of revenue administration. Altekar also thinks that the *lekhaka* was a village accountant.[42] We may add that he seems to be the counterpart of the *gopa* of the *Arthaśāstra*.

In the Gupta period, only two references to *lekhaka* are found. The Mandasor Pillar inscription of Kumāra Gupta and Bandhuvarman[43] bears the expressions *katṛ* (composer) and *lekhaka* (writer). It is evident that the latter's function was more or less clerical. A seventh century inscription of Samudrasena from the Kangra district of Punjab also mentions *lekhaka* in the sense of writer as opposed to the actual drafter of the grant.[44] It is, however, not clear whether the *lekhaka* of these records was responsible for the maintenance of village registers and accounts.

Several inscriptions of the Gupta period mention the term *divirapati*, which has been interpreted to mean an officer for

39. *AŚ*, II. 35.
40. *Lüder's List*, no. 209.
41. *Ibid.*, nos. 1037, 1045.
42. *Op. cit.*, pp. 12-13.
43. *CII*, III, no. 18, 1.24.
44. *Ibid.*, no. 80, 1.14.

keeping accounts.[45] The earliest reference to it is found in the Khoh Copper-plate inscription of the Ucchakalpa ruler Jayanātha, dated A.D. 496-97, which records a grant of land to the *divira* Sarvavāḍha.[46] But the term occurs somewhat frequently in the Maitraka inscriptions of Saurāṣṭra. In all these land grants, however, the word *divirapati* is used as a title, especially for the officers who draw up the *śāsanas*. This shows that the word denoted the holder of some office. Bühler quotes a passage from the *Lokaprakāśa* of Ksemendra, who belongs to a late period, to prove that *divira* meant a clerk or an accountant. In *Prakāśa* III of the above-named work, the author speaks of various classes of *diviras, gañjadiviras, nagaradiviras, grāmadiviras* and *khavāra diviras,* for whose benefit he explains all the documents according to the details of each.[47] On this basis, Bühler rightly holds that *diviras* had to do with writing and accounts.[48] This explanation is further supported by a Central Asian Kharoṣṭhī inscription which states that the receipt concerning the land of Mogata is to be carefully preserved by Ramshotsa, who was a *divira.*[49] Thus the *divirapati* of the Maitraka charters may mean an officer in charge of records and accounts, and may have been similar to the *lekhaka* of earlier records, though it is not possible to state his exact relationship with the village-headman.

Another officer *akṣapaṭalādhikṛta,* who is known from two Gupta inscriptions, seems also to have been associated with the fiscal administration. The spurious Nalanda Copper-plate inscription of Samudra Gupta of the year 5 mentions a *grāmaksa-patalādhikṛta.*[50] Again, the forged land grant of the same ruler from Gaya states : "This deed has been written by the order of the *dūta* Gopasvāmin, the *aksapatāladhikrta* of another village."[51]

---

45. Virji, *Ancient History of Saurāshtra,* p. 233.
46. *CII,* III, no. 27, 1.7.
47. *Prakāśa* III, quoted Bühler, "Additional Valabhī Grants," *IA,* VI. p. 10.
48. *Ibid.*
49. *Sel. Ins.,* p. 247, 11. 1-2; cf. *Ibid ,* p. 248. n. 3.
50. *Ibid.,* p. 264, 1.11
51. *CII,* III, no. 60, 1.15.

Since the above-cited charters are generally believed to have been forged probably in the seventh century, one may argue that the *akṣapaṭalādhikṛta* was not known during the time of the imperial Guptas. But at least in South India, this officer was familiar in the Gupta period; for the Bobilhi plates of Candravarman, palaeographically assignable to the first half of the 5th Century A.D., informs us that the edict was written at the command of the king himself, by the *deśākṣapaṭalādhikṛta* Rudradatta,[52] whose designation indicates that his rank was higher than that of the *akṣapaṭalādhikṛta* of the inscription referred to above. This officer is also found in the Alina Copper-plate inscription of Śilāditya VII, dated A.D. 766-67, which mentions one Siddhasena, who is described as a *mahākṣapaṭalika* and a member of the royal household.[53] But during our period none of the inscriptions of the Maitraka rulers refers to this officer. Possibly the office of the *akṣapaṭalādhikṛta* during the period under review was prevalent only in Eastern India, and parts of Eastern Deccan.

Akṣapaṭalādhikṛta is evidently derived from the term *akṣapaṭala*, which, according to Monier-Williams,[54] means a "court of law, or "a depository of legal documents." From this it follows that probably in the Gupta period copies of the records of the government relating to title deeds, royal grants etc., were kept in the village record office, which was under the charge of the *grāmākṣapaṭalādhikṛta*. Some idea of his functions may be formed from the *Harṣacarita* which states that during the king's stay in the village the *grāmākṣapaṭalika* appeared with his whole retinue of clerks, and saying, 'Let his majesty, whose edicts are never void, even now bestow upon us his commands for the day,' presented a newly made golden seal with a bull for its emblem.[55] It seems that the *grāmākṣapaṭalika* with his staff was expected to meet the king or his representative with a seal (*mudrā*) to legalise royal orders. In view of his association with the legal

52. *EI*, XXVIII, no. 8, 1.19
53. *CII*, III, no. 39, 1.76.
54. *Sanskrit-English Dictionary*, s.v. *akṣapaṭala*.
55. *Harṣacarita*, p. 203.

documents, it is most likely that the *grāmākṣapaṭalika* was a record-keeper who normally functioned at the village level.

While the above functionaries appear to have been connected with record keeping, there is evidence to show that a separate officer looked after land survey. The Indore plates of the Vākāṭaka king Pravasasena II mention the *rājuka* Koṭṭadeva as their writer.[56] *Rājuka* in the present context seems to have been an adaptation of the Aśokan *rājuka* (or *lajuka*), which also occurs in the *Jātaka* literature. In the *Kurudhamma Jātaka*[57] a *rajjugahakamācca*,[58] lit. the rope-holding minister, is seen measuring a *janapada* field by holding one end of the rope tied to a stick, the other being held by the owner of the field. Bühler[59] pointed out that the *rajjugahaka amacca* or *rajjuko* of the *Jātaka* and *rājuka* of the edicts of Aśoka[60] are identical. He also equated these with the *rajjuya* of the Jain *Kalpasūtra*, where Jacobi translated the term simply by a clerk or an accountant.[61] Bühler's view has been generally accepted by scholars, though some connect the word '*rājuka*' with the Pāli '*rāyu*' meaning a king.[62] But the question may now be considered as more or less settled as a result of further arguments, on sound philological grounds, given by Ghoshal and S. K. Chatterjee[63] in favour of Bühler.

An important point that merits attention is the fact that the *Jātakas* do not give anything more about the duties and functions than that he was connected with land measurement and survey. Again, no North Indian inscription of our period refers to this officer. Some South Indian epigraphs of the Sātavāhana period record gifts by individuals described as *rājukas*,[64] though

---

56. *EI*, XXIV, no. 10, 1.34.
57. *Jāt.*, II, pp. 366 ff.
58. Shortened in the *gāthā* into *rājjuko* (*Jāt.*, II, p. 367, *gāthā*.)
59. *ZDMG, XLVII*, pp. 466 ff.
60. Rock Edict, III; Pillar Edict, IV.
61. *EI*, II, p. 369.
62. Mookerji, *Corporate Life in Ancient India*, pp. 133-34.
63. *IHQ*, IV, pp. 424-31, 628.
64 *EI*, II, Sanchi inscriptions no. 230, p. 326 ; *Lüders' List*, no. 1195.

they do not give any data to ascertain their rank and functions. In the Gupta period, the Indore Copper-plate inscription of Pravarasena II cited above is the only record which alludes to this officer as its writer.[65] This would mean that one of the duties of the *rājuka* in the Vākāṭaka kingdom was to write the deeds of transfer of land. Since the *rājuka* is not mentioned in any other inscription of the Gupta period, it is not unlikely that his office tended to become less important than it was in earlier times and that his functions came to be distributed among the new officers who came in existence in course of time.

The inscriptions from the Gupta period onwards mention an officer called *āgrahārika,* who is not known from earlier sources. The term is recorded in the spurious Gaya Copper-plate inscription of Samudra Gupta,[66] as also in the Bihar Stone pillar inscription of Skanda Gupta.[67] In the Mallasarul Copper-plate inscription of Vijayasena, assignable to the 5th century A.D., the *āgrahārika* is referred to as one of the officers connected with the transaction of land.[68] The term *agrahāra,* from which this word is derived, means a piece of land or a village given to a brāhmaṇa for his subsistence or settlement therein, or for some religious purpose.[69] Thus Fleet rightly points out that *āgrahārika* is a technical official title, denoting probably 'an officer in special charge of an *agrahāra*'.[70] His administrative jurisdiction over the *agrahāras* may be inferred from the spurious Gaya plate of Samudra Gupta which states: "the taxpaying cultivators, artisans etc., of other villages should not be introduced by the *āgrahārika* [for the purpose of settling in it and carrying on their occupations] (for) otherwise there would certainly be a violation of the privileges of an *agrahāra*."[71] The *āgrahārika* is required

65. *Supra.*
66. *CII,* III, no. 60, l. 12.
67. *Ibid.,* no. 12, l. 29.
68. *EI,* XXIII, no. 24, l. 4.
69. S. C. Mukherjee, "Some observations on the Mallasarul Copper-plate," *JASB,* XXIV (Letters), p. 37.
70. *CII,* III, p. 52, n. 2.
71. *Ibid.,* no. 60, ll. 12-14.

not to allow the taxpaying people from other villages to settle in an *agrahāra* village evidently because this would entail a loss of income to the state. Thus it is reasonable to hold that this officer was perhaps in charge of tax-free gift-villages, fiscal and other administrative matters of which may have been his chief concern.[72] It may, however, be pointed out that the *āgrahārika* is not referred to in earlier inscriptions, even though the *Arthaśāstra* speaks of *agrahāra* grants to the brāhmaṇas. This may be due to the fact that in pre-Gupta times we do not have as many land grants as in the Gupta period, when with the increasing number of rent-free villages the creation of an officer like the *āgrahārika* may have become necessary.

Unlike the *āgrahārika*, the *śaulkika* seems to have been known throughout post-Maurya and Gupta times. The *Arthaśāstra* does not mention this officer. The term *śaulkika* occurs in the *Mahābhāṣya*[73] of Patañjali and the *Divyāvadāna*.[74] The *Milindapañho*[75] speaks of an officer styled *śulkādhyakṣa* who has been taken as a tax-gatherer.[76] Yājñavalkya refers to this officer in connection with ownerless property, but does not state his function.[77]

The term also occurs in some inscriptions of the Gupta and later periods. The Bihar Stone Pillar inscriptions of Skanda Gupta[78] uses the word *śaulkika*. Several Maitraka charters also refer to *śaulkika*[79] as one of the officers who are informed of land grants.

None of these references gives any indication of the precise duties and functions of *śaulkika*. But the term is obviously derived from *śulka*, which was an item of commercial tax. Fleet,

72. The word *āgrahārika* may also mean one who is the holder of an *agrahāra*.
73. *Mahābhāṣya*, IV. 2. 104. p. 295, 1. 15.
74. *Div.*, p. 276.
75. *Milinda*, p. 365.
76. *The Questions of King Milinda*, (Tr. SBE, XXXVI, pt. 2), p. 277.
77. *Yāj.*, II. 173.
78. CII, III, no. 12, 1. 29.
79. *IA*, V, p. 207 ; *JUB*, IV, p. 5 ; *EI*, XXX, no. 30, 1. 2.

therefore, rightly points out that the *śaulkika* was a superintendent of tolls and customs.[80]

Unlike *śaulkika, audraṅgika* is not mentioned frequently in contemporary records. The only inscription where it occurs in the list of officers is the Mallasarul Copper-plate of Vijayasena.[81] The term is evidently derived from *udraṅga,* which, as noted earlier, became an important item of land revenue in the Gupta period. Therefore, *audraṅgika* may indicate either a collector of the tax called *udraṅga,* or an enjoyer of the right to that tax. Sen interprets the term as the chief officer of the town, but does not adduce any argument in favour of his view.[82]

Although *audraṅgika* is not known from the records of the dynasties ruling in Central and Western India, the land grants of the Maitrakas of Saurāṣṭra often mention *drāṅgika* in the list of officers to be notified of the donations of land or village.[83] In the *Rājataraṅgiṇī*[84] *draṅga* is used in the sense of a 'watch-station ; and on this basis Maity suggests that *udraṅga* of the inscriptions may mean some kind of police-tax.[85] If this view is accepted *drāṅgika* would mean a collector of the tax known as *udraṅga,* and thus imply the same thing as indicated by *audraṅgika.* But the term *drāṅgika* also admits of another interpretation. Monier-Williams explains *draṅga* as a town or city.[86] Sircar points out that the word is used in the Jain literature in a similar sense.[87] Therefore, Bühler perhaps rightly translates *drāṅgika* as 'the head of a town.'[88] Besides, an inscription of Guhasena cited above records the grant of three villages situated in Maṇḍalī *draṅga.*[89] Here *draṅga* does not mean a watch-station,

80. *CII,* III, p. 52, n. 2.
81. *EI,* XXIII, no. 24, l. 4.
82. *Historical Aspects of the Inscriptions of Bengal,* p. 498.
83. *IA,* IV, pp. 105, 175 ; V, p. 205 ; *JUB,* (*NS*) I, pp. 30, 34, 68, etc.
84. *Rājataraṅgiṇī,* VIII, 2010, cf. Stein's tr. II, pp. 291ff.
85. Maity, *op. cit.,* p. 62.
86. *Op. cit., s.v. draṅga.*
87. *EI,* XXX, p. 167.
88. *IA,* IV, p. 106 ; cf. *CII,* III, p. 169, n. 6.
89. *IA,* IV, p. 175.

but a territorial unit, most probably a town or a township which forms the headquarters of several villages.[90] Therefore, *drāṅgika* perhaps signifies an officer in charge of a *draṅga,* in which capacity he may have been associated with the realisation of taxes levied from the local population.

The Mallasarul Copper-plate of Vijayasena mentions an important fiscal officer known as *hiraṇyasāmudāyika,* not known to any early or contemporary inscription. *Hiraṇya* was an item of royal income throughout our period, and hence the term may indicate an officer connected with its collection. *Sāmudāyika* is evidently a derivative from *samudāya,* which compounded with *hiraṇya* should mean *hiraṇya* and all other taxes of similar nature. Thus the term *hiraṇyasāmudāyika* may be explained as an officer entrusted with the collection of taxes in cash.[91]

Although the term discussed above is not recorded in any earlier or contemporary epigraph, *heraṇika* occurs in some pre-Gupta inscriptions. A Buddhist cave epigraph from Junar records the gift of a *caitya* by Sulasadatta, the son of a *heraṇika* (Sans. *hairaṇyika*).[92] Similarly two Buddhist sculpture inscriptions from Amarāvatī mention the *heraṇika* Buddhi[93] and the *heraṇika* Siddhārtha.[94] Lüders translates the term *heraṇika* as 'treasurer', but why he does so is not clear. The writings of the period do not refer to any officer by the title. Probably the *heraṇika* (*hairaṇyika*) of post-Maurya times was an officer appointed for the collection of the king's due technically known as *hiraṇya* and anticipated the *hiraṇyasāmudāyika* of the Gupta period.

The *dhruvādhikaraṇika* was also perhaps an officer directly connected with revenue administration. The officer, however, is mentioned only in the charters of the Maitrakas who ruled in the

90. *Supra.*

91. Sen explains the term as an officer in charge of taxes, both in money and in kind (*Historical Aspects of the Inscriptions of Bengal,* p. 498). Cf. *Sel. Ins.*, p. 360, n. 9.

92. *Lüders' List,* no. 1179.

93. *Ibid.*, no. 1239.

94. *Ibid.*, no. 1247.

Saurāṣṭra region, more or less contemporaneously with the Gupta kings.[95]

The expression *dhruvādhikaraṇika* has been explained by Fleet as 'one who has the superintendence of the *dhruvas*.'[96] The word *dhruva* means 'fixed', 'firm', 'certain', etc., and therefore, in the context of the land grants with fiscal immunities, it may be taken to denote the basic land tax, consisting of the king's fixed share of the grain. The association of *dhruva* with taxation is supported by Bühler, who pointed out long ago that the term was applied in Kathiawad and Cutch in his time to denote persons who superintended the collection of land revenue by the tax farmers on behalf of the king.[97] This leads Ghoshal to opine that the office of *dhruva* carries the method of farming of land revenue in Kathiawad back to the sixth and seventh centuries.[98] Ghoshal's contention does not seem to be sound, and it is more likely that the *dhruvādhikaraṇika* was an officer who superintended the realisation of land revenue by the king's collectors and not by the revenue farmers. An inscription of Viṣṇuṣeṇa[99] mentions the term *dhruvādhikaraṇa*, which, according to Sircar,[100] means the office of the *dhruva*. This implies that *dhruvādhikaraṇika* was an officer who had a department (*adhikaraṇa*) presumably of regular officers working under him.

Some Maitraka inscriptions have in place of *dhruvādhikaraṇika* the expressions *dhruvasthānādhikaraṇa*[101] or *dhruvasthānādhikaraṇika*[102] the import of which, according to Bühler,[103] is different from that of the first mentioned term. In his opinion the term *dhruvasthānādhikaraṇika* consists of two distinct titles, *sthānā-*

---

95. *EI*, XI, no. 5, 1.22; *CII*, III, no. 38, 1.20; *IA*, V, p. 207 VI p.,12 etc.
96. *CII*, III, p. 170, n. 1.
97. *IA*, V. p. 205. Cf. Sankalia, *The Archaeology of Gujarat*, p. 200, n. 5 and also *Sel. Ins.*, p. 404, n. 1
98. *HRS*, p. 221.
99. *EI*, XXX, no. 30, 1.3.
100. *Ibid.*, p. 168.
101. *IA*, V, p. 205.
102. *EI*, III, no. 46, 1.11; XIX, no. 55, l. 13.
103. *IA*, V. p. 205.

dhikaraṇika of the compound corresponding to the *thānādārs* of the present day, who in Kathiawad and Rajputana combined police and magisterial functions till recently.

Equally important and perhaps more controversial is the interpretation of the term *aṣṭakulādhikaraṇa,* which occurs in Gupta epigraphs from Eastern India. The Dhanaidaha inscription of the reign of Kumāra Gupta I, dated A.D. 432-33, states that the *kuṭumbins,* several brāhmaṇas named in the record, the *mahattaras* and others including the *aṣṭakulādhikaraṇa* in the village (*grāmāṣṭakulādhikaraṇa*) were informed by an officer, whose name ended with Viṣṇu, of some details of a plot of land.[104] Again, in the Damodarpur Copper-plate of the time of Budha Gupta (A.D. 482-83) a notification is addressed by the *aṣṭakulādhikaraṇa* and other people of Palāsavṛndaka to the brāhmaṇas and other inhabitants of Caṇḍagrāma for the sale and grant of a plot of land.[105] From these records it appears that *aṣṭakulādhikaraṇa* was associated with village administration and was consulted along with the *mahattaras, grāmikas* and *kuṭumbins* in matters pertaining to land administration, particularly regarding the purchase and sale of land in the village.

Much controversy has raged round the interpretation of the term *aṣṭakulādhikaraṇa.* According to R. D. Banerjee it means a local officer exercising authority over eight villages.[106] But this view is untenable, for there is no evidence to show that in the Gupta period eight villages constituted an administrative unit.[107] Nor does the word *kula* lend itself to the meaning 'village' being given to it.[108] Basak, however, takes the term to denote an officer in the village having supervisory authority over eight *kulas,* for which he offers two possible explanations. Relying on Kullūka's commentary on a passage of Manu,[109] he points out that

104. *EI,* XVII, no. 23, l. 6.
105. *Ibid.,* XV, no. 7(3), ll. 2-3.
106. *JASB,* (NS), V. p. 460.
107. The law-books also do not mention any unit consisting of eight villages.
108. Dikshitar, *op. cit.,* p. 273.
109. Kullūka on *Manu,* VII, 119.

kula perhaps means as much ground as can be ploughed by two ploughs, each drawn by six bulls. The alternative meaning of *kula*, according to him, may be 'family', in which case *aṣṭakulādhi-karaṇa* would be one in charge of eight families.[110] But Nirad-bandhu Sanyal rightly points out that the appointment of rural officers each for supervision of eight families or a small area of land in each village does not seem to be a practical proposition. Even if such a necessity existed, of which there is no indication, the purpose might well have been served by the *mahattaras*.[111] Moreover, if the term signifies a village officer for the supervision of different plots of lands and that of the households, the number of such officers in each village must have been more than one. But in the Dhanaidaha plate, the word *aṣṭakulādhikaraṇa* is used as a neuter singular form.

Again, according to Das Gupta the expression *aṣṭakulādhi-karaṇa* is similar to the phrase *jyeṣṭhādhikaraṇakadāmukha-pramukhaṁ adhikaraṇam*, which occurs in the Gugrahati grant of Samācāradeva.[112] He further equates the term with *aṭṭhakulaka*, used by Buddhaghoṣa in his commentary on the *Mahāparinibbāna Suttānta*, perhaps in the sense of a court composed of judges from all the eight castes.[113] On the basis of these parallelisms Das Gupta states that the term *aṣṭakulādhikaraṇa* means the *adhikaraṇa* or judicial court, which comprised more or less eight judges and functioned in the village.[114]

The contention of Das Gupta has been criticised by Saletore, who thinks that the inscriptions do not indicate that the *aṣṭakulādhikaraṇa* discharged judicial duties. According to Saletore,[115] although three of the Damodarpur Copper-plate charters imply that the *uparika*, the *viṣayapati*, the *nagara-śreṣṭhin*, the *sārthavāha*, the *prathamakulika* and the *prathama-*

---

110. *EI*, XV, p. 137, n. 2; cf. Saletore, *op. cit.*, p. 300.

111. *Ibid.*, XXXI, p. 61.

112. *Ibid.*, XVIII, no. 11, ll. 5-6.

113. *JASB* (NS), VII, pp. 993-94.

114. *IC*, V, pp. 110-111.

115. *Op. cit.*, pp. 299-300.

kāyastha[116] constituted the *adhikaraṇa*, the *aṣṭakulādhikaraṇa* is nowhere mentioned as its member. But this is a wrong argument. There is no reason why the *adhikaraṇa* functioning at the *viṣaya* headquarters should have as one of its constituents the *aṣṭakulādhikaraṇa*, which was perhaps connected with village administration.

The general error, committed by most writers in explaining the term, seems to have been that *aṣṭakulādhikaraṇa* has been taken to be an individual officer. As noted earlier, the word has been used as a neuter singular and thus does not indicate an officer for whom a masculine singular form would have been grammatically appropriate. If its use in the Dhanaidaha Copper-plate is correct the term *grāmāstakulālhikaraṇa* should signify the corporate body invested with definite administrative powers rather than an individual officer. Unlike Basak, according to whom the expression denotes an officer supervising over a small area of land or over eight families in each village,[117] Sircar explains it to mean a village-board representing eight or more families.[118] The former view is unacceptable for reasons adduced above, but the latter appears plausible. The interpretaion of *kula* as a certain area of land ploughed by six bulls[119] is not convincing for two reasons : first, this does not seem to fit in the context in which the term is used, and secondly, in the *Amarakośa*,[120] which is believed to be a work of the Gupta period, *kula* means 'family,' a meaning which suits the context where it occurs in the land-grants referred to above. The term *kula* is used in an identical sense in the contemporary law-books. In the opinion of Nārada[121] in addition to *śreṇī* (corporations), *gaṇa* (assemblies), certain persons appointed by the king, and *kulas* are invested with the power to decide the lawsuits. Passages from *Yājñavalkya*[122] and

116. *EI*, XV, no. 7, (1, 2, 3).

117. *Supra.*

118. *IHQ*, XIX, p. 16.

119. *Supra.*

120. *Amar.*, III. 3.207.

121. *Nārada*, I. 7.

122. *Yāj.*, II. 30.

Kātyāyana[123] may be cited to the same effect. Bṛhaspati, however, lays down that *kulas* should decide lawsuits, excepting those concerning violent crimes.[124]

The interpretation of *kula* occurring in the above-mentioned legal texts, however, has been an occasion for divergent opinion in later times. It is explained by the *Mitakṣara*[125] as groups of agnatic and cognatic relatives, whereas the *Vyavahāra Mātrikā* understands it to mean 'the family of the parties'[126] presumably involved in a suit. It is, however, reasonable to place greater reliance on the *Amarakośa* than on later writings because of its contemporaneity with the inscriptions in which the word is recorded. These facts, suggest that the *aṣṭakulādhikaraṇa* was some kind of corporate body consisting of representatives of eight families, and the contention of Das Gupta discussed above appears largely correct. But we may add that the *aṣṭakulādhikaraṇa* tried only civil cases and not the criminal ones, as can be inferred from the above-cited passage of Bṛhaspati. The judicial function of this organisation fits in well with the evidence furnished by the inscriptions where it is associated with land administration. In view of its association with land transactions, the possibility that *aṣṭakulādhikaraṇa* decided the lawsuits arising out of fiscal irregularities cannot be ruled out.

The term *aṣṭakulādhikaraṇa,* however, occurs neither in earlier nor in later sources. Even in the Gupta period, only the Dhanaidaha grant of Kumāra Gupta and the Damodarpur Copper-plate inscription of Budha Gupta mention it. This may imply that the body known as *aṣṭakulādhikaraṇa* was a peculiar administrative phenomenon which existed in an extremely limited area of Bengal during Gupta times.

Unlike the term *aṣṭakulādhikaraṇa,* which is found only in the land grants of Eastern India, the word *mahattara,* though not known from earlier North Indian inscriptions, finds frequent men-

123. *Kātyāyana,* verse 82.
124. *Bṛhaspati,* I. 92.
125. *Mit.,* on *Yāj., II.* 30.
126. Quoted Kane, *Kātyāyanasmṛtisāroddhāra,* p. 182n.

tion in the land grants of different parts of the country from the Gupta period onwards. Even among the South Indian records, there is at least one Sātavāhana epigraph which refers to *mahataraka*,[127] meaning perhaps the same thing as the *mahattara* of the Gupta and later periods.

Mahattara occurs in several Gupta land-sale charters from Bengal. It is stated in the Dhanaidaha Copper plate inscription that someone, whose name seems to have ended in Viṣṇu, approached the village householders (*kuṭumbins*), the *mahattaras* and the *aṣṭakuladhikaraṇa* and expressed to them his desire to purchase one *kulyavāpa* of cultivated land.[128] Again, in the Damodarpur Copper-plate of the time of Budha Gupta the *mahattaras* and others are described as informing the brāhmaṇas and the inhabitants of Caṇḍagrāma of the sale of a plot of land.[129] It can be inferred from these epigraphs that the *mahattaras* were often associated with land transactions.

The word *mahattara* is a comparative formation of '*mahat*' 'great' and is given by Monier-Williams in the special sense of 'the head or oldest man of a village.'[130] In the inscriptions, however, the plural form of it is used. The Dhanaidaha grant describes at least 12 persons as *mahattaras*.[131] This may mean that *mahattara* signified older and hence respectable inhabitants of a village. Pargiter seems to be right in regarding them as "men of position in the village or the leading men.[132]

It is strange that *mahattaras* are nowhere mentioned in the law-books of post-Maurya and Gupta times. Although they allow considerable authority to the senior inhabitants of a locality in deciding land disputes they do not use the word *mahattara*. In the law-books senior men of the place are conceded the right of deciding cases arising out of land disputes, presumably because they knew well the boundaries, titles, etc. of land of their area.

---

127. *Lüders' List*, no. 1340.
128. *EI*, *XVII*, no. 23. 1. 3.
129. *Ibid.*, XV, no. 7(3), 1.2.
130. *Op. cit.*, *s. v. mahattara.*
131. *EI*, XVII, no. 23, 11. 3-6.
132. *IA*, XXXIX, p. 213.

The mention of *mahattara* in the land-grants also may be due to the same reason. Therefore, it is quite likely that the expression signified what the law-books mention as senior or aged persons (*vṛddha*) of the locality.

Moreover, N. B. Sanyal[133] suggests that the compound *mahattarādyaṣṭakulādhikaraṇa* in the Damodarpur Copper-plate inscription indicates that the *mahattaras* formed at least one constituent of the *aṣṭakulādhikaraṇa*. This view appears to be of doubtful validity, because the Dhanaidaha grant uses the phrase *grāmāṣṭakulādhikaraṇa* and does not conjoin it with *mahattara*. Besides, no other inscription shows that the *mahattaras* were the members of the *aṣṭakulādhikaraṇa*.

Reference to the *mahattara* in the inscriptions of the Vākāṭaka rulers is rare,[134] but the Valabhī grants of the Maitraka dynasty frequently mention him in the list of persons who are informed of bestowal of land on the donees.[135] It appears that *mahattaras* in Saurāṣṭra, like those in the territories administered directly by the Guptas, were associated with land transaction. It is, however, not possible to show whether they had anything to do with revenue collection of their area.

The inscriptions of the Gupta age also mention *āyuktakas* and *viniyuktakas* in the list of officers who received notification of land grants. The term *āyuktaka*, unlike the *mahattara*, goes back to Pāṇini who alludes to *āyukta*.[136] The *Kāśikā* explains it as *vyāpṛta*, "engaged".[137] This may indicate that the term meant an officer who was engaged for a particular work. The word does not occur in the *Arthaśāstra* in this form, though Kauṭilya at one place lays down that in all departments, whoever, whether a *yukta* (officer), an *upayukta* (clerk), or a *tatpuruṣa* (servant), misappropriates sums from one to four *paṇas*, or any other valuable things, shall be punished with the first, middlemost, and highest

133. *EI*, XXXI, p. 61.
134. He is mentioned perhaps only in the Riṭhapur inscription of Prabhāvatī Guptā (*Sel. Ins.*, p. 417, l. 12.)
135. *IA*, IV, pp. 105, 175 ; V, p. 205; VII, p. 72, etc.
136. *Aṣṭādhyāyī*, II. 3. 40.
137. *EI*, XV, p. 140, n. 1.

amercement and death respectively.[138] If the *yukta* of the *Arthaśāstra* be taken to be identical with the *āyukta* of Pāṇini, it would seem that *āyuktas* were officers entrusted with the running of different state departments. The post-Maurya sources know of a solitary South Indian inscription which states that the village authorities (*grāmeyika ayutta*) were to grant a piece of land with all immunities.[139] The word *ayutta* qualified by *grāmeyika* means that the *āyukta* was generally a village officer. Nothing, however, can be said with certainty about the duties and functions discharged by him in post-Maurya times.

In the Gupta period the *āyukta* is first mentioned in the Allahabad *praśasti* of Samudra Gupta,[140] which records the expression *āyuktapuruṣa* in the sense of officers employed for restoring wealth of the various kings vanquished by Samudra Gupta. On this basis Sircar takes *āyuktapuruṣa* to indicate a treasury officer like the *yukta* of Aśokan inscription.[141] Although this interpretation seems to suit the context in which it occurs, this view is not supported by other contemporary inscriptions which record *āyuktaka* (*āyukta+ka*) and not *āyuktapuruṣa.* We learn from the Dhanaidaha Copper-plate inscription (A.D. 432-33) of Kumāra Gupta I that on behalf of one Varāhasvāmin, willing to purchase state land for religious purpose, the *āyuktaka* of the *viṣaya* placed the details of the case in the *adhiṣṭhānādhikaraṇa.*[142] This shows that the applicant for a plot of state land approached the *āyuktaka* who was perhaps informed of all the details of the area required. Thus this officer placed the whole case before the city-council, which considered it and came to a decision. Moreover, the particular plot of land that is sought to be granted in the Dhanaidaha inscription is described as situated in the Khāḍa(ṭa)pāra *viṣaya* and the *āyuktaka* is mentioned in the beginning of the record.[143] This may imply that he was the

138. *AŚ.* II. 5.
139. *Lüders' List,* no. 1327.
140. *CII,* III, no. 1, l. 26.
141. *Sel. Ins.,* p. 259, n. 2.
142. *EI,* XVII, no. 23, l. 11.
143. *Ibid.,* 1.7.

chief officer of this *viṣaya*. The term *āyuktaka* also occurs in the Paharpur inscription dated A.D. 479.[144] It is stated in this record that Nātha Śarman and his wife Rāmī approached the *āyuktaka* and the city council (*adhiṣṭhānādhikaraṇa*) headed by the *nagaraśreṣṭhin* at Puṇḍravardhana with the request that, in accordance with the procedure prevalent in the locality, they may be allowed to deposit three *dināras* in return for 1½ *kulyavāpas* of land distributed among four different villages.[145] From these two records it appears that the *āyuktaka* was an officer connected with the land administration. It is also known from a Damodarpur grant cited above that under the governorship of Jayadatta, the local administrator, for the *viṣaya* of *Koṭivarṣa*, was the *āyuktaka* Saṇḍaka[146] But this could not have been a general practice, for the inscriptions often refer to *viṣayapati* as ruling over a *viṣaya*. Nothing more is known from inscriptions about the duties and functions of an *āyuktaka*. But from a passage of the *Kāmasūtra*,[147] which mentions *āyuktaka* together with *grāmādhipati*, it can be inferred that the former lived upon a share of the agricultural produce of the village people, probably sending the major portion thus realised to the king.[148]

The office of the *āyuktaka* was no less important in Saurāṣṭra during the Gupta age. In a grant of Dhruvasena I the king is stated to have issued notification of a land-gift to *āyuktakas*, *mahattaras*, *drāṅgikas*, *cāṭas*, *bhaṭas*, etc.[149] The *āyuktaka* finds the first place in the list of officers not only in this but also in several other Maitraka inscriptions.[150] If the enumeration of officers in the inscription is in the descending order of importance, *āyuktaka* may have been an important official of the Maitraka kingdom.

144. *Ibid.*, XX, no. 5, 1.1.
145. *Ibid.*, 11. 3-6.
146. *Ibid.*, XV, no. 7(4), 1.3.
147. *Kāmasūtra*, V. 5.5.
148. Sharma. *Op. cit.*, p. 211.
149. *IA*, IV, p. 105.
150. *Ibid.*, p. 174; V, pp. 205, 207; VI, p. 12; *JUB* (NS). I,.pp. 17 19 23, 30, 34 etc.

In several epigraphs of the Gupta times *āyuktaka* is followed by the term *viniyuktaka* or *viṇiyukta*. A fragmentary grant of Īśvararāta from Kathiawad, palaeographically assignable to the 4th century A.D., states that the order in regard to the gift of land was issued from Prachakāśā to the brāhmaṇas and other villagers of Vindhyakūpikā*grāma* as well as to all his officers such as the *āyuktas*, *viniyuktas*, *kumarāmātyas*, *uparikas* etc.[151] Similarly in Maitraka records the *āyuktaka* is followed by the *viniyuktaka*.[152] Sircar, therefore, suggests that the latter was probably a subordinate officer under the *āyukta*,[153] though it is not possible to form any idea of his duties. A passage of the *Raghuvaṁśa*[154] uses the expression *koṣṭhāgāre niyuktaḥ*, which means an officer employed to administer the affairs of the treasury. Saletore equates the above term with *viniyukta* of the inscriptions.[155] This view, however, is untenable. In our opinion, Kālidāsa does not mention *koṣṭhāgāre niyuktaḥ* as a technical official designation, but in the sense of officers who were appointed to look after the matters of royal treasury. Here the term *niyuktaḥ* is not a noun as we have it in the inscriptions, but the past passive participle of the verb *ni+yuj*.

The Vākāṭaka inscriptions often refer to an officer known as *sarvādhyakṣa*, who is not known to the records of other contemporary dynasties. The land charters issued by the Vākāṭaka ruler Pravarasena II record the expression : *asmatsantakāsarvāddhyakṣaniyoganiyukta ājñāsañcārikulaputrādhikṛtāḥ bhaṭacchatraśca*",[156] which has been translated by Mirashi[157] as "our officials (*santakāḥ*) of noble birth (*kulaputrāḥ*), who are employed

151. *EI*, XXXIII, no. 56(1), 11. 2-4.
152. *IA*, IV, p. 174; v, p. 205, *EI*, XXI, no. 39, 1.16. etc. In a few inscriptions of the Maitrakas we come across *āyuktaniyukta* (*EI*, XVII, no. 7(A), 1.10). In all likelihood, *niyukta* is the same as *viniyuktaka*.
153. *EI*, XXXIII, p. 304.
154. *Raghu.*, V. 29.
155. *Op. cit.*, p. 261.
156. *EI*, XXII, no. 27, 11. 13-14; *CII*, III, no. 55, 11. 21-22.
157. *EI.*, XXII, p. 175.

by the order of the general superintendents (*sarvādhyakṣas*) and who exercise their authority by (our) command, (our) soldiers and umbrella-bearers". From this it appears that in the Vākāṭaka kingdom the *sarvādhyakṣa* was empowered to appoint all high officers of noble birth. Perhaps on this basis Altekar translates *sarvādhyakṣa* as prime minister.[158]

It is relevant to point out that Manu ordains that the king should appoint in each town a *sarvārthacintaka* (superintendent of all works) who should always personally supervise the work of other officers.[159] The *Śānti Parva* also states that *sarvārthacintaka* should be appointed over every town.[160] We do not know whether such superintendents were actually appointed in post-Maurya times, but the *sarvādhyakṣa* of the Vākāṭaka records reminds us of the *sarvārthacintaka* of Manu and the *Śānti Parva*. As regards the functions of this officer we only learn from the inscriptions that he was associated with land transactions. However, it may be guessed from the meaning of the word *sarvādhyakṣa* that he superintended all the departments of the government and hence exercised some supervisory control over fiscal administration as well.

The office of the *kumārāmātya* seems to have been an important feature of the administrative bureaucracy of the Gupta period, though, unlike *sarvādhyakṣa*, it is not mentioned in the Vākāṭaka inscription. Fleet takes the term *kumārāmātya* to mean 'minister of the Crown-prince'.[161] Bloch explains it as 'one who has been in the service of the king from the time when he was a boy.[162] Both these explanations are etymologically correct, but they are not supported by the internal evidence of the records in which the term is mentioned. *Kumārāmātya* may also be translated as 'princes as ministers'.[163] But the

158. Yazdani, *Early History of Deccan*, I, p. 193:
159. *Manu*, VII. 122.
160. *ŚP*, 88. 10.
161 *CII*, III, p. 16n ; cf. Marshall, *ASR*, 1911-12, p. 52 ; Sircar, *Sel. Ins.*, p. 360n.
162. *EI*, X, p. 50, n. 2.
163. Cf. Dikshitar, *Gupta Polity*, p. 152.

Karamdanda inscription of the time of Kumāra Gupta states that Śikharasvāmin and his son Pṛthvīsena, both of whom were *kumārāmātyas,* belonged to the brāhmaṇa caste. It is recorded that Kumāravyabhaṭṭa, the grandfather of Śikharasvāmin, was a teacher of the Chāndogya Veda and that his gotra was *Āsvāvāji*[164]. Evidently they did not belong to royal family.[165] Kumārāmātya, therefore, is to be treated as a technical official title which is difficult to explain on the basis of the literal meaning of the words *kumāra* or *amātya.*[166]

The true import of *kumārāmātya* in relation to the Gupta administrative system can only be understood in the light of the context in which it occurs. In the Allahabad *praśasti* of Samudra Gupta Hariṣeṇa, the composer, is described as the *sandhivigrahika kumārāmātya* and *mahādaṇḍanāyaka,* who was a servant of the emperor and had been attached to him (*paramabhaṭṭārakapādānudhyātakena*).[167] Similarly Śikharasvāmin and Pṛthvisena are mentioned as the *mantrī kumārāmātya* of Candra Gupta II and Kumāra Gupta respectively. Thus certain officers bearing the title *kumārāmātya* served directly under the emperor.

Another class of *kumārāmātyas* who functioned at the *viṣaya* level is known from the Damodarpur Copper-plates. Two inscriptions of the reign of Kumāra Gupta refer to a time when the *uparika mahārāja* Cirātadatta was governing the *bhukti* of Puṇḍravardhana and the *kumārāmātya* appointed by him was administering the *viṣaya* of Koṭivarṣa.[168] Two other near contemporary inscriptions from the same place inform us that the administration of Koṭivarṣa *viṣaya* was carried on by a *viṣayapati* and an *āyuktaka* respectively.[169] It may be inferred from these references that in North Bengal the *kumārāmātya* was discharging those functions which were later entrusted to the

164. *EI,* X, no. 15, 11. 4-5.
165. Cf. Majumdar & Altekar, *The Vākāṭaka-Gupta Age,* pp. 281-82.
166. Dikshitar, *op. cit.,* p. 152.
167. *CII,* III, no. 1, 11. 31-33.
168. *EI,* XV, no. 7 (1 & 2).
169. *Ibid.,* no. 7 (4 & 5).

viṣayapati.[170] The evidence of the Basarh seals belonging to the Gupta period shows that in North Bihar (Tīrabhukti) also the *kumārāmātya* was entrusted with the administration of *viṣaya* under an officer styled *uparika*.[171]

The legends on some of the Basarh seals throw further light on the office of the *kumārāmātya*. In Bloch's classified list, nos. 4, 5 and 9 bear the legend : *yuvarājapādīya-kumārāmātyādhikaraṇasya*, and nos. 6 and 7 have *śrīyuvarāja-bhaṭṭārakapādīya kumārāmātyādhikaraṇasya* and no. 8 reads *śrīparamabhaṭṭārakapādīyakumārāmātyādhikaraṇa*.[172] Bloch translates the first as "His Highness, the Yuvarāja, the Chief of Prince's Ministers", and the second as "seal of His Highness, the illustrious *Yuvarāja* and *Bhaṭṭāraka*, the Chief of Prince's Ministers". These versions, Ghoshal rightly points out, are contrary to the rules of grammatical constructions and the accepted meanings of the terms in questions,[173] and hence are not acceptable. R. D. Banerjee's explanation makes the confusion worse confounded. His view is based on a wrong interpretation of the term *pāda* occurring in the above-cited legends. He takes *pāda* to mean 'equal to' and *yuvarājabhaṭṭāraka* to signify "the real heir-apparent' as distinguished from the *yuvarājas* who were the younger princes of the royal family. From this he concludes that 'some of the *kumārāmātyas* were held to be equal in rank to the princes of the blood royal', and others were held to be 'equal to the heir of the Emperor', while still others were 'equal in rank to His Majesty the Emperor'.[174] It is not possible that the *kumārāmātya*, who served under the king, could have the same rank and status as was enjoyed by him and the princes.

One of the seals discovered by Marshall at Bhita records "*mahāśvapatimahādaṇḍanāyakaviṣṇurakṣitapādānudhyāta-*

170. Ghoshal, "New Light on the Gupta Administrative System", *Proceedings of the sixth All India Oriental Conference*, p. 212.

171. *Ibid.*, p. 212-13.

172. *ASR*, 1903-4, pp. 107-8.

173. Ghoshal, *op. cit.*, p. 213.

174. R. D. Banerjee, *The Age of the Imperial Guptas*, pp. 71-74.

kumārāmātyādhikaraṇasya".[175] Fleet points out that the term *pādānudhyāta* is frequently used in ancient Indian epigraphs to indicate the relation of a feudatory or an official to his suzerain, or that of a son or younger brother to his superior, or that of devotees to gods. Ghoshal thinks that this term in the present context carries the sense of father and son relationship, and thus in his opinion the above-quoted seal-inscription means that the *kumārāmātya* in question was the son of Viṣṇurakṣita, the chief cavalry-officer and commander-in-chief. Accordingly he adds that the legend *yuvarājapādīya-kumārāmātyādhikaraṇa* and the like on the Basarh seals refer to the *kumārāmātyas* who were related probably as sons to the crown-prince and the emperor.[177] Ghoshal's contention is of doubtful validity, for it appears from the Allahabad inscription of Samudra Gupta[178] that *kumārāmātya* Hariṣeṇa was perhaps attached to the king for a fairly long period of time and thus may have been promoted to the office of *mahādaṇḍanāyaka* and *mahāsandhivigrahika*. Similarly the Karamdanda inscription of Kumāra Gupta[179] states that Pṛthvīsena, the *kumārāmātya*, was subsequently promoted to the post of *mahādaṇḍanāyaka*, whose position was higher than that of the *kumārāmātya*. Moreover, the instances cited by Fleet[180] show that the expression *pādānu-dhyāta* is used in the inscriptions in respect of widely different kinds of relationship. It is, therefore, highly probable that the Bhita seal-legend implies that the *kumārāmātya* in question was attached to Viṣṇurakṣita, who combined in him the offices of *mahādaṇḍanāyaka* and *mahāsenāpati*. Similarly, the word *pādīya* in the Basarh seals may also indicate that the *kumārā-mātyas* were attached to the royal princes, the heir-apparent and the emperor. This is also supported by Ghoshal himself who, in course of refuting R. D. Banerjee's viewpoint, rightly points

175. *ASR*, 1911-12, p. 52.
176. *CII*, III, p. 17, n. 2.
177. Ghoshal, *op. cit.*, p. 215.
178. *CII*, III, no. 1, ll. 31-33.
179. *EI*, X, no. 15, ll. 7-8.
180. *CII*, III, p. 17, n. 2.

out that *pāda* means 'a little less than' and that the affix *cha* (*īya*) has a possessive sense. Thus in the dominions of the imperial Guptas the *kumārāmātya* functioned at different administrative levels, and he retained this title even when he was promoted to a higher rank. Hence the word *kumārāmātya* may have denoted a class of officers, belonging to a particular administrative cadre, and functioning in different capacities in different circumstances like the I.C.S. or I.A.S. officers of our times.[181]

Apart from the documents of the Guptas, there are references to *kumārāmātya* in the charters of the Maitraka kings, though they do not give any data about its meaning etc. In most inscriptions of Maitraka dynasty, the *kumārāmātya* occupies the last place among officers to whom the grant is addressed. This may suggest that the part played by the *kumārāmātya* in the sphere of land-administration in Saurāṣṭra was not very important. This is unlike Eastern India where he was sometimes placed at the head of the district headquarters in which capacity possibly he had to keep a supervisory control over the fiscal administration of the territory in his jurisdiction.

The term *bhogika* occurs frequently in the inscriptions of the Ucchakalpa rulers.[182] It is also recorded in the Gunaigarh inscription of Vainya Gupta (A.D. 507).[183] In the Mallasarul plates of Vijayasena we have *bhogapatika,* which may be identical with *bhogika.*[184] But these references do not furnish any data about the duties, functions and the administrative status of this officer. Fleet suggests that *bhogika* is a technical official title, possibly connected with the technical terms *bhoga* and *bhukti.*[185] But as has been shown earlier, *bhoga* as a territorial unit was not very much in fashion up to A.D. 550. The Bhumara Pillar inscription of Hastin and Sarvanātha, where *bhoga* is recorded, does not use

181. Dikshitar, *op. cit.*, p. 251 ; Majumdar & Altekar, *op. cit.*, p. 282.

182. *CII*, III, no. 21, l. 21 ; no. 22, l. 29 ; no. 23, l. 19 ; no. 26, l. 23 etc.

183. *Sel. Ins.*, p. 334, l. 17.

184. *EI*, XXIII, no. 24, l. 4.

185. *CII*, III, p. 100, n. 2.

it in the sense of an administrative division.[186] Even in the inscriptions of Bengal referred to above, *bhogika* or *bhogapatika* does not seem to have any connection with *bhoga* units. Thus there is nothing to suggest that *bhogika* had anything to do with the *bhoga* unit of administration, which came into existence in North India a little later than the period under study.

Sircar is of the opinion that *bhogika* may indicate an officer in charge of royal stables.[187] He opines that it may as well mean a *jāgirdār*.[188] *Bhoga* means possession, enjoyment of property, and therefore, the above explanation may appear plausible. But it is frequently used in the inscriptions of the Gupta period in the sense of an item of king's revenue,[189] and it is likely that *bhogika* originally may have had some connection with its realisation.[190]

The *dūtaka*, literally a messenger, appears to have been employed in connection with formal land grants from the Gupta period onwards. Thus the Khoh Copper-plate grant (A.D. 475-76) of Hastin mentions Bhāgraha as its *dūtaka*.[191] A similar reference to this officer is found in other epigraphs of Central and Western India.[192] In Eastern India the Gunaigarh inscription (A.D. 506) of Vainya Gupta mentions Vijayasena as the royal messenger.[193]

Earlier sources do not mention *dūtaka* but refer to *dūta*. The *Arthaśāstra*, Manu[194] and Yājñavalkya[195] speak of *dūta* more or less in the sense of a messenger, envoy or an ambassador. The earliest epigraphic reference to *dūta* is found in the Besnagar

186. *Supra.*
187. *Sel. Ins.*, p. 334, n. 1 : Cf. Monier-Williams, *op. cit.*, *s.v. bhogika.*
188. *EI*, XXXIII, p. 170 ; *Sel. Ins.*, p. 360, n. 9.
189. *Supra.*
190. Cf. Sen, *op. cit*, p. 556.
191. *CII*, III, no. 21, 1. 22.
192. *Ibid.*, no. 30, 1. 14 ; *EI*, XI, no. 17, 1. 34 ; XII, no. 7, 11. 32-33 ; XVII, no. 7(A), 1. 23 ; XIX, no. 55, 1. 27 etc.
193. *IHQ*, VI, p. 55.
194. *Manu*, VII. 63-65.
195. *Yāj.*, I. 328.

Vaiṣṇava Column inscription of Kāśīputra Bhāgabhadra, which refers to a Yavana *dūta* (ambassador) sent by Antialkidas to the former.[196] The ambassadorial function of the *dūta* (or *dūtaka*) does not appear to have any relevance to the land charters.

Kauṭilya, however, mentions a class af *dūta* whose duty was to convey the royal edicts. The *Mitakṣarā* on Yājñavalkya (1.328) enumerates three kinds of *dūta*, and one of these consists of conveyors of king's edicts. This aspect of the *dūta* seems to be relevant to the inscriptions which mention *dūtaka*.

The term *dūtaka*, evidently derived from *dūta*, first occurs in a passage of Bṛhaspati, who mentions the functionary as a kind of witness and defines him as a respectable man, esteemed and appointed by both parties.[197] Kātyāyana also mentions *dūtaka* as a proper type of witness in cases regarding deposits.[198] It appears that *dūtaka* could be one who was in the confidence of the parties involved in a dispute. Thus in the case of land grants it may be suggested that a *dūtaka* could be an individual or a royal officer who enjoyed the confidence of the king, the officers who were to execute the order, and the grantees.

All this, however, should not be taken to mean that the *dūtaka* carried the charter to the donees or to the officers of the locality in which land was granted. In some cases, the word *dūtaka* occurs in the inscriptions on stone,[199] and this may imply that this officer took to the donees, not the charter itself, but the king's sanction and order to the local officials whose duty it was to have the charter drawn up and delivered to the recipients of land grants.[200]

It can be inferred from the inscriptions that the duty of the *dūtaka* was considered to be of high importance. The Gunaigarh inscription referred to above states that Vijayasena, the *dūtaka* of the grant, held also other important offices such as those of the *mahāpratihāra* (royal chamberlain) *mahāpīlupati* (officer in charge

196. *Lüders' List*, no. 669.
197. *Bṛhaspati*, V. 11.
198. *Kātyāyana*, verse 353.
199. *IA*, IX, pp. 167, 168, 170, etc.
200. *CII*, III, p. 100, n. 3.

of elephants), *pañcādhikaraṇoparika* (?) and *purapāloparika*.[201] Similarly a Central Indian epigraph of A.D. 592 states that the *dūtaka* of the document was Bhaḍḍaka, who was the officer in charge of the department of war and peace (*sandhivigrahādhikaraṇādhikṛta*).[202] From the above it may be inferred that often high ranking officers acted as conveyors of the royal sanction regarding a land grant, presumably because they were supposed to be in the king's confidence.

Uparika is another official title known from the Gupta sources. It is mentioned in the Bihar Stone inscription of Skanda Gupta,[203] but due to its fragmentary nature no precise meaning of the term can be deduced. The five Damodarpur plates, which record sales of land for religious purposes, however, throw some light on the status of the *uparika*. The first two plates of this group of records, belonging to the reign of Kumāra Gupta I, state that the *uparika* Cirātadatta was in charge of Puṇḍravardhana *bhukti* and that he appointed the *kumārāmātya* Vetravarman to look after administration of Koṭivarṣa *viṣaya*.[204] But the Damodarpur plates nos. 3 and 4, of the time of Budha Gupta, mention the *uparika mahārājas* Brahmadatta and Jayadatta as the emperor's administering agents in the *bhukti* of Puṇḍravardhana.[205] The last inscription of the Damodarpur group, dated A.D. 543, refers to the *uparika mahārāja rājaputra* Devabhaṭṭāraka as the governor of the same *bhukti*.[206] The important point of resemblance in these records is the recurrence of the phrase *tadapādagṛhīta* which has been used as an adjective for the above named governors of the *bhukti*. This may mean that the *uparika*, who presided over the affairs of the *bhukti*, was directly responsible to the emperor and was perhaps appointed by him. Another significant point known from these inscriptions is that the *kumārāmātya* Vetravar-

201. *IHQ*, VI, p. 55.
202. *EI*, XXX, no. 30, l. 30.
203. *CII*, no. 12, l.27.
204. *EI*, XV, no. 7(1 & 2).
205. *Ibid.*, no. 7(3), l.2; no. 7(4), l.2.
206. *Ibid.*, no. 7(5), ll. 2-3.

man,[207] the *āyuktaka* Saṇḍaka[208] and the *viṣayapati* Svayambhūdeva[209] were under the *uparika* who was in charge of the *bhukti*. Moreover, the Damodarpur inscriptions reveal a gradual increase in the status and prestige of the *uparika*. In the plates of Kumāra Gupta the officer in charge of the *bhukti* is simply known as *uparika*, whereas in those of Budha Gupta and an unnamed Gupta ruler the title *mahārāja* is also appended to it. This implies that in course of time the office of the *uparika* tended to become more and more important. This is further supported by the fifth copper-plate from Damodarpur which mentions *rājaputra* Devabhaṭṭāraka as the *uparika mahārāja* of Puṇḍravardhana *bhukti*. The term *rājaputra* indicates that Devabhaṭṭāraka was either the son of the emperor or some member of the royal household. The appointment of a royal prince as the *uparika* of a *bhukti* proves that gradually much importance came to be attached to this office in course of time. Furthermore, the Damodarpur incriptions mention by name four *uparikas*, who administered Puṇḍravardhana *bhukti* perhaps successively in the time of Kumāra Gupta I, Budha Gupta and an unnamed Gupta monarch. The first three are Cirātadatta, Brahmadatta, Jayadatta, and the fourth is *rājaputra* Devabhaṭṭāraka. The names of the first three end in datta and thus may be taken to suggest that they belonged to the same family. It is likely that local families of consequence monopolised administrative power to the detriment of imperial interests. This is further borne out by the fact that Brahmadatta and Jayadatta used the title *māharāja* as an appendage to their official designation of *uparika*. Therefore, the deputation of the *rājaputra* Devabhaṭṭāraka of the royal household in the time of the Gupta ruler mentioned in the Damodarpur plate no. 5 may imply a conscious effort on the part of the emperor to assert himself against such individuals and families as were considered to be potential dangers to the imperial authority.

207. *EI*, no. 7, plates 1 & 2.

208. *Ibid.*, plate 4.

209. *Ibid.*, plate 5.

The association of the *uparika* with the *bhukti* administration is also attested by the seals discovered at Vaiśālī, two of which bear the legend : *tīrabhuktiuparikādhikaraṇasya.*[210] The expression implies that the seals belonged to the *uparika* of Tīra-*bhukti* (modern North Bihar), and the *uparika*, who is not named in the seal, was the executive head of Tīra*bhukti.*[211] Thus in some parts of Eastern India, the *uparika* administered the territorial division known as *bhukti.*

The *uparika,* however, is not always mentioned as ruling over a *bhukti.* In two grants of Jayanātha of the Ucchakalpa dynasty it is stated that the *dūtaka* was the *uparika* Sarvadatta.[212] On the basis of these two records, Vogel suggested some connection between the offices of *dūtaka* and *uparika.*[213] But this connection may have been due to the fact that the functions of two offices were combined in one officer, a feature of the Gupta administrative system.

Chhabra points out that Viśvarūpācārya in his commentary on Yājñavalkya quotes a verse from Bṛhaspati, according to whom a man who is resolute, sane, energetic, blissful, personable, generous, vigilant and capable of administering justice in legal disputes should be appointed as an *uparika* in order to maintain impartiality and morality[214] From this Chhabra infers that an *uparika* was invested with judicial as well as administrative authority. His office may, therefore, correspond to that of a magistrate.[215] In our opinion the use of the word 'magistrate' is a projection of a modern idea into the ancient period. The well-defined powers and functions of a modern magistrate may not apply to a functionary who existed more than 1500 years ago.

According to Saletore the office of the *uparika* owed its origin to the fiscal term *uparikara,* for the collection of which

210. *ASR,* 1903-4, no. 20.
211. Dikshitar, *op. cit.,* p. 162.
212. *CII,* III, no. 26, ll. 23-24; no. 27, ll. 23-24.
213. *The Antiquities of Chamba State,* p. 123.
214. *Bṛhaspati,* p. 484.
215. *D. R. Bhandarkar Comm. Volume,* pp. 231-33.

this officer may have been held responsible.[216] Although there is an apparent phonetic similarity between the words *uparika* and *uparikara*, it is not possible to state categorically that the one originated from the other. Again, there is nothing in the inscriptions to establish any connection between the *uparika* and the realisation of *uparikara*.

It is, however, probable that the word *uparika* is derived from *uparī* or *uprī*, meaning 'above,' which may also be the root of *uparikara*. And in view of this *uparika* may signify an officer who supervised over other officers under him. This would imply that his functions were similar to those of the *sarvādhyakṣas* of the Vākāṭaka records. Moreover, the passage of Bṛhaspati quoted above fits well in the context of inscription if the *uparika* is taken to be a senior officer with supervisory control over several departments and their officers.

Like the *uparika*, the *viṣayapati* was also an important officer from the Gupta period onwards, though the *viṣaya* units may have existed even in earlier times. The Damodarpur Copper-plate (A.D. 448-49) of Kumāra Gupta I referred to above, states that the *kumārāmātya* Vetravarman was appointed as *viṣayapati* by the *uparika* Cirātadatta.[217] Another inscription from Damodarpur of the time of Budha Gupta informs us that the *uparika mahārāja* Jayadatta, who was ruling over Puṇḍravardhana *bhukti*, appointed one Saṇḍaka as the officer in charge of Koṭivarṣa *viṣaya*.[218] But the Baigram Copper-plate of A.D. 448-49 bears the expression "*pañcanagaryyā bhaṭṭārakapādānudhyātaḥ kumārāmātyakulavṛddhiretad viṣayādhikaraṇam*.[219] The words *bhaṭṭāraka pādānudhyāta* literally mean "one meditating on the feet of His Majesty," and hence the entire sentence would indicate that the *viṣayapati* Kulavṛddhi, who ruled from his district office (*viṣayādhikaraṇa*) located at Pañcanagarī, paid his homage to the emperor. Paying homage directly to the emperor may imply

216. *Op. cit.*, p. 260.
217. *EI*, XV, no. 7 (2), l. 3.
218. *Ibid.*, no. 7 (4), l. 3.
219. *Ibid.*, XXI, no. 13, l. 1.

that the *viṣayapati* under reference was appointed by the former. This, however, contradicts what we gather from the Damodarpur records, according to which the *viṣayapati* owed his appointment to the *uparika* who was in charge of the *bhukti*, and not to the emperor. It is difficult to see how two different methods could have been adopted at the same time and almost in the same region with regard to the appointment of the officer in charge of a *viṣaya*. But this apparent contradiction may be resolved if we assume that the selection of the official was obviously made by the governor of the *bhukti* though his appointment was formalised by the emperor himself.[220]

The land grants often mention *viṣayapati* in connection with sale of land. In the plate nos. 1 and 2 of the Damodarpur inscriptions, *kumārāmātya* Vetravarman, the *viṣayapati* of Koṭivarṣa, is said to have been approached by two private individuals who were willing to purchase land for religious purposes. The plate no. 5 also states that one Amṛtadeva from Ayodhyā requested the *viṣayapati* Svayambhūdeva to allow him to purchase some land at the rate of three *dīnāras* for each *kulyavāpa* of land. From these instances it appears that no state-owned land could be sold without the consent of the *visayapati*, presumably because of the considerations of loss in revenue. Moreover, the *viṣayapati* perhaps exercised authority over other revenue officers functioning in a *viṣaya*, and thus may have served as a link between the emperor or the governor of the *bhukti* on the one hand and the officers of lower rank on the other.

Although the existence of the office of the *viṣayapati* beyond Bengal is attested by several inscriptions, his status does not appear to have been uniform everywhere. In a grant of the Maitraka Dharasena I, the *viṣayapati* is placed immediately after *dhruvādhikaraṇika* and before the *rājasthanīya*.[221] We have seen that the *dhruvādhikaraṇika* was connected with revenue administration of villages, and hence he could not have enjoyed

---

220. Dikshitar, *op. cit.*, p. 256.

221. *IA*, VI, p. 12.

a higher administrative status than the *viṣayapati*. Thus it is not possible to ascertain the administrative rank to which the *viṣayapati* in Central or Western India belonged.

With regard to Eastern India, however, some details about the administration of a *viṣaya* by the *viṣayapati* can be gathered from the Damodarpur Copper-plate charters referred to above. The plates of the time of Kumāra Gupta I state that *kumārāmātya* Vetravarman, the *viṣayapati* of Koṭivarṣa, administered the government of the locality in the company of Dhṛtipāla, the *nagaraśreṣṭhi*, Bandhumitra, the *sārthavāha*, Dhṛtimitra, the *prathamakulika*, and Sambapāla, the *prathamakāyastha*.[222] Another plate of Damodarpur of the time of Budha Gupta describes *āyuktaka* Saṇḍaka as governing Koṭivarṣa *viṣaya* in the company of the *nagaraśreṣṭhī* Ribhupāla, *sārthavāha* Vasumitra, *prathamakulika* Varadatta and *prathamakāyastha* Viprapāla.[223] A similar statement is available in still another Damodarpur plate dated A.D. 543.[224] It can be inferred from the above-mentioned facts that the *viṣayapati* carried the administration of a *viṣaya* in consultation with a board of advisers, consisting of the above-named persons who perhaps represented different classes of interests. The *nagaraśreṣṭhī* represented the various guilds or corporations in town or the rich urban population. The *sārthavāha* was a member of the *viṣayādhikaraṇa*, perhaps as the representative of the merchants of the *viṣaya*. We cannot be sure of the connotation of the term *prathamakulika*. The word *kulika* is shown as an alternative reading for *kulaka* in the *Amarakośa*.[225] The word *kulaka* is explained as the foremost in a company of artisans. The *prathamakulika* in the present context may mean the chief artisan who was the representative of various classes of artisans. The word *prathamakāyastha* may indicate the chief scribe who may have acted as chief secretary

222. *EI*, XV, no. 7 (1), ll. 4-6 ; no. 7 (2), ll. 3-5.
223. *Ibid.*, Plate 4, ll. 3-5.
224. *Ibid.*, Plate 5, ll. 4-6.
225. *Amar.*, II. 10. 5.

to the administrative board.[226] It is evident that the administrative board of the *viṣaya* consisted of persons who mostly represented the mercantile and industrial class. Although the functions of these representatives could not have been anything more than advisory, the fact that they were consulted in the administration of the *viṣaya* may indicate their importance.

The *viṣayapati* and his *adhikaraṇa* were assisted by the *pustapāla* in matters of land transactions.[227] The word *pusta* according to the *Medinīkośa* means both *lepyādikarma* (plastering, painting images, etc.) and books.[228] The officer *pustapāla* may be understood in the sense of an officer in charge of record-books containing boundaries, title etc., of land-holdings. Pargiter's translation of the term as record-keeper is, therefore, apt.[229] It is stated in the Damodarpur inscriptions that the application made to the *viṣayapati* for permission to purchase state lands was referred to *pustapālas* for necessary inquiries. This leads us to think that the government sanctioned sale of land only after the *pustapālas* had determined the title to the land under proposal of transfer.

From the foregoing account it is obvious that in Gupta times, unlike the post-Maurya period, the machinery for revenue administration was perhaps fairly well developed. Although it is not possible to precisely state the duties and functions of these officers, we gather the impression that most of them were associated with fiscal and land administration, some of them being entrusted with the task of general superintendence. It may further

---

226. The Faridpur plates B and C of the time of Dharmāditya (*IA*, XXXIX, pp. 199, 204) mention *jyeṣṭhakāyastha*, which Pargiter wrongly translates as the oldest *kāyastha* (*ibid.*, p. 211). But it seems that *prathamakāyastha* and *jyeṣṭhakāyastha* are identical in their meaning. For the interpretation of these words I have relied on Basak (*EI*, XV, p. 131 and notes).

227. EI, XV, no. 7 (1), l. 10; no. 7 (2), l. 7; no. 7 (3), l. 6; no. 7 (4), l. 9, no. 7 (5), l. 10.

228. *Ibid.*, p. 132, n. 3. Basak rightly points out that *pustapālas* of Bengal inscriptions may be the same as the *akṣapaṭalika* of other inscriptions.

229. *IA*, XXXIX, p. 213.

be assumed that the collection of revenue may have been more intensive—an important thing indeed, particularly in the context of the falling state income from the Gupta period onwards.

During our period, the administrative machinery came to be gradually manned by hereditary divisional and district officers, Although Kauṭilya lays down that officers (*amātyas*) and soldiers should be hereditary, we have hardly any contemporary epigraphic evidence to support this.[230] The first inscriptional reference to the hereditary nature of administrative posts is available in the post-Maurya period when we come across two generations of a *grāmika*.[231] The tendency, however, appears to have gathered further strength in the Gupta period. The Karamdanda Stone inscription of the time of Kumāra Gupta I refers to Pṛthvīsena, the minister, as being the son of Śikharasvāmin, the minister.[232] Similarly a seal from Vaiśālī mentions the *amātya* Bhadrika.[233] The Khoh and Majhgawan Copper-plate inscriptions of Hastin from Central India mention five generations of office holders in one family, of whom the first was *amātya*, the second and the third were *bhogikas*, and the fourth and fifth *mahāsandhivigrahikas*.[234] Two inscriptions of Jayanātha furnish instances of two and three generations of *bhogikas*.[235] More over, it has been shown earlier that the surname *datta* of the *uparika* in charge of Puṇḍravardhana *bhukti* suggests that they belonged to the same family. Although theoretically the emperor enjoyed the power of dismissing his officials, in practice they and their descendents continued to be in office because of their local strength.[236]

The officers may have further gained in power and influence because of the practice of combining several offices in the same person. The Allahabad inscription of Samudra Gupta states that

230. Sharma, *op. cit.*, pp. 210-11.
231. *Supra.*
232. *EI*, X, no. 15, 11. 6-7.
233. Dikshitar, *op. cit.*, p. 150; *ASR*, 1913-14, p. 134, no. 210.
234. *CII*, III, no. 22, 11. 28-30; no. 23, 11. 18-20.
235. *Ibid.*, no. 27, 11. 21-22; no. 26, 11. 22-23.
236. Sharma, *op. cit.*, p. 211.

Harisena besides being a *kumārāmātya* also held the offices of the *sandhivigrahika* and *mahādaṇḍanāyaka*.[237] The Khoh Copper-plate of Hastin mentions Naradatta, who was both *amātya* and *bhogika*.[238] Another grant from Central India refers to the *mahābalādhikṛta* Nāgasiṁha as its *dūtaka*. The Gunaigarh inscription from Bengal informs us that the *dūtaka* Vijayasena was also the *mahāpratīhāra* (royal chamberlain), the *mahāpīlupati* (officer is charge of elephants), *purapāloparika*, etc.[239] The combination of several offices in the same person perhaps added to the strength of the Gupta officers and with the power so derived they could often choose to oppress the people more for personal gains than in the interest of the royal exchequer.

Turning to the officer's remuneration, if we rely on the authority of Kauṭilya, it appears that in the Maurya period all the officers of the state from the highest to the lowest were paid in cash, the maximum salary being 48,000 *paṇas* and the minimum 60 *paṇas*, probably per month.[240] But in connection with the foundation of new settlements, Kauṭilya also prescribes that land may be granted as emoluments to superintendents of various departments, the accountants, the officers called *gopa* and *sthānika*, to officers in the army, physicians, horse-trainers, but without power to sell or mortgage.[241] Thus the principles of remunerating the state officials both in cash and through land-assignments are recognised by Kauṭilya, though from the detailed treatment of the former it appears that cash payment was perhaps comparatively more in practice.

The *Jātaka* evidence also indicates that usually the officers were paid in cash for their administrative services. The *Jātakas* generally use the term *bhatta-vetana* in the sense of remuneration. In the *Saṁvara Jātaka*, where the term occurs, *bhatta-vetana* has been translated as food-money.[242] But Horner renders *rañño-*

237. *CII*, III, no. 1, l. 32.
238. *Ibid.*, III, no. 23, l. 0.
239. *IHQ*, VI, p. 55.
240. *AŚ*, V. 3.
241. *Ibid.*, II. 1.
242. *Jat.*, IV, p. 132, Tr. IV. p. 84.

bhattavetanāhāro of the *Vinaya Piṭaka* as "living on a salary and food from a king."[243] Probably the latter meaning is correct. Apparently the term *vetana* cannot be taken literally as cash payment, but in the above-cited instance it can be safely presumed that there was no necessity of paying the officers again in kind if they were already given provisions.[244] Therefore Sharma rightly points out that the term *vetana* compounded with *bhatta* may be understood in the sense of cash payment.[245]

Besides, the cumulative evidence of the *Jātakas* is also in favour of cash payment. In the *Vidhurapaṇḍita Jātaka* there is a reference to the increase of *vetana* of his elephant-driver, or his life-guardsman, his chariot-soldier or his foot-soldier by the king.[246] This may imply that in this case salaries were paid in cash. The *Makhādeva Jātaka* refers to the grant of a village, yielding 1,000 pieces of money, to a barber[247] The *Padakusalamānava Jātaka* relates how a youth skilled in tracking footsteps enters the service of a king for 1000 pieces of money daily.[248] Similarly from the *Sarabhaṅga Jātaka* we learn of an archer who was employed by a king for the daily remuneration of 1000 pieces of money.[249] Evidently, whether it is the income of a village, or payment to a youth skilled in tracking footsteps or an archer, the amount stated in each case is a thousand pieces of money. Although this figure is conventional as is inevitable in folk literature, the above-mentioned instances seem to establish the possibility of payment in cash to the officers and employees of the king.

The term *bhogagāma* in the *Jātakas*,[250] however, has been interpreted to mean a village that was given to a minister for enjoyment as remuneration for his office.[251] But no *Jātaka*

---

243. *The Book of Discipline*, II. p. 67.
244. Sharma, *op. cit.*, p. 140.
245. *Ibid.*
246. *Jāt.*, IV, p. 295.
247. *Ibid.*, I, p. 138.
248. *Ibid.*, VII, p. 505.
249. *Ibid.*, V. p. 128.
250. *Ibid.*, *III*, p. 305; IV, pp. 453, 484; VI, p. 463.
251. Bose, *Social & Rural Economy*, I, p. 72.

passage can be cited to show that village was granted to ministers for their administrative functions. In fact, *bhogagāma* was a mark of favour bestowed by the king upon any body with whom he was pleased so that it could be conferred even upon a barber.[252] The term, according to Sharma, means a village given by the king to his favourites for enjoyment, and there is hardly anything to show that *bhogagāmas* were granted to officers for rendering administrative or other services to the state.[253] Thus the *Jātakas* largely support the practice of paying the state officials in cash and not in kind, which fits in well with the post-Maurya period when money-economy perhaps received a fillip from the flourishing trade with the West.

In the post-Maurya period the payment of officers in kind and through grants of land is recommended by Manu, who lays down certain interesting rules in this connection. According to him the headman of a village should obtain, presumably as his emoluments, those articles which the villagers have to furnish everyday to the king, viz., food drink, fuel and like.[254] The officer over ten villages should enjoy one *kula,* that over twenty villages five *kulas,* the superintendent of a hundred villages the revenue of one village and the high officer over a thousand villages the revenue of a town. This injunction, with minor variations, is also repeated in the *Śānti Parva*[255] which states that every headman should contribute his share for maintaining the lord of ten villages, and the latter should do the same for supporting the lord of twenty villages.[256] The *Sānti Parva* adds that the lord of a hundred villages should have for his support a large village, and that of a thousand should have a minor town for his maintenance.[257] This rule refers to the officers associated with local administration and not to those of the central government. This

252. *Jāt.,* I, 138.
253. For further discussion vide Sharma, *op. cit.,* pp. 138-139.
254. *Manu,* VII. 118.
255. *Ibid.,* 119.
256. *ŚP,* 87. 6.
257. *Ibid.,* 7-8.

may suggest that high ranking officials may have continued to be paid in terms of money. In any case, the payment of salaries in kind and through land-assignments was perhaps gaining ground in the post-Maurya period simultaneously with the practice of cash payment. The rule of Manu also occurs in the law-book of Bṛhaspati which may suggest that it continued to enjoy authority in the Gupta period.

The Chinese account may be considered, though it is not very clear on this point. Legge's translation of a passage of Fa-hsien reads : "the king's body-guards and attendants, all have regular salaries".[258] But Beal translates the passage thus : "the chief officers of the king have all allotted revenues;"[259] and a recent rendering by a Chinese scholar is as follows : "The king's attendants, guards, and retainers all receive emoluments and pensions".[260] If the last translation is accepted, the term emoluments, having a wider context, might include grants.[261] But even if we reject this interpretation of the crucial passage which is ambiguous, it is clear from Hsüan Tsang's report that during the time of Harṣavardhana high officers were not paid in cash for their services to the state, but one-fourth of the royal revenues was earmarked for the endowment of great public servants.[262] This may suggest that the practice of granting revenues to officers may have had its beginnings in earlier times and at least in the Gupta period.

Several epigraphic terms of the Gupta period also give the impression that officials were paid in kind. Some inscriptions of the rulers of Ucchakalpa mention the *bhogika* as *amātya*;[263] and it is no wonder that in such a case the office of the *bhogika* was meant to remunerate its holder for his functions pertaining to other office.[264] Again, the word *bhukti* means something intended

---

258. Legge, *A Record of Buddhistic Kingdoms,* Tr. p. 45.
259. Beal, *Travels of Fa-hian and Sung Yun,* p. 55.
260. Ho Chang-Chun, "Fa-hsien's Pilgrimage to Buddhist Countries," *Chinese Literature,* 1952, no. 3. p. 154.
261. Sharma, *op. cit.,* p. 27.
262. Watters, *On Yuan Chwang's Travels in India,* I, p. 176.
263. *CII,* III, no. 23, 11. 18-20; no. 26, 11. 22-23.
264. Sharma, *op. cit.,* p. 207.

for enjoyment. So it is not unlikely that the territorial unit called *bhukti* was meant for the enjoyment of the *uparika* under whose charge it was placed. Sharma interprets a phrase of the Damodarpur Copper-plate grants to suggest that even a *viṣaya* unit was meant for the enjoyment of district officers.[265] Thus it appears that the practice of paying the officers in kind was prevalent in the Gupta period on a considerable scale, though no epigraphic record directly referring to the grant of land to an officer for his administrative functions is available.

265. *Ibid.*, p. 209.

CHAPTER XIII

RECAPITULATION AND CONCLUSIONS

Although in theory taxes are often contemplated in the law-books as constituting the king's wages for hetprotection rendered by him to the people, in practice the idea of a king being the servant of his subjects does not appear to have worked. However, the literary texts of the Gupta period represent the king as the enjoyer of the earth, which apparently entitled him to taxes, a position that came to be legally recognised by Kātyāyana. To avoid the dangerous implications of this proposition the law-books of our times stress that taxes should be governed by the capacity of the people to pay and should not be oppressive and arbitrary These admirable precepts of taxation have been described as being far advanced from those of the classical antiquity and approaching the modern canons of taxation formulated in Europe during the 17th and 18 h centuries.[1] But as shown earlier the resemblance between the ancient Hindu principles of taxation and those of modern times is only superficial, and in their intents and purposes the two differ widely.

The principles set forth by the jurists of our period are symptomagic of a fairly developed revenue system, but they leave enough scope for fiscal oppression of the people by the king. In fact, the much appreciated Hindu tax-maxims cannot be reconciled with the divinity of the king leading to the belief in his infallibility. The king, if he so chose, could take advantage of the divine concept of monarchy to override the restrictions imposed on his power of taxation by the *Smṛtis*.

Our analysis of emergency financial measures laid down by our sources implies that the king could go to great lengths for

1. *HRS*, pp. 273-74.

raising funds in times of crisis. The *Arthaśāstra* of Kauṭilya recommends certain highly oppressive steps such as the realisation of benevolences (*praṇaya*) at exorbitant rates from the people, confiscation of temple treasures, setting up of new cults, and putting up of sudden miracles, for accumulating money in extraordinary circumstances. The levy of benevolences (*praṇaya*) is known from only a few inscriptions and so appears to have fallen in comparative deseutude in post-Maurya and Gupta times, whereas other measures prescribed by Kauṭilya are not referred to in our period. It is striking that the *Śānti Parva* gives a *carte blanche* to the king to confiscate the property of all except the ascetics and the brāhmaṇas, which is not done by any lawgiver of our period. The law-books prescribe only an increase in tax-rates so that the king could squeeze out of the people as much as possible. We do not know which of these measures found favour in practice, but there is no doubt that the Hindu monarch during the period under study was vested with the prerogative of levying burdensome taxes from his subjects. Panegyrics by their very nature cannot think of a king being an oppressor or a tyrant seizing the wealth of the people, but we have reasons to believe that the experience of excessive taxation was not altogether alien to ancient Indians.

The principal source of state revenue appears to have been land tax, which consisted most probably of the king's one-sixth share of produce, though its maximum rate in the Maurya period is one-fourth. The sources of the post-Maurya and Gupta periods often mention *bali*, *bhāga* and *kara* as items of land revenue. *Bali*, which is the oldest land revenue term used in different contexts in various works, is mentioned in the *Smṛtis* in the sense of basic land tax. Another term *bhāga*, which occurs first in the *Arthaśāstra*, is often recorded in the Gupta land grants in a similar sense. The solitary epigraphic record where *bali* and *bhāga* are distinguished is the Junagadh inscription of Rudradāman. In all other inscriptions of our period *bhāga* is used almost invariably to mean the basic land tax, which is indicated by the term *bali* in the non-epigraphic sources. The identification of *kara* is not possible in the present state of our knowledge, though according to the commentators' opinions it may have some connection with land revenues. The tax known as *hiraṇya*, which was perhaps realised in cash, was fairly widely prevalent from the Maurya period onwards.

From the time of the Guptas, inscriptions frequently mention two new land revenue terms, *udraṅga* and *uparikara*, which have been interpreted by Ghoshal to mean taxes on permanent and temporary tenants respectively. But in our opinion these terms indicate nothing more than some kind of extra tax over and above the king's normal grain share and their precise nature cannot be determined. In the Gupta charters we come across several land revenue terms which are not mentioned in earlier sources. Thus *meya*, *ditya* and *dhānya* are mentioned frequently in the inscriptions from the Gupta period onwards. Although the exact meaning of these terms is difficult to determine, their connotation seems to be wide enough to cover all revenues from land. Two land grants of the Ucchakalpa ruler Sarvanātha record another new land revenue term, *halikākara*, whose meaning is uncertain. Thus several new taxes came to be imposed in the Gupta period. On the other hand, some older taxes of Maurya times such as the water-tax (*udakabhāga*) gradually disappeared in our period because irrigation tended to become an individual or local concern. This naturally may have meant some relief to the peasants.

The *Smṛtis* refer more clearly than the earlier writings to the supply of the articles of daily use more or less in the nature of regular taxes, but the inscriptions of the Vākāṭakas mention it as miscellaneous contributions of provisions by the villagers to the officers on tour. Contemporary epigraphic records of North India mention the fiscal term *bhoga*, which is also known from the earlier sources and is probably the same as the supply of provisions recorded in the Vākāṭaka land charters. The supply of provisions to the officers may have imposed excessive financial burden on the common people because these could be realised as often as the king or his officers toured a particular area. The position of the people may have been further worsened by the levy of forced labour (*viṣṭi*) which was an important item of royal income. In the Maurya period forced labour (*viṣṭi*) was paid for as can be inferred from the *Artha-*

śāstra. There is, however, no evidence to suggest that impressed labour was paid in our period. According to the post-Mauryan law-books only śūdras, artisans and craftsmen were expected to render free service to the king in lieu of paying taxes. But it can be gleaned from the Gupta sources that in course of time even the free peasantry became liable to forced labour. In other words, forced labour tended to become oppressive. It became all the more so when from the Gupta period onwards the king's right to *viṣṭi* was transferred to the recipients of land grants.

A considerable bulk of royal revenue resources consisted of commercial taxes, the principal item under this head being the *śulka* with which the earlier sources are also familiar. From the Gupta period onwards several inscriptions of the Kathiawad region refer to *bhūtavātapratyāya,* which Ghoshal[2] wrongly interprets as the revenue derived from the elements and the winds and which according to us has the same connotation as the term *śulka.* Ferry charges of earlier times continued to be realised during the period under review. *Klṛpta* and *upaklṛpta,* however, appear for the first time in the Gupta epigraphs. Although Ghoshal holds that tax on liquor, an important source of the royal exchequer under the Mauryas, disappeared under the Guptas, there is no evidence to show that the policy of prohibition was followed.

We may mention some miscellaneous sources of revenue, e.g., fines, resumption of heirless property, treasure troves, and booty and tributes from the vanquished kings. Whereas the king received a part of his total income from these sources, war-booty and tributes became more and more important because of frequent wars in the period of our study. Moreover, the crown lands, forests, mines, and similar other royal monopolies provided a considerable income to the king.

All the taxes enumerated above may not have been payable by the same individual, but there is nothing to show that the burden was equitably distributed among all sections of the tax-payers. The frequent grants of land to the brāhmaṇas clearly indicate that the donees were immune from the payment of taxes;

2. *HRS,* p. 291.

the privilege may also have been enjoyed by the learned brāhmaṇas who were not donees. The epigraphs from the 5th century A.D. testify to the fact that often the ruler made over his right to mines to the beneficiaries, which not only undermined his political power but also adversely affected his total revenue receipts. The loss in the royal income may have been compensated by throwing the maximum weight of taxation on the non-brāhmaṇas who do not seem to have enjoyed any exemption from taxation. On the other hand what was lost in revenue by the state was gained by the priests, whose improved economic condition placed them in a superior position in relation to the ordinary villagers. The difference between the priestly class and the lower castes may have been further accelerated in Saurāṣṭra, where the non-brāhmaṇas were subjected to the payment of a tithe known as *brāhmaṇaviṁśati* for the support of the brāhmaṇas.

We notice some changes in the fiscal units of our times. *Grāma* continued to be the smallest unit of administration. *Āhāra,* which appears for the first time in the Aśokan epigraphs, was a popular fiscal unit in the Sātāvāhana dominions, and in the Gupta period it remained confined to the same areas. The antiquity of *viṣaya* goes back to the time of Aśoka, and this unit obviously obtained in the post-Maurya period for we have numerous references to it in Gupta times. The provenance of the Gupta inscriptions referring to *viṣaya* suggests that it was an important unit of fiscal administration in Bengal, Gujarat and Central India, though the actual expanse of the territory covered by it is difficult to ascertain.

The Gupta sources, however, refer to many new administrative units which possibly served the purposes of fiscal administration as well. These are *bhukti, vīthī, pura, sthalī, paṭṭa, peṭha, padraka, deśa, maṇḍala* etc. But these were not prevalent in all parts of the country; nor could their size in every region have been uniform. These units are mostly mentioned in the inscriptions, whereas the *Smṛtis* generally provide for the division of the kingdom into units based on the decimal system, which is supported by epigraphic evidence from the 7th or the 8th century.

Although the revenue officers mentioned by Kauṭilya do not generally occur in our sources, some of them seem to have existed in our period. *Grāmika* of the *Arthaśāstra* finds mention also in later sources. Two officers of the *Arthaśāstra* can be equated with their counterparts found in the Gupta records, the *śulkādhyakṣa* with the *śaulkika* and the *āyukta* with the *āyuktaka.* Although *akṣapaṭala* in the sense of records office is known to Kauṭilya the officer in charge of it appears in inscriptions only from the Gupta period onwards. Similarly, *hiraṇya* as an item of revenue figures in the *Arthaśāstra,* but the officer who collected it first appears in the Gupta inscriptions. *Dūtaka* of the Gupta land grants is reminiscent of the *dūta* of the *Arthaśāstra.* In addition to the officers referred to above, our sources mention a number of officers, e.g., *lekhaka, divirapati, āgrahārika, audraṅgika* or *drāṅgika, dhruvādhikaraṇika, viniyuktaka, sarvādhyakṣa, kumārāmātya, bhogika, uparika,* and *viṣayapati.* But it is not possible to delienate their duties and functions with precision. In the time of the Guptas the number of officers associated directly or remotely with revenue administration was far greater than in post-Maurya times. Besides, most of these functionaries tended to become hereditary, and several functions were combined in the same person.

BIBLIOGRAPHY

(A) Primary Sources

(i) *Original Texts and Translations*

Abhiiñāna-śākuntalam of Kālidāsa — Nirnayasagar Press. Bombay, 1947.

Āpastamba Dharmasūtra — Ed. by G. Bühler, Bombay, 1932. Trs. of *Āpastamba, Gautama, Vasistha* and *Baudhāyana* by G. Bühler in SBE, Vols II and XIV, Oxford, 1879-82.

Aitareya Brāhmana — Ed. Th. Aufrecht, Bonn, 1879.

Arthaśāstra of Kautilya — Ed. by R. Shama Sastry, 3rd. End., Mysore, 1924. Tr. R. Sharma Sastry, 7th Edn., Mysore, 1961. Ed. with commentary by T. Ganapati Sastri, 3 vols., Trivandrum, 1924-25.

(i) Commentaries on the *Arthaśāstra Jayamaṅgalā* (runs up to the end of the Book I of the *AŚ* with gaps), Ed. by G. Harihar Sastri, *JORM,* XX-XXIII.

(ii) *Pratipada-pancikā* by Bhaṭṭasvamin (on Book II from section 8), Ed. by K. P. Jayaswal and A. Banerji-Sastri, *JBORS,* XI-XII.

(iii) *Naya Candrikā* by Mādhava Yajva (on Books VII-XII), Ed. by Udayavira Sastri, Lahore, 1924.

Atharva Veda Saṁhitā — Ed. by C. R. Lanman, Tr. W. D. Whitney, *HOS,* VII and VIII, Harvard University, 1905.

Aṭṭhaśālinī — Ed. by E. Muller. PTS. London, 1879. Eng. Tr. (*The Expositor*) by Maung Tin, London, 1920-21

Avadānaśatakam — Ed. by J. Speyer
Ed. by P. L. Vaidya. Darbhanga, 1958.

Baudhāyana Gṛhyasūtra — Ed. by R. Sharma Sastry, Mysore, 1927.

Bṛhajjātaka of Varāhamihira — With an Eng. trans. and notes, by V. Subrahmanya Sastri. Mysore, 1929. With Bhaṭṭotpala's Commentary Ed. by Sita Rama Jha. Benares, 1934.

Bṛhaspati-smṛti — Reconstructed by K. V. R. Aiyangar, GOS. Baroda, 1941. Eng. Tr. by Jolly, SBE, Oxford, 1889.

Bṛhatsaṁhitā of Varāhamihira — Ed. by H. Kern, Bibliotheca Indica, Calcutta, 1865. Eng. tr. by H. Kern. *JRAS*, 1870-1875; Parts 1-5. London, 1870-73. Ed. with Eng. trans. and notes by V. Subrahmanya Sastri and M. Ramakrishna Bhat, 2 vols., Bangalore, 1947.

Buddhacarita of Aśvaghoṣa — Ed. & Tr. E. H. Johnston, (Punjab University Oriental Publication, No. 31) Lahore, 1935.

Caraka-saṁhitā — Ed. by J. Vidyasagar, 2nd Edn. Calcutta, 1896.

Dhammapada Commentary — Ed. by H. C. Norman, 5 vols., PTS., London, 1906-15. Eng. Tr. (*Buddhist Legends*) by E. W. Burlingame, 3 vols., HOS, Cambridge, Massachusetts, 1921.

Dīgha Nikāya — Ed. by T. W. Rhys Davids and J. E. Carpenter. 3 Vols., PTS, London, 1890-1911. Eng. Tr. (*Dialogues of the Buddha*) by T. W. Rhys Davids, 3 vols., London, 1899-1921.

Divyāvadāna — Ed. by E. B. Cowell and R. A. Neil, Cambridge, 1886.

Gāthāsaptaśatī of Hāla — Ed. & Tr. by N. Chaturvedi, Benares, 1961.

Gautama Dharmasūtra — Ed. A. S. Stenzler, London, 1876. With the commentary of Maskarin, Ed. L. Srinivasacharya, Mysore, 1917.

Harṣacarita of Bāṇa — Ed. by K. P. Parab & Wasudeva Laxman Sastri Pansikar, Nirnayasagar Press, Bombay 1937.

Jātakamālā of Āryasūra — Ed. by H. Kern, Boston, 1871. Eng. Tr. J. Speyer, London, 1895.

Kāmandakīyanītisāra	Ed. and trans. in Hindi by Jwalaprasad Mishra, Venkateswar Press, Sake 1826. Eng. trans. by M. N. Datta, Calcutta, 1896.
Kāmasūtra of Vātsyāyana	Nirnayasagar Press, Bombay, 1900. Eng. trans. by K. R. Iyengar, Lahore, 1921.
Kathāsaritsāgara of Somadeva	Eng. Tr. (*The Ocean of story*) by C. H. Tawney, and ed. by N. M. Panzer, 10 vols, London, 1924.
Kātyāyana-smṛti-sāroddhāra	*Kātyāyana-smṛti on Vyavahāra, Law and Procedure*), Ed. with reconstituted text, trans. notes and introduction by P. V. Kane, Bombay, 1933.
Kumārasaṁbhava of Kālidāsa	Nirnayasagar Press, Bombay.
Lalitavistara,	Ed. by S. Leffmann, Halle, 1902-8.
Mahābhārata	*Śānti Parva,* Critical Edn. by S. K. Belvalkar, Poona, 1949-54. For all other chapters reference is to the Eng. tr. by K. M. Ganguli. Published by P. C. Roy, Calcutta, 1884-96.
Mahābhāṣya of Patañjali	Ed. by F. Kielhorn, 3 vols., Bombay, 1892-1909.
Mahāvaṁsa	Ed. by W. Geiger, PTS, London, 1908. Eng. Tr. W. Geiger (*The Great Chronicles of Ceylon*) London, 1912.
Mahāvastu,	Ed. by E. Senart, 3 vols., Paris, 1882-97.
Mālavikāgnimitra of Kālidāsa	Nirnayasagar Press, Bombay, 1950.
Mānava Dharmaśāstra (or *Manusmṛti*)	Ed. by J. Jolly, London, 1887. Eng. Tr. by G. Bühler, SBE, Oxford, 1886. Eng. Tr. by G. Jha, 5 vols., Calcutta, 1922-29.
Milindapañho	Ed. by V. Trenckner, London, 1880. Eng. Tr. by T. W. Rhys Davids, SBE, Oxford, 1890-94.
Mṛcchakaṭika of Śūdraka	Bombay Sanskrit Series, Vol. I, Bombay, 1896.

Mudrārākṣasa of Viśākhadatta — Ed. by K. T. Telang. Revised by V. S. Ghate. 5th Edn., Nirnayasagar Press, Bombay, 1945. Eng. Trans. by R. S. Pandit (*The Signet Ring*), Bombay, 1944.

Nāmaliṅgānuśāsanam of Amarasiṁha (*Amarkośa*) — With the commentary of Kṣīrasvāmī Ed. H. D. Sharma and N. G. Sardesai, Poona, 1941.

Nāradasmṛti — Ed. by J. Jolly, Calcutta, 1885 Eng. tr. J. Jolly, SBE, XXXIII, Oxford, 1889.

Pañcatantra — Ed. F. Edgerton, Poona, 1930. *Pāṇinisutra Pāṭha* and *pariśiṣṭas* with Word Index, compiled by S. Pathak and S. Chitrao, Poona, 1935.

Raghuvaṃśa of Kālidāsa — Nirnayasagar Press, Bombay, 1929.

Rājanītiprakāśa

Rājataraṅgiṇī — Ed. M. A. Stein, Bombay, 1892. Eng. Tr. M. A. Stein, London, 1900.

Ritusaṃhāra of Kālidāsa — Nirnayasagar Press, Bombay, 1952.

Saṁyutta Nikāya — Ed. Leon Freer, PTS, London, 1884-98. Eng. Tr. (*Book of the Kindred Sayings*) by Mrs. Rhys Davids and F. L. Woodward, PTS, London, 1917-30.

Śatapatha Brāhmaṇa — Ed. A. Weber, London, 1855.

Saundaranandakāvya of Aśvaghoṣa — Ed. by E. H. Johnston, London, 1928. Eng. Tr. by E. H. Johnston (*Nanda The Fair*), 2 vols, London, 1932.

Sumaṅgala-Vilāsinī (Commentary to *Dīgha Nikāya*) — Ed. T. W. Rhys Davids and others, 3 vols., PTS, London, 1886-1932.

Śusruta-saṁhitā — Ed. by J. Vidyasagara, 3rd. Edn., Calcutta. 1889.

Vaiṣṇava Dharmaśāstra (*Viṣṇusmṛti*) — Ed. by J. Jolly, Calcutta, 1881 Eng. Tr. J. Jolly, SBE, VII. Oxford, 1880.

Vasiṣṭha Dharmaśāstra — Ed. A. A. Fuhrer, Bombay, 1916.

Vicitrakarṇikavadanoddhṛta — Ed. & Tr. by Hans Jorgensen. London, 1931.

Vikramorvaśīyam of Kalidāsa — Nirnayasagar Press. Bombay, 1942.

Vinaya Piṭaka — Ed. H. Oldenberg, 5 vols., London, 1870-1883. *The Book of Discipline,* Tr., I. B. Horner, 5 parts, London, 1938-52.

Viṣṇudharmottara Purāṇa — Venkatesvara Press, Bombay, 1912.

Viṣṇu Purāṇa — With Hindi tr. by Munilal Gupta. Gita Press, Gorakhpur. V. S. 1990.

Yājñvalkyasmṛti — With *Vīramitrodaya* and *Mitākṣarā,* Chowk-*hamba* Sanskrit Series, Benares, 1930.

Yuga Purāṇa, — Ed. D. R. Mankad, Vallabhvidyanagar, 1951.

(ii) *Coins and inscriptions*

Allan, J., — *Catalogue of the coins of the Gupta Dynasties and of Śasāṅka, king of Gauḍa,* London, 1914.

Epigraphia Carnatica.

Epigraphia Indica.

Fleet, J. F., — *Inscriptions of the Early Gupta Kings, CII,* III, London, 1888.

Gnoli, R., — *Nepalese Inscriptions in Gupta character,* Pt. I. Text. Rome, 1956.

Konow, S., — *Kharoṣṭhī Inscriptions, CII,* II, Part I. 1929. *Lüders' List of Brāhmī Inscriptions* (being a supplement to *Epigraphia Indica,* Vol. X.

Mirashi, V. V., — *Inscriptions of the Kalacuri-Cedi Era, CII,* IV (in two parts), Ootacamund, 1955.

Sircar, D. C., — *Select Inscriptions bearing on Indian History and Civilisation,* I, Calcutta, 1942.

(iii) *Non-Indian Sources*

Beal, S., *Si-Yu-ki. Buddhist Records of the Western world.* Tr. from the Chinese of Hsüan Tsang, 2 vols., London, 1906.

Giles, H. A., *The Travels of Fa-hsien* or *Record of Buddhistic Kingdoms,* Cambridge, 1923.

Legge, J. H., *Record of the Buddhistic Kingdoms,* being an account of the Chinese monk Fa-hsien's travels, Oxford, 1886

McCrindle J. W., *Ancient India as Described in Classical Literature,* Westminster, 1901.

.... *Ancient India as Described by Megasthenese and Arrian,* Calcutta, 1926.

Schoff, W. H. (Tr.) *The Periplus of the Erythraean Sea,* London, 1912.

Watters, T., *On Yuan Chwang's Travels in India,* Ed. by T. W. Rhys Davids and S. W. Bushell. 2 vols., London, 1904, 1905.

(B) Modern Works

Adhya, G. L., *Early Indian Economics,* Bombay, 1966.

Agarwala, V. S., *Harsacarita-ek Sanskritik Adhyayana* (in Hindi), Patna, 1953.

.... *India as known to Pāṇini,* Lucknow, 1953.

Altekar, A. S., *A History of Village Communities in Western India,* Madras, 1927.

.... *The Rāṣṭrakūṭas and their Times,* Poona, 1934.

.... *State and Government in Ancient India,* Benares, 1949.

Aiyangar, K. V. R., *Aspects of Ancient Indian Economic Thought* (Manindra Chandra Lectures 1927, Benares Hindu University), Benares, 1934.

Aiyangar, K. V. R. *Indian Cameralism,* Madras, 1949.

.... *Rājadharma,* Madras, 1941.

Aiyangar, S. K., *Studies in Gupta History,* Madras, 1928.

.... *Evolution of Hindu Administrative Institutions in South India,* Madras, 1931.

Baden-Powell, B. H., *The Land-Systems of British India,* I, 1892.

Bandopadhyaya, N. C. *Kauṭilya,* Calcutta, 1927.

.... *Development of Hindu Polity and Political Theories,* 2 vols., Calcutta, 1927-38.

Banerjea, P. N., *Public Administration in Ancient India,* London, 1916.

Banerji, R. D., *The Age of the Imperial Guptas,* Benares, 1933.

Beni Prasad, *The State in Ancient India,* Allahabad, 1928.

Basak, R. G., *History of North-Eastern India,* Calcutta, 1934.

Basham, A. L., *The Wonder that was India,* London, 1954.

Bastable, *Public Finance,* London, 1903.

Bhandarkar, D. R., *Carmichael Lectuers,* 1918.

.... *Some Aspects of Ancient Hindu Polity,* Benares, 1929.

Bloch, Marc, *Feudal Society,* London, 1961.

Campbell, *Modern India,* London, 1852.

Chapot, Victor, *The Roman World* (Translated from French by E. A. Parker), London, 1928.

Charlesworth, M. P., *The Roman Empire,* Oxford University Press, 1951.

Coomaraswamy, A. K., *Spiritual Authority and Temporal Power in the Indian Theory of Government* (American Oriental Society Series, Volume 22), New Haven, 1942,

Coulborn, R. (Ed.), *Feudalism in History,* Princeton University Press, 1956.

Dandekar, R. N., *History of the Guptas,* Poona, 1941.

Das, S. K., *The Economic History of Ancient India,* Calcutta, 1929.

Datta, B. N., *Studies in Indian Social Polity,* First Edn., Calcutta, 1944.

.... *Dialectics of Land-Economics of India,* Calcutta, 1952.

Dikshitar, V.R.R., *Hindu Administrative Institutions,* Madras, 1929.

.... *Mauryan Polity,* Madras 1932.

.... *Gupta Polity,* Madras, 1952.

Fick, R., *The Social Organisation in North-East India in Buddha's time.* Calcutta, 1920.

Ghoshal, U. N., *A History of Hindu Political Theories,* Calcutta, 1923.

.... *The Agrarian System in Ancient India,* Calcutta, 1930.

.... *The Beginnings of Indian Historiography and othher Essays.* Calcutta, 1944.

.... *Contributions to the History of Hindu Revenue System,* Calcutta, 1929.

Gopal, L., *Economic life of Northern India, (c. A.B. 700-720)*, Baneras, 1965.

Gupta, K. M., *Land System in South India,* Lahore, 1933.

Heesterman, J. C., *The Ancient Indian Royal Consecration,* The Hague, 1957.

Heichelheim, F. M., *An Ancient Economic History,* 2 Vols., (English tr. by Mrs. Joyce Stevens), Leiden, 1958-64.

Jain, J. C. *Life in Ancient India as Depicted in the Jain Canons,* Bombay, 1947.

Jayaswal, K. P. — *Hindu Polity*, third Edn. Bangalore, 1955.

Jha, G. N., — *Notes on Manusmṛti,* 3 vols., Calcutta, 1924-1929.

Jolly, J. — *Recht und Sitte,* Strassburg, 1896. (Eng. trans. by B. K. Ghosh, *Hindu Law and Custom,* Calcutta, 1928.

Jouveau-Dubreiul, G., — *Ancient History of the Deccan* (trans. from the Franch by V. S. Svaminadha Dikshitar), Pondichery, 1920.

Kanakasabhai Pillai, V., — *Tamils Eighteen Hundred Years Ago.,* Madras, 1904.

Kane, P. V. — *History of Dharmaśāstra,* 3 vols., Poona, 1930-46.

Kosambi, D. D., — *An Introduction to the Study of Indian History,* Bombay, 1956.

.... — *The Culture and Civilisation of Ancient India in Historical outline,* London, 1965.

Law, B. C., — *History of Pali Literature,* 2 vols., London, 1933.

.... — *India as Described in Early Texts of Buddhism and Jainism.* London, 1941.

Macdonell, A. A., and Keith, A. B., — *Vedic Index of Names and Subjects,* 2 vols., London, 1912.

Maine, H. S., — *Village Communities in East and West,* London, 1890.

Maity, S. K.. — *Economic Life of Northern India in the Gupta Period.* Calcutta, 1957.

Majumdar, R. C., — *Corporate Life in Ancient India,* Second Edition, Calcutta, 1922.

......& Altekar, A. S., — *The Vakāṭaka-Gupta Age,* Benares, 1954.

Mehta, R. N., — *Pre-Buddhist India,* Bombay, 1939.

Mookherji, R. K., *A History of Indian Shipping and Maritime Activity*, London, 1912.

.... *Local Government in Ancient India*, Oxford, 1919.

.... *The Gupta Empire*, Bombay, 1948.

Motichandra *Sārthavāha* (in Hindi) Patna, 1953.

Musgrave, *The Theory of Public Finance*, McGraw-Hill Press, 1961.

Nath, Pran, *A Study of the Economic Condition of Ancient India*, London, 1929.

Niyogi, Puspa, *Contribution to the Economic History of Northern India* (from 10 to 12 Centuries) Calcutta, 1962.

Olmstead, A. T., *History of Assyria*, London, 1923.

Paul, P. L., *The Early History of Bengal*, 2 vols., Calcutta, 1939.

Pires, E., *The Maukharis*, Madras, 1934.

Prasad, B., *Theory of Government in Ancient India*, Allahabad, 1927.

.... *The State in Ancient India*, Allahabad, 1928.

Puri, B. N., *India in the Time of Patañjali*, Bombay, 1957.

Rapson, E. J., *The Cambridge History of India*, *I*, Cambridge, 1922.

Rawlinson, H. G., *Intercourse Between India and the Western World*, Cambridge 1926.

Raychaudhuri, H. C., *Political History of Ancient India*, Sixth Edition, Calcutta, 1953.

Rhys David, T. W., *Buddhist India*, London, 1905.

Rostovtzeoff, M., *The Social and Economic History of the Hellenistic World*, 3 vols., Oxford, 1941.

Saletore, R. N., *Life in the Gupta Age*, Bombay, 1943.

Sammadar, J. N., *Economic Condition of Ancient India*, Calcutta, 1922.

Sankalia, H. D., *The Archaeology of Gujarat,* Bombay, 1941.

.... *Studies in the Historical and Cultural Geography and Ethnography of Gujarat,* Poona, 1949.

Sarkar, B. K., *Political Institutions and Theories of the Hindus,* Calcutta, 1939.

Sarkar, U. C., *Epochs in Hindu Legal History,* Hoshiarpur, 1958.

Sen, B. C., *Some Historical Aspects of the Inscriptions of Bengal,* Calcutta, 1942.

Sharma, R. S., *Some Economic Aspects of the Caste System in Ancient India,* Patna, 1952.

.... *Śūdras in Ancient India,* Delhi, 1958.

.... *Aspects of Political Ideas and Institutions in Ancient India.* Delhi, 1959.

.... *Indian Feudalism* : *c.* 300-1200, Calcutta, 1965.

.... *Light on Early Indian Society and Economy,* Bombay, 1966.

Sircar, D. C., *The Successors of the Sātavāhanas in the Lower Deccan,* Calcutta, 1939.

Smith, Adam, *The Wealth of Nations,* Ed. E. Cannan, New York, 1904.

Smith, V. A., *Early History of India,* Fourth Edn., Oxford, 1924.

Subha Rao, N. S., *Economic and Political Condition in Ancient India,* Mysore, 1911.

Subramanya Aiyer, K. V., *Historical Sketches of Dekhan,* Madras, 1917.

Thapar, R., *Aśoka And the Deline of the Mauryas,* Oxford University Press, 1961.

.... *History of India,* vol., Palican, 1966.

Upadhyaya, B. S., *India in Kālidāsa.* Allahabad, 1947.

Van Lohuizen de Leeuw, J. E., *The "Scythian" Period,* London, 1949.

Vinogradoff, P., *Outlines of Historical Jurisprudence.* 2 Vols. *Oxford,* 1920.

Virji, K. G., *Ancient History of Saurāṣṭra,* Bombay, 1955.

Vogel, J. Ph., *Antiquities of Chamba State,* Calcutta, 1911.

Warmington, E. H., *The Commerce Between the Roman Empire and India,* Cambridge, 1928.

Wilson, H. H., *Glosary of Indian Terms.*

Winternitz, M., *History of Indian Literature* (Eng. Trans. by Mrs. S. Ketkar), Vols., I and II, Calcutta, 1927-33.

Yazdani, G., (Ed.), *The Early History of Decan,* 2 vols., Oxford, 1960.

(C) JOURNALS, COMMEMORATIVE VOLUMES AND PROCEEDINGS

Annual Reports of the Archaeological Survey of India.

Archaeological Survey of Western India, Annual Reports.

Archiv Orientalni, Prague.

Ashutosh Mookerjee Silver Jubilee Volumes, 3 volumes in 4 parts, Calcutta, 1922-28.

B. C. Law Volume, 2 Parts, Calcutta, 1945-46.

Bulletin of the School of Oriental and African Studies, London.

Chinese Literature, Peking.

D. R. Bhandarkar Volume, Calcutta, 1940.

Enquiry, Delhi.

Indian Antiquary, Bombay.

Indian Culture, Calcutta.

Indian Historical Quarterly, Calcutta.

J. N. Bannerjea Volume, Calcutta, 1960.

Journal of the American Oriental Society, Baltimore, Maryland (U.S.A..

Journale Asiatique, Paris.

Journal of the Asiatic Society Bengal, Calcutta.

Journal of the Bombay Branch of the Royal Asiatic Society, Bombay.

Journal of Bihar and Orissa Research Society, Patna.

Journal of Bihar Research Society, Patna.

Journal of the Economic and Social History of the Orient, Leiden.

Journal of the Numismatic Society of India, Banaras.

Journal of Oriental Research, Madras.

Journal of Pali Text Society, London.

Journal of the Royal Asiatic Society of Great Britain and Ireland, London.

Journal of the University of Bombay, Bombay.

K. V. Rangaswamy Aiyangar Commemoration Volume, Madras, 1940.

Proceedings of the Indian History Congress.

Proceedings of the All-India Oriental Conference.

S. K. Aiyangar Commemoration Volume, Madras, 1936.

Sukthankar Memorial Edition, 2 vols., Bombay, 1945.

Zeitschrift der Deutschen Morgenlandischen Gesellschaft,

(D) DICTIONARIES

Dharmakośa, I (in three parts), Laxmanshastri Joshi, Wai, District Satara, 1937-41.

Kannaḍa English Dictionary, by Kittel, Mangalore, 1894.

Pāli-English Dictionary, by Rhys Davids, T. W. and Stede, W., PTS. London, 1921.

Śabdakalpadruma, by Radhakanta Deva, Saka Era, 1743.

Sanskrit-Wörterbuch, 7 volumes, Bothlingk, O., and Roth, R., St Petersburg, 1855-75.

Vācaspatyam, by Taranath Tarkavacaspati, Calcutta, 1873.

INDEX

A

O

P

R

T

AFTERWORD: THE *ARTHAŚĀSTRA* SCHOLARSHIP – PAST AND PRESENT

The reprinting of the *Revenue System* is to be welcomed not merely for its substantive value that was discussed in the Foreword. It may equally be celebrated for its symbolism, as one good example (among a number of not-so-good as well as outstanding ones, e.g. the works of Kosambi, our author's all-time ideal) of the need to keep going back to older productions, as a regular part of research strategy. The Afterword is being presented as an essay in this celebration.

We have increasingly paid less attention to the semantic issues in our sources. For the good part, it would appear to be a case, not so much of opting out, as of shying away from it. In the prevalent disposition of self-satisfaction among practising historians of India, it may perhaps be salutary to visit some sobering reflections (we can seek defence behind the exaggerations in the quotes that follow, but only to our own peril). In 1980, the prevailing trend in the field seemed to D.C. Sircar to be one of rapidly deteriorating competence. A 'dearth of people capable of reading and interpreting not only a lengthy Kāvya-type inscription in Sanskrit and Prakrit', he lamented in his General President's Address to the Indian History Congress, 'but even a small epigraph in the early script has now become shocking'.[1]

No signs of recovery are yet to be reported; little notice indeed seems to have been taken of Sircar's pervasive sense of crisis in

1. Sircar 1980: 8-9. A somewhat misplaced use of 'efficiency' in the address takes nothing away from the truth of his observations. Professor Sircar's reputation for plain speaking was legendary; it would never fail to bring a smile to Sharmaji's face. A good sample is available in print in Sircar's no-nonsense, non-nostalgic reminiscences about his teachers (Sircar 1969: 363-9).

his discipline. Instead, some three decades later the situation had become alarming, or so was thought by Sheldon Pollock:

> At the time of independence in 1947, India was home to scholars whose historical and philological expertise made them the peer of any in the world. They were the heirs of the longest continuous multicultural literary tradition in the world, and produced editions and literary and historical studies of texts in Apabhramsha, Assamese, Bangla, Brajbhasha, Gujarati, Kannada, Malayalam, Marathi, Oriya, Persian, Prakrit, Sanskrit, Tamil, Telugu, Urdu—the list could go on because the list of Indian languages goes on—that are still used today. Two generations later their works have not been replaced not because they are irreplaceable—*it is in the nature of scholarship that later knowledge should supersede earlier*—but because there is no one capable of replacing them. And this is a sign of what people should be worrying about: if Indian education and scholarship continue along their current trajectory, the number of citizens capable of reading and understanding the texts and documents of the classical era—or precolonial or premodern or pre-1800 era … —will very soon approach a statistical zero. India is about to become the only major world culture whose literary patrimony, and indeed history, are in the custodianship of scholars outside the country: in Berkeley, Chicago; and New York; Oxford, Paris, and Vienna. This would not be healthy either for India or for the rest of the world that cares about India.[2] (Emphasis added)

It shall be our argument here that supersession, even when it is real and not simply a matter of posterior publication, is not the same thing as wholesale discarding, so that superseded works may yet remain irreplaceable in more than one way for a fresh round of evaluation. After all, we cannot be sure that we have (a) learned, or (b) learned correctly, all that needed to be carried forward from the authoritative works of the past generations, and; (c) that we have not made any mistakes of our own with regard to our opinions of their views, that we are necessarily correct in offering our own alternatives to theirs. We need to bring these considerations to bear on our practice, if only for the reason that our own work gets its due when the turn is ours: one good turn, we may then hope, will deserve another!

About the promise of terminological studies – that it is possible,

2. Pollock 2011: 21-2.

required, and rewarding to return to much-used translated sources for an alteration, a refinement at least, of the current picture – we can take heart from a series of recent re-translations of ancient texts, including of the works we thought we did not need to worry about, above all by the redoubtable Patrick Olivelle. He has put us all under debt once again by rethinking the *Arthaśāstra* (*AŚ*) through translation over a period of five years – admittedly the 'most difficult translation project … [he has] ever undertaken.'[3] I seek to pay mine by exploring the new vistas of terminological research that his enterprise provokes forth, discovering in the process that the new vistas are much illumined by the beacons of pre-Olivelle scholarship, including even those harnessed by him.

The *AŚ* is a key text used in D.N. Jha's *Revenue System*, which however relied on R. Shamasastry's edition and translation without being able to use R.P. Kangle, whose landmark three-part work has since been the indispensable reference. Among other things, his numbering of the passages made it supremely convenient to refer to the freshly-edited text based on the larger numbers of manuscripts and commentaries available at his time,[4] but his supreme achievement

3. Olivelle 2013: xiii. Apparently that has remained so till date, through his subsequent translation projects.
4. Precision of reference used to be a big problem, especially for the larger chapters, in the earlier dual book-chapter referencing system followed by Shamasastry and T. Ganapati Sastri. The unease about this inability to refer exactly to the passage under discussion was felt by everyone, and is seen on the occasions when persons like Kosambi would try to help the readers, as in the following: '*Arth[aśāstra*]. 2.24 *(just after the reference to ardhasītikas*)' (Kosambi 1956: 215, emphasis added); 'preservation of the *janapada* unit would enable local custom to be allowed for, as in A[rthaśāstra] 3.7, *end*' (Kosambi 1952: 205, emphasis added).

   The numbering of passages was done earlier by Udayaveer Shastri for his Hindi translation of the text (Shastri 1925).

   It is unfortunate that Kosambi should have been so uncharitably hostile, to his own loss no doubt, to Kangle's work, just because Kangle preferred (mistakenly, as many others like T. Burrow (1968: 24-6) also thought and as I do; cf. Olivelle 2019: 31-6) Kauṭilya to Kauṭalya (Kosambi 1978-9: 277-8 n2). I await the building up of some kind of consensus – it can be a small part of the agenda of any one of the international gatherings of

lay in the extremely rich, learned and illuminating footnotes to the English translation in Part II. This Part has been taken over since 2013 by the lavishly-annotated translation of Olivelle, who however continues to base himself on Kangle's edition of the text (with the exception of some eighty passages, where Olivelle has preferred alternative readings[5]).

Apart from the main reason of it being an excellent locus of discussion for the issues at hand, there is another one for the choice of the *Arthaśāstra* of Kauṭilya (without prejudice to Kauṭalya) as an appendage to a work on post-Mauryan and Gupta periods that treats it as a Mauryan source (by and large correctly in my view). This is the great promise of a flexible synchronic approach to the sources. Several considerations suggest this. Not only were the sources composed over long periods and could contain substantial carry-overs from the past and interpolations by posterity, they could represent significant continuity as much as significant change. One does not have to be a votary of *l'histoire immobile* to appreciate this. Especially important are the hazards of arguing for change on negative evidence from the fragments of information in the ancient sources. Unless it be a case of head-on contradiction, a fragment from a predominantly Mauryan source may profitably be used to fill the missing part of a picture from, say, a Gupta source, and vice versa. The principles of extrapolation ought surely to be applicable even more to the data nearer in time/space than they are with respect to anthropology/comparative history.

At all events, Kauṭilya's is a text to which all ancient Indianists (not least Jha in the *Revenue System*) keep returning almost as a force of habit, no less for the fun of (even undergraduate) teaching than for the ardours of advanced research. In so doing, the teacher/researcher has often run into certain issues both of the text and the translation in Kangle's work. It was often impossible to read the splendidly edited text and translation by Kangle without doing some research of one's own, demanded inter alia by inconsistency of

experts – before switching over to Kauṭalya from the currently predominant Kauṭilya.

5. Olivelle 2013: xvii, Table 0.6.

translation as well as the greater historical sense of what occur as mere variants in the footnotes of the main textual body. It is thus seen that a crucial term with a fixed technical sense in Kauṭilya has been translated in more than one way, apparently for the sake of English idiom. Thus the term *adhyaksha*, after which one whole book is named, is translated in a majority of cases as 'Superintendent' but quite often by other words. Thus *lavaṇ-ādhyaksha* (2.12.28) is rendered as 'Salt Commissioner'; *lakshaṇ-ādhyaksha* (2.6.2, 2.12.24) as 'Mint Master'; *sīt-ādhyaksha* (2.15.2, 2.24) as 'Director of Agriculture'; *nāvadhyaksha* (2.28) as 'Controller of Shipping'; *paṇy-ādhyaksha* (2.16) as 'Director of Trade'; *kupy-ādhyaksha* (2.17) as 'Director of Forests; *sur-ādhyaksha* (2.25) as 'Controller of Spirituous Liquors, and; *śulkādhyaksha* (2.21-22) as 'Collector of Customs'/'Collector of Customs and Tolls'. They all, including the Superintendents, are alternately 'Heads of Departments', which is how *adhyaksha* in the heading of Book II ('*Adhyaksha-Prachāra*) is rendered.

Also, as one followed a lead to the text, one found the reading not in the main body of Kangle's edition, but in the footnote as a variant reading, and then saw that historically it was the variant that made better sense. Thus, after a prolonged use for lecture-notes of Kosambi's reference to the *AŚ* provision of the state seizing the property of goldsmiths in financial emergencies,[6] one fine morning the curious teacher looks up the text (5.2.24-25) to find something very different: 'They shall recover a tax in cash from those skilled in work, and shall not overlook any offence of theirs. For, these might sell (something) by representing it as not belonging to them' (Kangle (K.).) 'Goldsmith' is here 'tax in cash' (*hiraṇya-kara*), the reference to claiming to sell 'something not belonging to them' is still more perplexing, and the explanations given by Kangle in the footnote seem convoluted and do not help. But in the place of *aparigṛihīta*, 'something not belonging to them' in the main body of the text, the reading in a manuscript, given as variant, is *a-para-gṛihīta*, 'not taken from others'. This makes much better sense as an obvious reference to the open secret about the recirculation of

6. E.g. Kosambi 1956: 211.

stolen or robbed precious goods, especially jewellery, in the market through unscrupulous goldsmiths. The editor, the humble outsider feels, might have treated the whole thing as one more of the numerous cases of text-corruption, and attempted a restoration that could vindicate Kosambi's understanding.

The publication of Olivelle's work has thus come as a tremendous fulfilment of a much-felt need. My appreciation must begin with *pāshaṇḍa*, which had so far been taken to mean a non-Brahmanical heretical sect in the *AŚ*, whereas its Prakrit form in Aśoka's inscriptions (*pāsaṃḍa/prashaṃḍa*) had the clear sense of a religious sect.[7] The incongruity between the two sources in this respect is now gone, as the term in the *AŚ* is rendered, quite rightly, as a 'religious order', to which much solid support has come from the evidence marshalled by Joel Brereton.[8] Equally welcome is the correction at several places of the earlier work's literalism. The *mātṛikā* of a courtesan establishment (2.27.5, 17) is now more properly 'madam' rather than 'mother' (as in Kangle's translation). Likewise, *uchchhid* means 'to exterminate', and is to be taken precisely in that sense at several places, as when issuing a warning about the extermination of people if there is a transgression (or mixture) of castes (1.3.15) or when one divulging secret counsel is to be exterminated (1.15.6). However, it is surely odd to read about a king that, after he has been 'exterminated by both' (K.) (*dvābhyām=uchchhinno*), 'he should find shelter with' some other kings or kings (7.2.23), having given up the ghost! The appropriate word in English here is of course 'vanquished', supplied by Olivelle (O.). But I should like to venture further and suggest that the fuller sense, as demanded by the context, is not just of vanquishing but of annexation after defeat (hence 'extermination').

Unlike K., Olivelle decided to dispense with the use of

7. Such was the contradiction that in providing the Sanskritized version of the Aśokan inscriptions, Sircar would not dare to Sanskritize it as *pāshaṇḍa*, and thought that in Sanskrit it was *pārshada*, generally meaning 'a member of a society or assembly' (*parishad*) but here 'people following particular doctrines' or 'different religious sects'(Sircar 1965: 32 fn2 and 33-4).
8. Brereton 2019.

parentheses, 'except in the rarest of cases' and provide translations for the numerous varieties of flora and fauna that K. had left untranslated.[9] However, his most important task, O. explains in the Note to the Translation, is removal of K.'s inconsistencies of translation: 'One problem with Kangle's translation is the inconsistency in rendering technical terms into English. As much as possible, *I have tried to use a single English term for each technical term of the AŚ.*'[10]

Thus *adhyaksha* is to be translated *only* as a 'superintendent'. This was quite a heartening relief from the problems one had been noting all these years. But then one paused at *kara* (Table 0.5), to wonder, in disbelief, whether it was to be rendered only as 'tax' and as nothing else. One had known this revenue termall these years to have had quite distinct meanings in different contexts. In the context of our Foreword, it is the first major issue on which one has to disagree with O. The meaning of *kara* as tax in general is unexceptionable when the term occurs singly to represent all kinds of payments to the state (2.4.32); likewise, when there are only two words, one *daṇḍa* and the other *kara*, it is of course 'fines and taxes' (e.g. 1.13.3, 8, 19; 2.1.7), as also when *kara* occurs (2.1.37) with *daṇḍa* (fines) and *vishṭi* (forced labour); the same meaning of tax in general is there in *kara-da* (2.1.8), 'the giver of taxes' or taxpayer. But it has to be a more specific source of state income when *kara* is clubbed with other such specific items. It makes no sense to translate *sītā* (income from state agriculture farms), *bhāga*, *bali*, and *kara* in 2.6.3 as 'agriculture, share, tribute, tax', as is done by O.; apart from the inaccurate rendering of *sītā* (along with allied others, to be discussed later), the remaining three are three types of the *kara* of the previous references. The same for 2.15.3 where *kara* is one of the different types of *kara*.

I should like to present it as the price that Olivelle has paid for neglecting to consult works like those by U.N. Ghoshal or D.N. Jha. The latter does not make the grade for a place in his bibliography as the *Contributions* does, which however does not

9. Olivelle 2013: xiii.
10. Ibid.: xiv. Emphasis added.

seem to have been actually consulted, for it is cited only once at second hand, from the work of H. Scharfe.[11] One of his major findings, as Ghoshal puts it in the Preface, was how 'terms, such as *bhāga*, *bali* and *kara*, have been shown to have borne a multiplicity of meanings, the connotation varying according to different authorities or *even within the range of the same authorities*'.[12] Jha provides an elaborate confirmation of this dictum, with his own inputs of course, including qualifications of Ghoshal's specific interpretations of evidence.

This, or anything else that will presently be said in this connection, must not be allowed to obscure the fact that Professor Olivelle has made a most sincere attempt to dig as far back as he could, and recognize any and all kinds of contributions that other works have made to his own. He takes legitimate pride, for instance, in restoring Harihara Sastri his rightful place in the *AŚ* studies: 'Harihara Sastri is an unsung hero in Arthaśāstric scholarship; his edition of the most significant commentary and insightful introductions were of enormous help'.[13] What this discovery has meant for the excellence of his book may be seen in the numerous acknowledgments of Sastri's work, alike for translation, interpretation, and text-criticism leading to emendation.[14]

---

11. Olivelle 2013: 481.
12. Ghoshal 1929: x (emphasis added).
13. Olivelle 2013: ix.
14. However, it is difficult to agree with an emendation suggested by Harihara Sastri that has been accepted by O., that it should be *kāntāra-param* ('someone who haunts wild tracts') in place of *kāntā-param* (4.6.2), which is found in all manuscripts and editions, and was translated by K. as 'one devoted to a beloved' (Olivelle 2013: 634). *Kāntāra* has been preferred to *kāntā* on the following grounds: a. The passage is about all kinds of people 'doing odd things', and it is difficult to see how one 'being devoted to a beloved' can be an odd thing; and b. (In contrast to *kāntāra*, a term of frequent occurrence) '*kāntā* as woman is found nowhere else in the *AŚ*' (ibid.) The second objection is easily dismissed, for, as the three-volume *Index Verborum* of the text shows (Shamasastry 1924-5), the *AŚ* has no dearth of words that occur only once, and single reference can hardly be an objection to so familiar a Sanskrit word on which moreover all the manuscripts agree; for good measure, O. himself refers to several such hapaxes in the text (Olivelle 2013: 500, 503, 539, 540, etc.). As to

Again, far from making Kangle's (1963) the starting point for his own translation, O. has regularly consulted the much earlier German translation by J.J. Meyer (1926), treating it at par, and, on a point of dispute, giving his own alternative only when he cannot choose one out of the given two. Thus when *gaṇikā-dāsī* in 2.27.8 is taken to mean 'a female slave of a courtesan' by K., but had been interpreted as 'a courtesan who is a female slave' by Meyer, O. decides to side with the latter on the following ground: 'This [view of K.] seems unlikely, *as this chapter [2.27] does not deal with such a slave anywhere else*, and it seems odd that that topic is introduced here'[15] (emphasis added). This is patently too hasty: the chapter does mention the female slave, more than once and as distinct from the courtesan (2.27.17, 18); together with the reference to the courtesan's daughter (to which K. had drawn attention in favour of his interpretation[16] but is ignored by O.), this simply rules out Meyer's and O.'s view. A vital principle is established by O. nonetheless: the superseded is not to be left out of consideration in any fresh application of mind.

It must also redound to the credit of O., although he does not see it this way, to have justly elevated Ganapati Sastri to a higher prominence than he has had so far. Ganapati Sastri's Sanskrit Commentary, named *Śrīmūla*, represents a modern scholar's understanding of the *AŚ*. His work, however, is bracketed with the traditional commentaries, abbreviated Cs (i.e. the Commentary *Śrīmūla*), by K., who refers to his *work in this short form* throughout in the notes to his translation, generally only to criticize *its* views

---

the first objection, it is true that *kāntā-param* occurs as an item in a long list of various types of people who were naturally suspect in the eyes of the Arthaśāstra state, but its other items too may amaze *us* equally, e.g. 'someone with a low occupation or caste'. And the reference is probably not simply to any beloved but to a mistress, a standard meaning of *kāntā*. Combined with the other standard meaning of the frequently-used *para* as 'given up to (i.e. yielding oneself to a particular feeling or influence)', a person given up to his mistress would fit the bill nicely.

Except for this and one more passage (2.4.21), we have not gone in this essay into the emendations that O. has made to K.'s text.

15. Ibid.: 568 (emphasis added).
16. Kangle 1963: 183n8.

(e.g. notes to 1.1.19, 1.12.4, 6, 25; 1.13.8; 1.16.8; 1.17.12), though every so often also in acknowledgement (e.g. notes to 1.14.3; 2.7.36; 2.10.43). While other authorities are mentioned by name (e.g. Kane, Ghoshal, Meyer), the name of the Sastri is shrouded by Cs. Thus as against Meyer, whose name appears scores of times, that of Ganapati Sastri perhaps not even once in these notes. As a result, his contributions have tended to be undervalued by all except those with the keenest eye for detail.

O.'s work has rescued Ganapati Sastri from a near-anonymous commentator of Cs to a leading modern interpreter of the *AŚ*, on a par with Shamasastry, Meyer and Kangle. In fact, the contribution of Ganapati Sastri would seem to run much deeper than seen in the explicit references to his work, whether by name or by the abbreviation. I have not been able to do a full-scale check, but it appears that a good deal of the non-discussed differences between Kangle and Olivelle on one hand and Shamasastry on the other may originate in the word commentary of Ganapati Sastri.[17] I noticed it first in the important case of *udara-dāsa* (3.13.1). Shamasastry thought it meant 'born slave' (from the meaning of *udara* as 'womb'). K. takes it to mean 'slave for livelihood' (from the 'stomach' meaning of *udara*): 'he is one who, in distress, lives with another person in better circumstances and works as a slave in return for food. A minor may be so handed over for his maintenance. There is no actual sale in this case, only stay for the time being.' O. goes along with this meaning, but rephrases it as 'subsistence slave': 'This is an individual who becomes a slave in order to obtain maintenance. Thus, no sale takes place.' We note here, for a fuller discussion later, O. repeating K.'s views with a bit of rephrasing. But was it K. who first gave this alternative

17. It must be considered unfortunate that, in the revised edition of his translation, Shamasastry was not able to take into account the alternatives offered by Ganapati Sastri, as he did, however imperfectly, the work of Meyer. In the first revision (1923) he regretted that the 'long-advertised' work being done by Ganapati Sastri was not yet available (Shamasastry 1956: xxiii). In the second revision (1929), however, he is altogether silent on the matter.

interpretation of *udara-dāsa*? Not quite, for one finds Dev Raj Chanana (alias Devaraj) too having the same opinion in 1957.[18] In fact, both K. and Chanana evidently took this from the same source, i.e. the Sanskrit commentary of Ganapati Sastri, and both missed to acknowledge their source, inadvertently of course.

DĀSA, *UDARA-DĀSA*, AND *ĀRYA*

We would like to go along with Shamasastry (and Kane[19]) rather than with the others in seeing *udara-dāsa* as a 'born slave'. Our argument however is predicated upon, and must therefore tail the elaboration of, a meaning of *ārya* in the relevant portions that was pointed out severally by Kosambi and V.S. Agrawala, but has unfortunately not been noticed by the translators as well as the general run of the historians of early India. As they pointed out, *ārya* is best translated at a number of places as 'free', as against the servile categories of *dāsa* and *āhitaka*. Kosambi pointed out that at an early date the term *ārya* came also to mean 'a free individual', including in the *AŚ*, and criticized Meyer for his inability to see that *ārya-prāṇa* (3.13.1, 19) must mean 'living as a free individual'.[20] A few years later, in his classic *India as Known to Pāṇini* Agrawala pointedly brought out the meaning in Pāṇini as well as Kauṭilya of *ārya* as a free person, with such clear-cut statements as the following: 'Kauṭilya takes *Ārya* to mean a free man as opposed to *Dāsa* who had lost his freedom, e.g. "The offspring of a man who has sold himself off as a slave shall be an Ārya ...".'[21] Although he closely followed Kosambi's works, Chanana missed this, and he did not notice it in Agrawala either, although he cited from the same page of his work where this

18. Devaraj Chanana, *L'esclavage dans L'Inde Ancienne* (Institut Francais d' Indologie, Pondicherry, 1957), p. 72, cited in Chakravarti 1971: 126 and fn26. In the English translation (Chanana 1960), it occurs on p. 87 fnb.
19. Kane 1941: 183.
20. Kosambi 1952: 181 fn2.
21. Agrawala 1953: 79.

meaning is elucidated.[22] O. too, like K., remains unaware of this suggestion of Kosambi (who never tired of pointing it out, including in his *Culture and Civilisation in Ancient India in Historical Outline*, listed – just listed – in O.'s bibliography) at the same time as he, like K. again, refers to Agrawala for other things, not this one. Ironically, Chanana came upon this meaning of *ārya* on his own in other contexts, when he interpreted *ārya-bhāva* in the *AŚ* as 'state of freedom' or just 'freedom'.[23] For his part, O. too almost gets there in 3.13.15, where he thinks that the term *āryatva* 'probably means freedom from slavery, rather than the condition of being an Ārya'[24]; he still does not see that '*ārya*' itself can means a free person, so that, despite this doubt, he, like all previous translators, stays with the rendering 'Ārya status' for it[25], not only here but also in 3.13.21 – 'anyone who does not make a slave an Ārya' (*dāsam ... āryam-akurvato*) – where *ārya cannot possibly* mean anything else than a free person.[26]

In other contexts we do come across the other meaning of the term. The Ārya-Śūdra distinction may be seen in the opposition of Āryas to 'low' (*nīcha*) persons/Chaṇḍālas/Śvapākas (1.14.10; 3.20.16; 4.13.35), as well as in a revealing four-tier hierarchy of

---

22. Chanana 1960: 91 fns n and o.
23. Chanana 1960: 80, 99.
24. Olivelle 2013: 614.
25. In the following somewhat longwinded translation of *mūlyena ch=āryatvaṃ gachchhet*: 'He can get back his Ārya status, moreover, by paying the original price.' Kangle I think brings it out better: 'And he shall become an Ārya by paying the price.'
26. In *A Dictionary of Law and Statecraft* Olivelle and his collaborators, David Brick and Mark McClish, finally settle on the meaning of Ārya as a free person in the *AŚ*: 'in the AŚ, however, *ārya* often refers to a free person as opposed to a slave' (Olivelle et al 2015: 86). In a reversal, however, in a most recent study McClish would not recognize this sense of the word at all, interpret the Ārya in the *AŚ* as 'a respectable person' (McClish 2019: 177) and remain perplexed about 'the well-known passage ascribing Ārya status to Śūdras, something that is anathema to all dharma texts' (ibid.: 204, also 177 fn6), unable not only to see that here it means a free person, but also to notice the passages in the *ĀŚ* that distinguish the Ārya from the Śūdra, as discussed by us above. The completeness of the reversal is confirmed in the entry 'Śūdra as *ārya* (respectable person)' in the Index (ibid.: 273).

quantity of meals, combining the social with the biological, with the largest quantity for Ārya males, followed by (males of) lower-class (*nīcha*), women, and children in that order (2.15.43-6). When there are references to the *mlechchhas* or the *aṭavīs* as the Other (e.g. 3.13.3; 9.2.18), the Ārya is of course a member of the caste-based society, including the Śūdra. Nobility of status is implicit in 1.17.35 in the distinction of Ārya women with the 'filthy' or 'impure' ones (*amedhyā*). But when an *ārya* woman is distinguished from a slave one (4.9.26), or an *ārya* female prisoner from one who is a slave or a pledge (4.9.24), it cannot but denote free status.

Coming back to the meaning of *udara-dāsa*, the purpose of the first five passages of Chapter 13 of Book Three where it occurs is legislation against abuse of minors. There one is prohibited, on pain of fines and/or punishment including execution (for the seller as well as the purchaser and the witnesses), from taking away (*nayataḥ*: this crucial word is omitted in all translations) a minor for sale or pledge. The only exception is the minor who is an *udara-dāsa* and who could be taken away for sale or pledge. That is to say, the law allowed one to sell/pledge a minor who was a 'born slave', but not other minors. The oft-quoted dictum from the text (3.13.4) – 'An Ārya, however, can never be reduced to slavery' – actually pertains to this context, as a clarification of the preceding passage that allows the mlechchhas to sell or pledge their offspring. If we remember the context and read the two passage together, we can scarcely doubt that the reference is to an Ārya offspring: 'It is not an offence for Mlechchhas to sell an offspring or keep it as a pledge. But there shall be no slavery for an Ārya (offspring) in any circumstances whatsoever.'

Here of course the distinction is between *ārya* and *mlechchha*. Everything is made crystal-clear, obviating further discussion, when the two meanings of *ārya* come together in 3.13.13: 'The progeny of one who sells himself shall be known as Ārya' (K.): It is an Ārya, i.e. a non-*mlechchha*, who is selling himself (and becoming a *dāsa* or unfree), but his offspring remain Āryas, i.e. free persons.

The construction of the statement in this passage ('the progeny of one selling himself') shows that this refers only to those born before the sale. Here we have a further clue to the meaning of *udara-dāsa*: he was the one who was born after the sale, of one who was already a *dāsa* or *dāsī*.[27] From 3.13.20, 23 and 3.20.17 we learn of female slaves conceiving and bearing children as well as that the child sired by the owner would not be a slave, implying that any child born of a *dāsī* and not fathered by the owner was to become the *dāsa* of the owner, i.e. the born slave or *udara-dāsa*. Further, as against the above-mentioned case of (male) minors (i.e. of those below 16 years as per the definitions in 3.3.1) who could not be taken away for sale or pledge with the sole exception of *udara-dāsas*, in 3.13.20 protection against doing 'lowly' (*nīcha*) work or being sent out to work in 'foreign' land (*videśa*) is extended to all four kinds of child *dāsas* below eight years of age, those who were without kin (*vibandhu*) and unwilling to do the work; no exception is allowed in case of these orphaned kinless kids, meaning that in such cases the *udara-dāsa* too had the protection. The four types are specified as slaves born in the house (*gṛihe-jāta*), followed by the inherited, gifted and purchased ones. Thus the *gṛihe-jāta* ('house-born') is seen to be the same as the *udara-dāsa*.[28]

We may pause here for the implications for our concerns of the discussion on the *udara-dāsa*. I have chosen Shamasastry's interpretation over Ganapati Sastri's in this case, but on a reasoning which is entirely mine; they gave none. It was by noticing the alternatives and thus a problem that I was led into the whole exercise. It is possible that I may have undertaken it all on my own, but then equally that I may well not have. The debt to the original stimulus, to how it got started and has moved thence, has

27. The statement (3.13.16) that 'by that are explained the *udara-dāsa* and the *āhitaka* (the pledged one)' is of little direct help for deducing the definition of either from the preceding passages of the chapter.

28. Contrary to what historians have tended to assume, the various categories of *dāsas* in the thirteenth chapter of Book Three of the *AŚ* come from no single, but rather more than one, scheme of classification, and so are often overlapping, to the point of being identical. Uma Chakravarti has listed nine categories as representing 'nine separate types of *dasas*' (Chakravarti 1985: 39), but the overlap/subsumption in many cases is pretty obvious. The ninth category of 'those who sold themselves as *dasas'*, for instance, is a subset of the fourth one of 'those who were purchased', and most of the other members of this category would equally belong to the first one of 'persons captured in battle'.

to be acknowledged in as many words. We will find it practised by all our ideals. My sources of inspiration have been A.A. Macdonell and A.B. Keith, Karl Marx, and Kauṭilya himself (the constraints of space do not allow elaboration, which would moreover have meant, quite justifiably, an unnecessary digression to many).

PRAKRAYA AND *AVAKRAYA*

It can of course hardly be the case that Ghoshal or Jha in their understanding of the *AŚ* do not stand corrected by the works of K. or O. For instance, they take *bhāga-bhoga* in 3.9.36 to be one word, meaning 'a specified share of the ... produce' and thus similar to *bhāga* that occurs elsewhere in the text as the king's claim to (normally) the sixth share of the produce.[29] It is a difficult passage, the basic sense of which could not be grasped by Shamasastry. But there was never any warrant for Ghoshal's clearly forced interpretation: the phrase refers to two of the several distinct conditions on any one of which water for irrigation is to be provided for use by others by privately-owned waterworks: for a share of the produce (*bhāga*); or for free, i.e. as *bhoga* (literally 'enjoyment', meaning 'authorization/permission for use'). The passage fixes the responsibility for the maintenance of the waterworks on the users, not the providers.

But there remains a need to go beyond the renderings provided by K. and O. The passage also refers to *prakraya*, a new word that has not been traced in any other text (not even in the lexicons), as one more condition on which the water may be provided. Its import is readily given away in the twelfth chapter of Book II, where it occurs twice, especially by the context in 2.12.22: 'He (i.e. the Superintendent of Mines) should give out on lease a mine demanding heavy expenses and labour (*vyaya-kriyā-bhārikam=ākaram*) either by share (*bhāga*) or by *prakraya*; one demanding light (expenses and labour) (*lāghavikam*), he should work himself.' Since the contrast is with working a mine oneself, the verb *dā* here should

29. Ghoshal 1929: 214; Jha 1967: 64. Ghoshal thinks it to be the same as the *bhāga-bhoga-kara* of inscriptions, with which Jha differs.

mean not just 'give', but 'give on lease'. If one form of rental was a 'share' of the produce, the other – *prakraya* – was most likely a 'money-rent'. Moreover, since this money-rent would be fixed on the basis of an estimated, not actual, volume or price of the actual produce, it would also be a 'fixed rent'. So Shamasastry was right in translating it alternately as 'fixed rent' once and 'money rent' next in that chapter. K. gives us exactly this reasoning about the meaning of *prakraya* in his note to 2.12.22, but has preferred to render it as 'lease' or 'lease-rent'. In his table as well as in the twelfth chapter, O. has 'fixed rent' for it.

However, the term had a more specific meaning than fixed rent or lease. This is seen in 3.9.36, where *avakraya* figures together with *bhāga*, *bhoga*, and *prakraya* (and some more terms) as a condition on which the water could be provided for use. *Avakraya* is an old word for rent that recurs several times in the *AŚ* so that when *prakraya* and *avakraya* occur together, they cannot have the same sense. By not coming to terms with it, our translators falter: 'at a stipulated price (*prakraya*), or for annual rent (*avakraya*)' (Shamasastry); 'on lease [*prakraya*], on hire [*avakraya*] (K.); 'on lease [*prakraya*], on fixed rent [*avakraya*]' (O.).

2.36.23 refers to the *avakrayin* or tenant and his house-owner (*gṛiha-svāmin*). In 3.8.24-25, we see again the tenant paying house-rent, and also learn that it was a yearly arrangement: if the *avakrayin* chose to leave midway, he was liable to pay the remainder of the yearly rental (*varsh-āvakraya-śeshaṃ*).[30] *Prakraya* was obviously coined by the *Arthaśāstra* authors to represent a more lasting arrangement, a long-term lease as distinct from the yearly renewal of *avakraya*: the state did not lease a mine to be worked for just one (or some more) year(s), but presumably would have made it a lasting arrangement under normal circumstances; and persons using water on rent for their fields, gardens, etc., had the option of entering into a long-term understanding on payment of *prakraya*, or on a yearly basis on *avakraya* payment.

30. The term was used figuratively too to describe a kind of treaty ('avakraya' treaty), in which the defeated kingdom was freed on condition of paying the produce of the land (as tribute) (7.3.34).

SAMĀJA AND *PRAHAVAṆA*

We now discuss two more terms – *samāja* and *janapada* – where the non-consultation of previous scholarship has affected O.'s work, not just in respect of the two but of other related terms as well.

The term *samāja* in Rock Edict I of Aśoka had bothered scholars for some time before the discovery of the *AŚ*. 'Even in the latest translations', G. Bühler wrote in 1883,'the prohibition on keeping *samājas* is, I think, misunderstood'. What exactly were the *samājas* that the king banned there *along with* sacrificial killing of animals, and what were those which he found good and encouraged? This is not the place to go into the detail. In sum, Bühler ranged wide, drawing upon early Indian literature, a Nasik inscription of Gautamīputra Śātakarṇi, comparative history, and his own knowledge of traditional India, to see them as gatherings in various religious contexts, whether connected with 'high feasts of the gods' or 'what is now called in the vernacular *melā* or *melāo* (in poor Sanskrit *melāpāka*) and what the Anglo-Indian calls "fairs" denotes': 'These *melās* or fairs are solemn assemblies associated with markets, displays, and other folk entertainments, and are held in honour of the various gods on the great holidays.'[31] Some of these *samājas* are seen to be objectionable, apparently on moral grounds, even in the *Dharmasūtras*. It was thus natural, Bühler concluded, that the great moralist Aśoka should have disapproved of them, but also that the great Buddhist king should have targeted only the Brahmanical *samājas* but looked favourably upon and encouraged Buddhist, Jaina, and other non-Brahmanical ones.[32] D.R. Bhandarkar saw the prohibited ones as those where meat was freely consumed, and the others as those where it was not;[33] Sircar found support in some literary evidence that the latter kind of *samāja* was a synod for religious discourses.[34] F.W. Thomas invoked evidence suggesting that the bad ones were the spectacles involving bloody animal fights

31. Bühler 1883: 93.
32. Ibid.: 93-4.
33. Bhandarkar 1904: 395-6; idem 1913: 255-7; idem 1932: 20-1, 142, 144, 157-8.
34. Sircar 1965: 16 fn3; idem 1967: 23.

while the good ones were like those which Asoka refers to in Rock Edict IV.[35] At times a new suggestion could be made that was based on a rather improbable reading of the relevant part of the edict, did not seek any support in the literary sources, and, most fatally, conflated the *samāja* with the *maṅgala* (ceremony) of Aśoka's edicts.[36] All these authorities were not always properly attentive to, or even aware of, one another's views;[37] particularly unfortunate was Bühler's flat rendering 'festive gathering' in *Epigraphia Indica*, which came to be widely adopted, as it concealed the just-discussed nuances and insights of the 1883 annotation in German.[38] At all events, one was free to form one's own opinion – or to stay confused, for that matter – about the issue, but could scarcely fail to recognize the special technical sense of the term.

Kosambi brought the *AŚ* to the centre-stage in its interpretation, and argued that it was the *AŚ* kind of *samāja* – 'some sort of saturnalia' with 'freedom to drink for three [sic!] days', which was 'forbidden altogether in the army' – that was banned by the Mauryan.[39] Given the privileged status of King Aśoka in early Indian and of Kosambi in the *AŚ* studies, it is surprising as well as distressing to find the translators so carefree with the term, to significant additional costs.

A consideration of these writings would likely have provided a deeper, at least a less imprecise, understanding also of a few more allied terms, especially *prahavaṇa*, which is one of the most

35. Thomas 1914: 392-4.
36. Bose 1928: 111-13, 117-22.
37. Thus Bhandarkar would maintain till the end that 'the real sense of *samāja* was unknown to scholars till it was first pointed out by me in 1902 in *JBBRAS*' (Bhandarkar 1932: 298 n5).
38. While editing, translating and annotating the inscriptions of Aśoka in the second volume of the *Epigraphia Indica*, Bühler indicated that he had left out all the terms which he had already annotated in his earlier articles (Bühler 1894: 466 fn1).
39. Kosambi 1952: 211 fn21. This was regularly noted by him in his later writings right up to the *Culture* (Kosambi 1956: 189; idem 1965: 162). It is clear that Kosambi was unaware of the previous discussions, which in fact anticipate and offer much support to his basically correct, if somewhat excessive and not-always-accurate, reading of the *AŚ* evidence.

significant terms in the text but has somehow been almost completely neglected (as far as I can tell). As it happens, an inattention to these studies *and* the textual contexts on this count has resulted in a near-wanton rendering of these and allied terms by our translators. I begin with 2.25.35-7 as translated by Kangle and Olivelle respectively, inserting the terms in square brackets and highlighting them and the translations:

Householders should be free to manufacture white liquor on festive occasions [*kṛityeshu*] or an *arishṭa* for medicinal use, or other (spirituous preparations). On the occasions of festivals [*utsava*], gatherings [*samāja*] and fairs [*yātrā*], permission to manufacture and sell liquor should be granted for four days. On those days, he should charge a penalty per day from those not permitted, till the end of the festivity [*prahavaṇa*]. [K.]

Householders should be permitted to produce white Surā-liquor during festive occasions [*kṛityeshu*], and for medicinal purposes Arishṭa or other kinds. During festivals [*utsava*], fairs [*samāja*], and excursions [*yātrā*], he should grant a Surā-liquor license for four days. During those days, he should collect a daily penalty from those who are unauthorized until the end of the festivities [*prahavaṇa*]. (O.)

Thus *kṛitya*, *utsava*, and *prahavaṇa* are equally festivals or festivities for both, while *samāja* is 'gathering' for Kangle but 'fair' for Olivelle and *yātrā* is 'fair' for one but 'excursion' for the other. Moreover, they do not wonder, though the reader might, that, for the *kṛitya* 'festivity' and for medicinal purposes, it is permissible to manufacture liquor freely, but for the other two 'festivities', 'gathering'/'fair', as well as 'fair'/'excursion' only on a license, only for four days, on pain of penalty. If the householders were allowed to make one kind of beverage for medicinal use and to make another kind for *kṛityas*, the *kṛitya* here most likely stood for the magic rituals, comprising spells and incantations, which were as regularly used for treating patients as were medicines. And once we begin to worry about their precise imports, we will detect at once a classificatory scheme of the terms in the combined testimony of the last two sentences, namely, that *prahavaṇa* was a general category to which *utsava, samāja*, and *yātrā* belonged. This in turn helps us to see that *yātrā-samāja-utsava-prahavaṇāni* in 1.21.28 refers to these three types of *prahavaṇa* rather than four things. Their close and regular association with communal religious practices is clear enough from the available literary evidence, e.g. the *yātrā* being a religious procession. We will attempt to demonstrate the same for *prahavaṇa*. Before that, we need to note, however briefly, the damage that the neglect has done to the current translations of the *Arthaśāstra*.

When *utsava* and *prahavaṇa* occur together (1.21.28), since *utsavas* are 'festivals', *prahavaṇas* become 'parties' for Kangle; having decided to retain the latter as 'festivity', Olivelle has now 'feast' for *utsava*. In 13.3.56 *utsava-samāja* are no longer two distinct things for Kangle, but together become 'festive gatherings'. When this is overturned as *utsava* comes after *samāja* in the phrase *deśa-daivata-samāja-utsava-vihāreshu* (13.5.8), the business becomes trickier. *Samāja* is no longer 'gathering' for Kangle and 'fair' for Olivelle, but 'festival' for both: *deśa-daivata-samāja* is 'festivals in honour of deities/gods of the country/region'! Here they also agree on *utsava* and *vihāra*: 'festive gatherings and sportive amusements'/'festivities and recreational activities'.

As to *prahavaṇa*, its congregational/communal religious character is clearly seen in more than one passage. In 7.17.44, it occurs as the third of the following threefold combination: on the occasion (*nimittam*) of (a) offerings to gods (*daivat-opahāra*), (b) worship of or offerings to manes (*śrāddha*), and *prahavaṇa*. All three are furthermore big occasions watched by teams of guards (*ārakshin*). Then we have 13.2.15, where a secret agent in the guise of a holy person (*siddha-vyañjano*), is advised first to find shelter in (the temple of) the region's god (*deśa-devatā*), and then to win over the leading subjects (*prakṛiti-mukhyān*) by means of *prahavaṇas* before outwitting/overreaching the kind himself. Again, *prahavaṇa-karman* can hardly refer to anything else than the rituals of *prahavaṇa* in 13.3.54, where an agent appearing as an ascetic with a shaven head (*muṇḍa*) or with matted locks (*jaṭila*) and posing as a devotee of god Saṅkarshaṇa, should overreach (the forest robbers) by using a stupefying liquid in the *prahavaṇa* ritual. In 3.10.36 *prahavaṇa* occurs as a generic name for all kinds of communal gatherings of the village in which each villager (family) had to contribute its share of food and drink. These, it is clear from the next passage, were distinguished from shows or spectacles (*prekshā*), towards which too contributions had to be given. On this basis, *prekshā* is to be distinguished from *prahavaṇa* in 13.2.04 (rather than being made a part of it, as is done by K. and O.). In 3.10.44 the privileges as well as the active participation of the brahmin are seen. In general, people contributing their share were also to receive theirs. The term is *aṃśa* for both (what you give and what you get). But nothing is said of their doing any work in these *prahavaṇa*. The brahmin, however, was expected to do work, for which he was to receive his share. Here it is specified that even if he was not willing to do any work, he was still to be given his share. In 13.4.26 it is also distinguished from drinking sessions, so that *madya-prahavaṇa* in 3.12.38 must have been something else than a routine 'drinking bout'/drinking party' as Olivelle and Kangle would have it. These considerations may then be applied to the several other passages where the meaning of the term is not clarified by the context.

JANAPADA

Kosambi was probably the first to argue with proper evidence that 'the Arthaśāstra State' (as he called it) was composed of several *janapadas*. 'The *janapada*, which most of us mistake for the whole country at a first reading of the Arthaśāstra, is really the natural unit of administration.'[40] Kangle however argued that there was no mistake here and that *janapada* meant the entirety of a very small state, where the king could look personally into the affairs of all his subjects; which had as the maximum no more than 800 villages; which was so small as to have had just one *samāhartṛi* who divided the *janapada* into four parts for revenue collection; and, finally, that *janapada* as one of the seven organs of the state would denote the entire territory of the state rather than just one of its territorial units of administration.[41] This critique by Kangle was based on just

40. Kosambi 1952: 205. He was preceded by Bernhardt Breloer and Pran Nath in seeing the *janapada* as a constituent territorial element of the state rather than the state itself. However, as we shall see, they did little by way of adducing specific *AŚ* evidence in support.
41. Kangle 1965: 121.

one, the already-cited general statement of Kosambi in his 1952 article ('Ancient Kosala and Magadha'), and ignored a considerable body of his other statements on the issue, including in the article.

Unlike Kangle, who insisted on only a single usage of *janapada* in the *AŚ*, Kosambi did recognize the multiple meanings of the term. Even in 'Ancient Kosala and Magadha', he would implicitly assume a small *janapada* state in referring to kings as developing from 'the tribal chiefs of a *janapada*'.[42] More commonly, however, he noted how the system of cash payments do imply a much larger area: 'It is incredible that this scheme of cash payments, unparalleled in a country where feudal tenure is not yet forgotten, should be purely imaginary or designed for a mere *janapada* king.'[43] Elsewhere too, before describing the *Arthaśāstra* state in terms of what he thought was the principal meaning of *janapada*, he would underline the multiplicity of its meanings: 'The word *janapada*, literally "foothold of a tribe", is later used for "country", "state", or even "district"....'[44] This suggestion of the state as consisting of multiple *janapada* units then comes through his discussions. For instance, in the *Introduction to the Study of Indian History*, Kosambi developed the argument that Kauṭilya's 'first five books consolidate the internal administration of the state in *janapada* units, each with its ministerial overseers for every department'.[45] Thus, we learn that 'besides obeying regulation of weights and measures, the merchants had to pay tolls at both ends whenever their merchandise went from one *janapada* to another'.[46]

This meaning of *janapada* as a territorial unit of a state ('tribal district') recurs quite frequently in several of Kosambi's writings.[47] All this is bypassed by O., who, unlike the previous scholars, insists on taking it to mean 'countryside' – at most, by extension, 'people

42. Kangle 1952: 205.
43. Ibid.: 209.
44. Kosambi 1965: 122.
45. Kosambi 1956: 205.
46. Ibid.: 207.
47. E.g. Kosambi 1964: 34 ('scattered *janapada* units separated by extensive tracts of forest and wasteland' being 'the norm of settlement' in the *Arthaśāstra*).

of the countryside' – only. Once, however, O. refers approvingly to Scharfe's discussion of the term, and argues that although the term '*often does* refer to the people' in the text (emphasis added) as pointed out by Scharfe, he would still adhere to his own preferred rendering of 'countryside' for it in this particular case (2.3.2).[48]

It is imperative to pause here for two major points of our interest. First, O.'s agreement with Scharfe that *janapada* in the *AŚ* does often mean people is limited to this statement alone and means nothing for his actual translations. In practice, O. continues insistently with his belief that *janapada* must mean only 'countryside'/'people of the countryside', never people in their entirety. Thus when 7.1.32 refers to an enemy's *janapada* being 'oppressed by [some other] enemy' and coming to the king, O. does not take it to mean people in general as Scharfe does, but as 'people of the countryside'. Likewise for 7.1.33 (the conqueror carrying off people from the defeated kingdom) and 4.3.19 (in times of famine the king taking his people to some other region), where there can scarcely be any doubt about the reference being to people as a whole as Scharfe argues so persuasively and with which O. agrees in theory, in the translations it is 'people of the countryside'. Even Kangle, who quite impossibly spoke of the 'region' (*janapada*) coming to the king and being carried off by the conqueror, does refer to 'people' in the last instance.

Second, Scharfe offers detailed arguments[49] that elaborately refute the view of 'most scholars working with the Arthaśāstra [who] have taken for granted that the state described in this work comprised only one such *janapada*, headed by the chief fiscal officer (*samāhartṛi*).'[50] In his view, it is only when we think of the state in the *AŚ* as consisting of 'several provinces called *janapada*' that 'the difficulties [of interpreting the *AŚ*] diminish, or even disappear'.[51] Although he mentions neither in this context, we can see that he is just re-establishing Kosambi's standpoint as against Kangle's critique, invoking in the process some of the same

48. Olivelle 2013: 497.
49. Scharfe 1993: 120 ff., 155 ff.
50. Ibid.: 121.
51. Ibid.: 122.

evidence as the former did, e.g. the reference that '(only) with a sealed pass shall a person be entitled to enter or leave a *janapada*'.[52] He mentions Breloer and Pran Nath as the exceptions who also had this view of the *janapada* as territorial units of the state, but points out how the former offered as evidence nothing from the *AŚ* itself, but from seventeenth-eighteenth century Maharashtra under the Peshwas;[53] an inadequate lack of the required empirical support is seen in the case of Pran Nath too, who relied less assuredly on the *AŚ* than on the other texts for arguing his case.[54] The work of Scharfe is referred to a number of times by O. Yet it will be found that he could have made a much more profitable use of it, and not just for *janapada* and the allied/synonymous terms such as *deśa* and *vishaya.*

We will now proceed to see, necessarily briefly for illustrative purposes, how, with reference to the *Sanskrit-English Dictionary* (*MW*) of Monier-Williams and his collaborators (Monier-Williams in short) and the translation of Kangle, a closer reading and wider consultation could have saved O.'s great work from more than one pitfall of omission and commission.

MŪLA AND BHAKSHYA-BHOJYA

For interpreting the meaning of *mūla* (14.1.29) as 'a vegetable in the group *pañchamūla*', Olivelle refers us to Maria Macri's study of Suśruta.[55] I have not yet been able to consult the cited work, but this suggestion of *mūla* being any one of a given group of five *vegetables* is in all likelihood quite misleading, going by the details furnished by Monier-Williams. It could be any among five groups of five *plants* each, i.e. twenty-five plants, e.g. five kinds of creepers and five of grasses; there were sub-groups too, a group of two being known as *dvi-pañchamūla*, i.e. ten *mūlas* with reference to Suśruta and others, Monier-Williams summed it all up in the entry

52. Ibid.: 123.
53. Ibid.: 121-2 and fn115.
54. Nath 1929: 45-52.
55. Olivelle 2013: 447; *Lexicon Phytonimicum (Therapeutica ex Suśrutasaṃhitā*). Pubblicazioni del CESMEO, Torino, 1988.

'*pañchamūla*' (besides providing detailed information for the specific compounds in separate entries), as follows: '*pañcha-mūla* n. (also *-laka*) and (*ī*) f. a class or group of 5 roots or plants with tuberous roots (according to Suśr. there are 5 classes each containing 5 medicinal plant, viz. *kanīyas* or *alpam* or *kshudrakam*, *mahat*, *vallī-saṃjñaḥ* [sc. *gaṇaḥ*], *kaṇṭakas-*, and *tṛiṇas-* i.e. the smaller and the larger classes, the creepers, the thorny plants and the 5 kinds of grass; other groups are also enumerated) Suśr. Bhpr. &c.'

MW has been referred to by O. very, very occasionally, its potential barely scratched. A likely reason of neglect is the kind of attack that has been mounted on it, together with works such as the translation of the *Manusmṛiti* by G. Bühler, over recent decades, though it has to be said that, unlike others, O. has been very genuinely and comprehensively appreciative of the latter in his *magnum opus* on Manu.

To give one more example, O. translated *bhakshya-bhojana* as 'food and delicacies' (4.6.2, 5.1.30), as against K.'s 'eating of food'/'food', and explained his new meaning by referencing an article by Toru Yagi (1994): 'Although both terms, as also the related *bhojya*, can refer simply to food, as Yagi (1994) has shown, when the two are used together or contrasted, *bhakshya* refers to food that needs mastication, while *bhojya* (*bhojana*) refers to less dense food, perhaps delicacies that are soft and melt in the mouth.'[56]

It does no injury to Yagi's insightful and informative piece, however, to point out that the particular meanings of the two terms had almost always been known, and are given as such by Bühler ('various [kinds of] hard food which require mastication, and of soft food')[57] as well as in *MW* (*bhakshya*:'anything eaten, food (esp. such as requires mastication)); *bhojya*: '*to be enjoyed* or eaten, eatable, *what is enjoyed* or eaten, (esp.) what may be eaten without mastication', emphases added).[58] The two terms have had in fact a complex historiography of translation. We just note here, as suggested here by the italicized parts of the dictionary meaning of

56. Olivelle 2013: 633, note to 4.6.2
57. Bühler 1886: On Manu 3.227.
58. *MW*: sv.

bhojya, that for some time before O.'s translation of 'food and delicacies' for *bhakshya-bhojana/bhojya*, it has been understood precisely as such. Thus J.A.B. van Buitenen in his translation of the *Mahābhārata* ('food, delicacies'/'food and delicacies'), and thus Wendy Doniger and Brian K. Smith in their translation of the *Manusmṛiti* ('foods that are eaten and enjoyed').[59]

APAVĀHANA, SATTRA, AND *VIRĀTRA*

Of the greatest significance for our theses is Patrick Olivelle's assimilation of R.P. Kangle. Even a hurried comparison will show that O.'s debts to, as well as departures from, K. are much more substantial than could be specified as such. This is only to be expected between two such exercises on the same theme, and most of the time the non-mention is quite unexceptionable; the tedium would otherwise have been equally agonizing for the reader. It has to be underlined all the same that the massive notes in K.'s translation – by far his real *tour de force* – continue to remain for a very large part almost as solid a basis of O.'s translation as is his edited text. O.'s notes, for all their invaluable inputs, not only remain significantly smaller and less succinct than but also substantially overlap K.'s.

On more than a crucial count, moreover, O. hasn't got K. right. We discuss this with reference to the following three terms: *apavāhana*, *sattra*, and *virātra*.

The term *apavāhana* in 2.1.1 is translated by Kangle as 'bringing in' people from elsewhere for settling a territory. Olivelle does it differently, on the following grounds: 'The term *apavāhana* is translated by Kangle as "bringing in" and by Meyer as "Herbeiziehung." Scharfe (1993, 122) sees a stronger intent here and thinks that the foreign population was abducted to settle the countryside. I think Scharfe is correct, especially because this term and its verbal equivalent (*apavāhayet*) occur frequently within

59. Van Buitenen 1973: 397, 414; Doniger and Smith 1991: on Manu 3.227.

contexts that imply the forcible removal of a population, 7.1.33; 7.16.16; 8.2.8; 8.4.15; 9.4.8; 11.1.16, 53; 12.3.14; 13.5.18.'[60]

Accordingly he takes it to mean 'forcing people out' rather than bringing them in. An immediate objection would be that 'forcing out', i.e. driving or chasing away, gives the very opposite of the intended sense of 'abduction', i.e. taking (persons) along by force (O. can actually translate the verb as 'depopulate' in 8.2.8). Far more important for our purposes is the oversight about K.'s deep insight here in calling it simply 'bringing in' (whether forced or induced), on the ground given in the appended note: '*apavāhana* includes the idea of enticement as well as displacement by force'. This observation of the term denoting the idea of inducement is seen to be based on 7.16.16, where *apavāhita* is translated as 'enticed away' by K. In doing it as 'lured away', O. not only concurs (while being phrasally different), but also makes a point of it in the note: '*lured away*: That is, a person who has been lured away from the enemy's side and has come over to his. For this meaning of *apavāhita*, see 12.3.14.' In rejecting flatly K.'s translation 'bringing in', O. obviously did not remember his own rendering of 7.16.16 and patently missed K.'s insight. (It is not at all clear if that is the sense also in 12.3.14; at least it is not rendered as such there.) *Whenever* the context as he saw it warranted, Kangle would translate *apavāhana* as 'carrying off' with the implication of compulsion; he thought 2.1.1 as open to either of the two senses, hence the neutral 'bringing in'.

As to *sattra*, Olivelle makes a dual allegation: While Kangle interprets the term, wrongly, as a 'sacrificial session' in 7.15.22, 'elsewhere, he translates it as hiding place'. As against this, Olivelle points out that most of the time, including in 7.15.22, *sattra* is 'used with the meaning of a secure location that is also good as a hideout or escape from danger (perhaps also fortified) and as a place of ambush at 7.5.46; 7.17.56–57; 8.4.41 (where it probably means ambush); 8.5.11, 19; 10.2.15, etc.'; additionally, it means 'a rest house at 2.35.3'.[61] It is a huge misrepresentation of Kangle's

60. Olivelle 2013: 492.
61. Olivelle 2013: 668.

work. We begin with 2.35.3, where Kangle too takes it to mean a rest-house, so that Olivelle follows rather than departs from Kangle here. In so taking *sattra* as a rest-house Olivelle repeats in fact what is clearly an error committed by Kangle, who furnished no reason for departing from the meaning 'feeding houses' given by Shamasastry. In view of the juxtaposition of *sattra* in 2.35.3 with *prapā*, which means 'sheds for drinking water' (rephrased, somewhat curiously, as 'water-dispensing sheds' by Olivelle), it is pretty obvious that *sattra* means a feeding house here; as Ganapati Sastri explains, one is *anna-dāna-śālā*, the other *pānīya-śālā*.

It is indeed difficult to see how O. could miss that like him, K. too had noted the regular sense of 'ambush' for the term, inherent indeed in its etymology. In the note to 1.12.1 Kangle states: '*sattrin* is apparently derived from *sattra* frequently used in the sense of "an ambush" from *sad* "to sit in ambush or to lie in wait unseen"; cf. 7.17.56; 10.2.15; 8.5.11 etc.' And again in the note to 7.5.46: '*sattrād*: for *sattra* "ambush" as a dangerous situation, cf. 10.3.24.' (A little reflection may have persuaded O. to give up his 'secure location' for K.'s 'dangerous situation' in his following translation of 7.5.46: 'he should make every effort to flee from a secure location'.) Again in 8.4.41, 8.5.11, 8.5.19 (also note the Russian translation of Kangle's work given as 'Additional Notes'), 10.3.15 and 10.3.24, K. has the same or similar rendering of the term. For instance, for *iti sattrāṇi* in 10.3.24, Kangle wrote 'these are places for ambush'; Olivelle 'the following are places for an ambush'.

Equally unfortunate is the lapse in the case of *virātra*. In his note to 4.6.2, O. argues in some detail how Ganapati Sastri, Meyer, Kangle as well as van Buitenen have all been wrong in rendering *virātra* as 'mid-night', the correct one being 'day-break' of 'night's end', 'end of the night, that is, daybreak or possibly just before dawn':

> *Night's end* (*virātra*): Both Meyer and Kangle, following Gaṇapati Śāstrī (glossed as *ardha-rātre*), take the term here and at 4.13.6 to mean the middle of the night or midnight. But I think B-R [Böhtlingh and Roth, *Sanskrit-Wörterbuch*] is correct in taking the term to mean end of the night, that is, daybreak or possibly just before dawn. It makes little sense

to think that someone can walk in the shadows of a wall in the middle of the night. The term is found in *Mbh* 3.282.28, 32; 10.3.33; 13.91.8; *Rām* 5.16.2. Johnson (1998; *Mbh* 10.3.33) translates it as the darkness before dawn, and Goldman (1984–2009; *Rām* 5.16.2) translates it as daybreak; these translations fit the contexts well. I think they are correct in their interpretation; van Buitenen's (1973–1978) rendering 'dead of night' (*Mbh* 3.282.28, 32) is incorrect.[62]

But in 4.6.2 on which O. offers the above note *virātra* is *not* translated as 'the middle of the night' by K., as alleged, but as 'an odd hour of the night'. This is surely the best thing to do here. The dictionaries admit both the meanings of the term (midnight and night's end or daybreak) in different contexts, and as there is no indication in this passage of which part of the night is being meant, K. calls it 'an odd hour of the night'.[63] It is only when the context makes it quite clear in 4.13.6 that K. translates it as 'midnight' ('for *virātra* here is obviously midnight'[64]). This passage makes it an offence for a person to 'climb ... over the perimeter wall of his own house' *after virātra* (*virātrāt*), and it is difficult to see how that can be if you do it 'after the end of night' as O. would have it.

PARENTHESES

In line with an established practice among Indologists, Kangle was consistently attentive to putting in round brackets the parts of his English rendering that have no counterpart in the original text but are implied. As I also believe that it makes good sense to use parentheses to denote the translator's insertions as distinct from the words of the text, we need to argue our case vis-à-vis O., who has been a firm believer in their non-use, in line with an ascendant vogue in some of the more creative of Indological circles.

It is in two ways that O. has by and large dispensed with the

62. Ibid.: 634.
63. In this sense, *virātra* has survived in my mother tongue Maithili in the expression '*rāti-birāti*' (pronounced *rāit-birāit*).
64. Kangle 1963: note to 4.13.6. He also invokes here a comparison with 4.6.1.

practice of using parentheses in his translation of the *AŚ*. First, he enters seamlessly his own words, clauses and phrases amidst the English equivalents of the Sanskrit original in order to clarify the intended meaning of the Sanskrit text. Alternatively, he would adhere strictly to a translation of the text alone, supplying nothing from his own side. The first may be seen in the rendering of *sabhy-opakāribhyaḥ* (2.16.13) – a compound of *sabhya* and *upakārin* – as 'those who are members or associates of *local* corporate bodies' (emphasis added). However, *sabhya* means 'a member of *sabhā* or a corporate body', and *upakārin* 'an associate'; 'local' forms no inherent part of the meaning of either. The context shows that the reference is to members of private as distinct from state-owned/operated bodies, which O. seeks to denote by the word 'local'. Putting 'local' in brackets would have both conveyed the exact character of the original expression and clarified exactly what was being meant.

An insertion from the translator, whether with or without brackets, is again called for in the very next passage (2.16.14); this time, by keeping to the text alone, Olivelle's rendering tends to mislead the reader. The just-quoted passage about *sabhyas* and others as well as the previous two passages (2.16.11-12) are about private traders, but everything before in the chapter pertains to state-owned goods or commodities (*rāja-paṇya*). It is these royal commodities that are brought back into discussion in 2.16.14-16, where *paṇya* in *paṇy-ādhishṭhātṛi* can *only* refer to *rāja-paṇya*. K. accordingly translates the term as 'officers in charge of (royal) goods'; to render it literally as 'overseers of commodities' without the explanatory 'royal', coming as it does after the references to the private traders, is to create an unnecessary confusion.

Lastly, we note through a simplest of examples how the omission of an explanatory insertion in the translation of following passage bears vitally on our knowledge of foresters in early India (the passage is critical also for establishing the meaning of *janapada* as a territorial unit of the state, as well as the persistence in early historical India of the tribe-caste continuum for the case of the Chaṇḍālas):

teshām antarāṇi vāgurika-śabara-pulinda-chaṇḍāla-araṇyacharā raksheyuḥ (2.1.6).
'Trappers, Śabaras, Pulindas, Chaṇḍālas *and forest-dwellers* should guard the intervening regions between them [i.e. the *janapadas*].' (K.) (Emphasis added.)
'Areas between them [i.e. the *janapadas*] should be guarded by trappers, tribals, mountaineers, Chaṇḍālas, *and forest dwellers*.' (O.) (Emphasis added.)

These translations can only mean that the Śabaras and the Pulindas, among others, were distinct from forest-dwellers! The intended meaning would have come right through with a simple addition, from the translators' side, of 'other' before 'forest-dwellers'; and greater accuracy would have been achieved, with no corresponding injury to readability, by putting it in brackets. An equally good alternative is of course a re-translation ('Forest-dwellers (such as) trappers, Śabaras, Pulindas and Chaṇḍālas ….').

SOME MORE ISSUES

One is also called upon to engage with O. according to one's own lights, without the benefit of the available beacons. We may begin with the most cherished of his principles, i.e. 'a single English term for each technical term of the *AŚ*'.[65] As the cardinal tenet on which the new translation is based, the Note to the Translation presents a full elaboration of this point, with a total of eighty-three such terms arranged in five tables for the following categories: state officials (Table 0.1); secret agents (Table 0.2); elements of the *maṇḍala* policies of the would-be conqueror (*vijigīshu*) (Table 0.3); religious personnel (Table 0.4), and; economic and revenue vocabulary (Table 0.5). Each term is represented by a precise English equivalent, with just one exception where three such technical terms – *tāpasa*, *yati*, and *liṅgin* – are recognized as synonyms, to be rendered as 'ascetic'.

However, O. has not always been able to follow this precept.

65. Olivelle 2013: xiv.

To cite just three technical terms (*adhyaksha, mudrā,* and *āya*): *Lakshaṇ-ādhyaksha* is translated first as 'director of the mint' (2.6.2), then as 'the Superintendent of the Mint' (2.12.24); *mudr-ādhyaksha* as 'director of passports' (2.6.2) as well as 'the Superintendent of Passes' (1.1.4, 2.34.1), and; *āya*, for which only 'income' was proposed to be used (Table 0.5), is sometimes 'income' (e.g. 1.19.9), 'revenue' otherwise, and indeed alternately 'corpus of revenue (*āya-śarīra*)' and 'income' as parts of the discussion of one and the same thing (2.6.9-22),[66] sacrificing the consistent renderings of K. ('corpus of income' and 'income'). The slip in the use of 'revenue' for *āya* is particularly unfortunate here as well as in passages such as 2.7.3, where various calculations of revenue (e.g. estimated revenue, outstanding revenue, current revenue, etc.) have to be distinguished from *āya.* As a technical term incorporating and heading a complex system of accounting, *āya* must also be capitalized in English, as Income, along with other such technical terms. We may recall Moreland's elucidation about such a usage,[67] and would be more consistent if we speak of Income as we do of the Superintendents, Collectors, etc. Using 'Income' for *āya* would also usefully distinguish it from the non-technical uses of 'income' in the text, as for instance for *artha* in 1.8.13.

Next, as has already been seen in the case of *kara*, a technical term could also be a homonym. Another good example is *rāshṭra* (some others will be seen presently). *Rāshṭra*, when distinguished sharply from *sītā* (produce of crown lands) (2.15.1), is a smaller, therefore different, entity than when *sītā* is described as one of its constituents (2.6.3).

Third, it is well known that the *AŚ* teachers drew upon several sources for their vocabulary, so that different technical terms that have been treated as different in meaning and so given different English equivalents actually stood for one and the same thing, i.e. were synonyms. Fourth, there is a problem with O.'s lone recognition

---

66. Cf. Olivelle: 511 (note to 2.6.9).
67. 'The terms which I have selected for use are printed throughout with an initial capital letter, as a tacit reminder, to the reader that they bear the definite sense which has been explained at their first mention.' (Moreland 1929: v.)

of the presence in the *AŚ* of synonyms in the three terms, i.e. *liṅgin*, *tāpasa* and *yati*: the former had a wide range of meanings, all derived from the basic one of a person having identifying marks or emblems, so that it could both be the same as and different from the other two well-known words for 'ascetic'. However, *tāpasa* and *yati* were parts of a much larger group of synonyms, a number of which have been treated as distinct in meaning by O. and thus given different English equivalents. We discuss these first as we combine the third and the fourth objections to O.'s cardinal principle, before returning to *liṅgin*.

In Table 0.4 (followed by and large faithfully in the translation), where *tāpasa* and *yati* are translated as 'ascetic', they are also treated as distinct in meaning from *bhikshu(ka)* or 'mendicant', *tapasvin* or 'recluse', *pravrajita* or 'renouncer', and *parivrājaka* or 'wandering ascetic'; the literal meanings (which have always been known) are now taken to be the actual ones, so that each category is now treated as different from the other. No attempt is made by O. to show, on the basis of the *AŚ*, the meaning of any of these terms, or their mutual distinctiveness, from the context. I do not think it is generally possible either. For a person who has studied in such great detail religious specialists of ancient India, much of which has been collected in his *Ascetics and Brahmins: Studies in Ideologies and Institutions* (2006), we naturally thought that he derived these definitions from his analyses of other texts. The collection is a monument to his labour of love on the subject of asceticism over nearly three decades, ranging *inter alia* from a comprehensive definition of the ascetic in English language[68] to a most formidable documentation of its Sanskrit and Prakrit equivalents, when he refers to a variety of terms in a large number of texts, including in the *AŚ*, *as synonyms*. In an early piece (1984) he collected a very large body of references from the Dharmaśāstras (including the *Dharmasūtras*), which 'use several terms for a renouncer', including *bhikshu, pravrajita, parivrājaka,* and *yati.*[69] This was subsequently reinforced from other sources: the Pāli

68. Olivelle 2006: 28-32.
69. Ibid: 271-272fn1.

literature 'has parallels for all common Sanskrit terms for a renouncer and renunciation', e.g. *bhikkhu*, *yati*, *pabbajita*, and *paribbajaka*; Pāṇini and Patañjali have *parivrājaka, śramaṇa, bhikkhu, yati,* and *maskarin* for the renouncer; then we have 'the *Arthaśāstra*, the *Kāmasūtra,* and the *Pañchatantra*, all of which use several terms for a renouncer' (which in the *AŚ* are *pravrajita, parivrājaka, bhikshu,* and *yati*), and; the *Rāmāyaṇa* has as synonyms *parivrājaka, bhikshu, śramaṇa, and śramaṇī.*[70] However, in the Preface to that book, O. refers in general to his evolution over time: 'It is quite natural that as one matures both in years and, hopefully, in wisdom, one's approaches and theoretical models change.'[71] Is it the case then O. changed his views in our work? It is likelier that he did not keep in mind his previous works, just as he was to forget his Table 0.4 in his later translation of the *Yājñavalkya Smṛiti.* There, in the opening verses of the topic *yati-dharma-prakaraṇa*, we read that the 'renouncer' (*yati*), after he has 'become a wandering ascetic' (*parivrajya*), is a 'mendicant' (*bhikshuka*) who is enjoined to seek food in villages according to certain norms, in one of the prescribed types of 'bowls of ascetics' (*yati-pātra*).[72] Further, here the *tapasvin*, who in the *Arthaśāstra* is a 'recluse' different from all these beings ('ascetic', 'renouncer', etc.), is an ascetic,[73] as he was in O.'s translation of *Manu* (4.162).[74]

The one-time aberration in the *AŚ* can be explained only in terms of a steadfast observance of his one-time cardinal principle there about one English equivalent for one technical term, with its implicit denial of any homonymy or synonymy of the technical terms. The whole exercise amounts to a demonstration of how theoretical-methodological presuppositions can influence one's empirical observations, erasing in the process all memory that would come in the way of the new theory.

We now come to *liṅgin*. It is known to occur in a number of

70. Ibid.: 129 and fn8, 130 fn13, 131 and fn18-19.
71. Ibid.: 9.
72. Olivelle 2019: 3.58-60, 62.
73. Ibid.: 2.70.
74. The renderings are 'individual given to ascetic toils' and a person 'given to austerities' respectively.

texts, including *Manu* and the *Mbh*, in a variety of contexts, and the meaning has not always been clear, or at least agreed upon. Thus in *Manu*, 4.200, it is taken to mean 'a student' by Bühler, but as a member 'of a religious profession' by O., who however underlined the difficulties, as follows: '... the term *liṅgin* is ambiguous. It refers to a person who bears a distinguishing mark or emblem. Generally, this refers to the emblems of a religious professional, such as a vedic student, a forest hermit, or an ascetic. Medhātithi and Nārāyaṇa, correctly I think, take it with a broad meaning, whereas Govinda and Kullūka restrict it to a vedic student.'[75]

In the *AŚ*, however, O. is positive that the *liṅgin* is always an ascetic. We differ, and propose to proceed by keeping in mind the basic meaning of a person sporting identity marks or emblems (*liṅga*) and bringing in relevant evidence from *Manu* and *Mbh*. In a caste society people wore their identity marks on the body; these caste-marks would be *liṅgas*. Thus the *Manusmṛiti* refers to the *śūdras* assuming the marks of the twice-born (*śūdrāṃś cha dvija-liṅginaḥ*, *Manu*, 9.224), or a non-Arya wearing those of the Āryas (*anāryān=āryaliṅginaḥ*, *Manu*, 9.260). So when Kauṭilya, in a list of persons to be arrested on suspicion (4.6.2), refers to *liṅgen-āliṅginaṃ liṅginaṃ vā bhinn-āchāram* – i.e. one who is sporting emblems (*liṅga*) of one, but is not a *liṅgin*, or one whose conduct or behaviour pattern (*āchāra*) does not conform to that of the people whose emblems he sports – he could be speaking of all social groups in general rather than specifically of religious groups, still less of ascetic orders alone (as K. and O. assume).

In 2.28.20 the reference is to the *pravrajitas* who are also *liṅgins*, a difficult situation for O. for whom the two technical terms denote two different kinds of religious specialists, 'renouncers' and 'ascetics' respectively. He gets around it by taking the *liṅgins* here to mean simply a person with identifying emblems, divesting it of any specific meaning: 'a renouncer with emblems that he has just put on or without any emblem'. This is just right, though the expression – *sadyo-gṛihīta-liṅginam=aliṅginaṃ vā pravrajitam* –

75. Olivelle 2005: 275, note to 4.200.

refers more precisely to a *pravrajita* who has just turned a *liṅgin* or one who is not a *liṅgin.* The context of this passage shows that a renouncer (*pravrajita*) who was not a *liṅgin* was suspect and had to be arrested; the same for one who had just put on the marks of a *liṅgin.* This presumes the general existence of several orders of ascetics, each with its own distinctive marks, where a renouncer without any such marks was an obvious suspect. The point is, here *liṅgin means a pravrajita.* However, it appears to be a larger category subsuming the renouncers in 13.3.48, which refers to *liṅgins* who are *pravrajitas* (*pravrajita-liṅgibhiḥ*), implying those who are not. The term probably means here religious personnel in general, as in the *Mbh*, 12.61.12, which refers to a pious donor who is generous to all the *liṅgins* without distinction (*sarva-liṅgi-pradātṛi*) as well as the *Mbh*, 12.66.7, which draws a distinction between religious people (*liṅgin*) and common folk (*loka*) in the reference to an ideal king honouring the *mukhyas* (the foremost or prominent) of both (*loka-mukhyeshu ... liṅgi-mukhyeshu*).

In fact, representing the fact that there were identity marks for all kinds of sets and subsets of social groups, the bearer of the marks at any level could be called the *liṅgin*; the intended meaning would be understood from the context, which would also exclude the non-intended connotations. Thus *Manu*, 8.407 distinguishes between *pravrajita* ('wandering ascetic'), *muni* ('sage'), and *liṅgin* (a person 'wearing the insignia of a religious profession'). A narrower meaning of the term as a member of a non-ascetic religious order/sect is also there in the *Mbh,* 12.65.25, which distinguished *liṅgins* from *bhikshu.* It may likewise be the case that the *liṅgin* brāhmaṇas in the *Mbh*,13.23.1-2 were members of such sects, while the brāhmaṇa who is stated to be non-*liṅgin* (*brāhmaṇam ... aliṅginam*, ibid.) was a non-sectarian *smārta* one (the context excludes any reference to his other kinds of identity marks, say as an Ārya).

ON CHOICE OF WORDS

Even when there is no disagreement on meaning with the extant translations, O. likes, as we have had occasions to note before, to have his own phraseological preferences. This is only to be expected from a practised stylist, and welcome for the variety it introduces and the monotony it breaks. Except when it (a) results in what can only be regarded as avoidable slips, or (b) impedes a more meaningful engagement with the text. A range of terms will need to be discussed here to convey the kind of alternatives O. has provided all through and throughout.

Thus in place of Kangle's perfect 'spiritual brother' for *dharma-bhrātṛi* in 3.16.37, Olivelle has 'brother in the Law', which is rather confusing and which he rightly abandons for 'spiritual brother' in his recent rendering of the slightly modified version of this passage in *Yājñavalkya Smṛiti*, 2.141.[76]

Further, *pradakshiṇ-odakaṃ* (2.3.3) is translated as 'clockwise' after the literal meaning ('circumambulating water') in place of K.'s 'left to right'. However, in this case *pradakshiṇā* cannot possibly mean any circular clockwise movement, but connotes simply an auspicious left to right movement. The reference is to the building site of an administrative centre. The site, it is stated, should be located at the confluence of rivers, or on the bank of some other water body. 'Clockwise' flow of the rivers would have required the site to be surrounded by them, not located at their confluence. So, as K. had explained in the note to his translation: '*pradakshiṇodakam,* i.e., in effect on the right bank of the river'. In fact, as O.'s own note shows, he means as much (which, in effect, amounts to a confession of the folly of substituting 'clockwise' for 'left to right'):

76. Olivelle 2019: 158-9. In other editions, it is *Yājñavalkya Smṛiti* 2.137. It is a slightly modified version of the *AŚ* passage. Thus there is now 'virtuous pupil' in place of simply '*pupil*', and *eka-tīrthin* in place of *samāna-tīrthya.* However, having rightly translated the last one (same as the *sa-tīrthya* of the *Mālatī-Mādhava*) as 'fellow student'. Olivelle now takes its obvious synonym to mean 'someone belonging to one's own order', i.e. *saha-tīrthika* as opposed to the *para-tīrthika* of Lexicons (*MW*, sv *para-tīrthika*).
Aside from the rendering 'brother in the Law', O. has also offered a qualitatively different understanding of 3.16.37, without a word on why he does not accept Kangle's reasons for taking *krameṇa* to mean 'respectively' rather than 'in this order'.

'The water should be moving from the left to the right as one faces it from the city. This is, of course, the auspicious direction of movement.'[77]

Likewise in 2.3.6, it is too much of unnecessary and misleading innovation – as against K.'s innovations that I think generally come *only* after a clear-headed and hard-nosed review – to have 'dirt', 'cavities', and 'royal residence' in place of 'earth', 'low places', and 'palace grounds'. The context in this and the previous passages is the uses to be made of the huge quantities of earth from the excavation of three moats around the administrative centre. The earth should be used, Kauṭilya says, first for building a rampart, and then for filling up *vāstu-chhidra* (literally, 'holes in residential areas', combined as *vāstuchchhidraṃ* in the original) 'or *rāja-bhavana* (literally 'the king's house'). K. perceptively noted that *vāstu-chhidra* 'refers to areas in the city unsuitable for building purposes because they are not level' and so translated it and *rāja-bhavana* as 'the low places in the residential areas or palace grounds' that were to be filled up 'with the remainder of the earth'. On the other hand, O., having rendered it in the previous passage as the 'earth' being used for the rampart construction, refers now to 'the remainder of the dirt' being used to fill 'cavities' not only in the 'building sites' but also in 'the royal residence'!

After K., Dieter Schlingloff too in his admirable study (*Fortified Cities of Ancient India*)[78] had understood *vāstu-chhidra* as 'irregularities in the building area'.[79] Yet when the term occurs again in 2.4.16 – the context is the location of the houses of guilds and foreign traders in *vāstu-chhidra* area along the city walls[80] – K. forgets his own explanation about it being an uneven residential land, and translates the term as 'non-residential areas'! This time, O. agrees, but substitutes his own 'area … [that is] unsuitable as

77. Olivelle 2013: 497.
78. O. has regularly referred to his original German piece in his translation, while its English translation is acknowledged to have been revised and edited by O.
79. Schlingloff 2013: 69.
80. 'In enclosures' according to K.; corrected as 'along the walls' by Schlingloff (ibid.: 45 fn155).

a building site' for it. There is in fact no reason why the term's previous sense of uneven residential area should not be applicable here as well.

Prākāra in two successive passages, 2.3.31 and 2.3.32 means two different things, first a wall or rampart and next the area enclosed by it. Although the second meaning is well attested, with *MW* giving 'enclosure', yet in the second instance too *prākāra* has been taken to mean a wall by K. as well as O., following Shamasastry, without realizing that it leads to impossible results. The two passages describe several types of gates. The first passage (2.31.31) refers to a gate called *gopura*, which is to be constructed at an opening in the *prākāra* (rampart) that is equal to its width. The next one refers to two gates by name – the 'Lotus-Pond Gate' (*pushkariṇī-dvāra*) having a *vāpī*, and the 'Muṇḍaka Gate' (*muṇḍaka-dvāra*) having a two-storeyed building; and probably also to a third gate by implication, the Princess Fort (Gate) (*kumārī-pura*) having a building with four rooms (*chatuḥ-śālā*). This second passage about these three structure-complexes, each having a gate, begins with the term *prākāra-madhye* ('in the midst of the *prākāra*, which has been taken to mean 'in the midst of the wall/parapet (*sic!*)' in the translations) and ends with the clause *bhūmi-dravya-vaśena*, 'depending on (the availability of) *land* and materials' (emphasis added); a single common verb *niveśayet* is used to describe all the constructions. 'In the midst of *prākāra*' should be thus applicable to all the three complexes, otherwise the whereabouts of the latter two would remain unknown. If so, and keeping in mind the reference to availability of land, all three complexes could hardly have been accommodated in the midst of the wall, for which the land is already given (as the land 'in the midst of the *prākāra*').[81] The space would in fact be rather inadequate even for the first complex, which comprises a *vāpī* with the Lotus-Pond Gate.

81. It is really curious that the later translators and commentators should have missed to pause at this impossibility of having so many things in the midst of a rampart, which leaps to the eye even in the first rendering by Shamasastry, as follows: 'In the centre of the parapets, there shall be constructed a deep lotus pool; a rectangular building of four compartments, one within the other; an abode of the Goddess Kumārī ... having its

Prākāra has thus to be understood as an 'enclosure', the area enclosed by the fort wall, and *prākāra-madhye* as 'in the midst of the fort area'). While the *gopura* was the gate of the fort, the other three complexes were constructed at the centre of the fort area. Actually, 2.4.2 speaks of the ideal of 12 such gates for the residential area of the fortified city.

The term *vāpī* of the preceding paragraph occurs elsewhere in the text too; each time it has been rendered as a trench or hole, even when it has been translated as a 'well'. Thus K.: 'the *vāpī* would appear to be a sort of hollow into which the enemy soldiers would be trapped' (2.3.32 note). However, once it is seen that the Lotus-Pond Gate with a *vāpī* was located in the midst of the fort area, it becomes obvious that a step-well is being meant, as part of the provisions of water-supply within the fort to which Kauṭilya refers elsewhere (2.4.2, 8). In a special circumstance, i.e. for making an underground chamber, when 2.5.2 refers to the digging of a *vāpī*, it takes care to specify that it should be without water (*an-udaka*); thus unless specified otherwise, the term would mean a source of water, i.e. a step-well.

Next, in place of K.'s 'cremation ground' for *śmaśāna*, O. gives us 'cemetery' (e.g. 2.4.4, 21, 23; 2.35.3; 2.36.13, 33; 3.9.23; 3.10.5; 3.19.29; 4.3.15; 13.2.29; 14.2.44) without discussion. One wonders if this is more accurate, attesting the continuation of the term's meaning in the later Vedic literature, where the *śmaśāna* was 'the name of the "burial mound" in which the bones of the dead man were laid to rest',[82] so that the term in the Vedic period may be understood as cemetery, as a burying-ground of the bones or ashes of the cremated body,[83] but probably also of body burials, a familiar practice of the times. For equally consistently, O. reserves 'cremation spot'/ 'cremation ground' (14.3.29, 32-3, 49) for another, equally ancient term *ādahana*.

---

external area one-and-a-half times as broad as that of its innermost room; a circular building with an archway ....' (Shamasastry 1956: 52.) Schlingloff (2013: 81) guessed that *prākāra-madhye* denoted the area 'between the two brick rows of the wall'.

82. *VI*, II: 397.
83. *MW*: sv *śmaśayana, śmaśāna*; *VI*, I: 9.

However, the different wording is actually a matter only of style, without realizing that something very different is being meant thereby. That *śmaśāna* was also a cremation ground is proved by 2.36.33 which prescribes a fine for depositing or burning a corpse anywhere else than a *śmaśāna* (*śmaśānād anyatra nyāse dahane cha*). 'Depositing' (*nyāsa*) something is different from burying, for which other terms were used (e.g. *nikhānayet*, 14.3.55). That the *śmaśāna* was a place where corpses could simply be thrown in, instead of being ceremonially disposed is seen later too, as in the account of Faxian: 'North of the vihāra two or three le there was the Śmaśānam, which name means in Chinese "the field of graves into which the dead are thrown".'[84] In fact, a Buddhist text translated in Chinese in the sixth-century AD refers to all kinds of corpse-disposal – exposure, cremation, collecting and preserving the bones in various ways, hanging dead bodies from the trees, as well as burials, all in the same area.[85] In view of these, it seems best to render *śmaśāna* as charnel-ground in the wider sense of an area of corpse-disposal (by whatever means). There were no different charnel-grounds for different *varṇas*, as one variant of *AŚ* 2.4.21 preferred by K. would lead us to suppose; as O. has demonstrated, K.'s text must be emended for the variant which refers to bodies of different *varṇas* being taken out of the city in the prescribed directions through the respective gates, a practice well-attested in *Manu* 5.92;[86] e.g. the southern gate for the *śūdras*.[87]

Next, *vyādhi* has uniformly been translated as 'disease' by both K. and O. There are places, however, where 'epidemic disease' or 'pestilence' suits the context better. For example, when *vyādhi* and *maraka* figure together (4.3.16), the first is of course 'disease', the

84. Legge 1886: 84.
85. Beal 1875: 159-60. These details were linked with specifically Tibetan or Mongoloid practices by Vincent Smith as he argued, notoriously enough, for the insignificance of non-monarchical forms of government in ancient India (Smith 1903).
86. Olivelle 2013: 506-7.
87. The continuity of the southern association for the lowest castes right into our times has recently been graphically demonstrated by Professor P.K. Basant (Basant 2019).

other 'epidemic'.[88] However, when *vyādhi* in 4.3.13 *is explained in the next sentence* as *maraka* (*tena marako vyākhyātaḥ*), it has to be rendered as 'pestilence'. Also, when Kauṭilya explains *vyādhi* as something that afflicts a single region or *deśa*, and contrasts it with famine (*durbhiksha*) that afflicts all the *deśas* (8.4.6), he is referring to no ordinary disease but to an epidemic one.

Śauṇḍika is translated more safely as 'vintner' (K.) rather than as 'tavern keeper' (O.), as the contexts (12.4.4, 13.3.56) have him visiting military camps, ritual sites, *samājas*, etc., to sell alcoholic beverages; a tavern keeper does not visit, but is visited by, his customers. The term for tavern in the text is *pānāgāra*.

K. preferring 'theurgist' or 'thaumaturgic ascetic' for *siddha* and *siddha-tāpasa*, in place of O.'s 'holy man', would expect us to believe that the *AŚ* shows them performing miracles or some other kind of magic. This however is not the case; 1.11.16ff, for instance, shows him rather as an omniscient seer.

For *antapāla* O. has substituted 'frontier commander' for K.'s 'frontier chief/officer'. The military character of the post is indeed very evident in passages such as 2.1.5, 2.4.29-31. Yet the office seems to have represented a wider range of authority, connected as much with non-military administration as with military ones, as in 2.21.24-6, where *antapāla* is seen discharging all kinds of customs-related duties. The oddity of O.'s alternative is striking in these passages:

> The Frontier Commander should collect a road levy of one and a quarter Paṇas for a vehicle loaded with goods, one Paṇa for a one-hoofed animal, half a Paṇa each for farm animals, a quarter Paṇa each for small farm animals, and one Māshika for a man carrying a load on his shoulder. He should, moreover, pay compensation for anything that is lost or stolen. He should dispatch to the Superintendent any foreign caravan after examining its goods of high and low value and providing an identity card and a seal.

Frontier Officer/Chief/Protector rather than Frontier Commander would thus convey better the all-encompassing nature of the officer's charge.

---

88. In Sanskrit there are probably no distinctions as between endemic, epidemic, and pandemic.

To render *Śabara* and *Pulinda* as 'tribals' and 'mountaineers' respectively (2.1.6) is to blur and erase, without warrant, their distinctly ethnic identity as Śabaras and Pulindas. As the authors of *The Vedic Index* noted quite some time ago, 'Śabara is the name of a wild tribe who in the *Aitareya Brāhmaṇa* are classed as Dasyus, with the Andhras, Pulindas, Mūtibas, and Puṇḍras'.[89] That they retained their meaning of an ethnic group later too (instead of becoming a generic name for something else) comes right through our texts, e.g. the *Mbh*; epigraphic substantiation for the Pulindas comes from the Aśokan inscriptions.

A TRIBUTE TO THE PIONEER

In the end we revisit for its generally unrecognized merits the English translation by Shamasastry, on which the prevalent opinion has been that it 'leaves much to be desired' (to quote Kosambi).[90] It redounds to the credit of O. again that he should have consulted it all the time and duly acknowledged the correctness of his renderings as against those of others. For many terms this was only to be expected: whatever can be the justification for replacing the precise 'collector-general'/'revenue collector' for *samāhartṛi* (Shamasastry) with 'administrator' (K.), a designation so general as to have almost no meaning (how is a 'superintendent' not an 'administrator'?); it is another matter though that, having restored 'collector', O. should, giving in to literalism, render the equally specific *prasāstṛi* as 'administrator'. Also Shamasastry was often able to get (what I have argued is) the correct sense of *prahavaṇa*, as in 3.10.44 ('the combined performance of any sacrifice of his village') or 1.21.28 ('sacrificial performances'), though once, quite imaginatively, he went really off the mark, in taking *prahavaṇa-nimittam* (1.10.09) as 'with the intention of sailing on a commercial vessel'!

It also needs to be pointed out, because it has not yet been, that another significant and really necessary departure from K. in

89. *VI*, ii: 354.
90. Kosambi 1956: xi. Contrast this with his unstinted praise and complete dependence on Shamasastry's three-volume *Index Verborum*.

the new translation is in fact a restoration of Shamasastry's practice. In Appendix I, it is observed by O.: 'One problem with Kangle's translation is that he has made no effort to identify the flora and fauna mentioned in the *AŚ*.'[91]He may have added how Shamasastry would take all possible pains to provide the identifications for the flora, fauna and other technical terms.

Above all, however, we have considerable scope for imbibing Shamasastry's habits, *as a translator*, of critical self-awareness and self-doubt, and conveying it by the way he did, i.e. by providing the original Sanskrit words in parentheses. No doubt he often did it excessively, i.e. unnecessarily, as in giving '(*kumāra*)' after prince, and also omitted to do it sometimes when it would be called for. The inherent merit of his practice is however easily illustrated. For the meaning of *piṇḍa-kara* in 2.15.3, O. is persuaded by the arguments of Bernhard Kölver to translate it as 'subsistence tax', as against Kangle's suggestion that it was 'a tax given by a village as a whole, as opposed to individual cultivators'.[92] He goes along with Kölver even in thinking that this was probably the same levy as the (unnamed) one described in *Manu* 7.118. There is of course no independent basis for the identification of *piṇḍa-kara* with this passage in *Manu*, which had so far been taken to represent, with a matching lack of support, the *bhoga* of epigraphs, following Bühler.[93] The fact is, as O. himself notes while giving it as 'subsistence tax', that 'the meaning is unclear'.[94] Such indeed was his self-doubt that two years later, in his *Sanskrit Dictionary of Law and Statecraft*, O. is converted back, as the term now is defined in K.'s words: 'aggregate tax on an entire group, such as a village'.[95] So Shamasastry, who thought the term meant 'taxes that

91. Olivelle 2013: 439. This is by and large, but not wholly, correct. For instance, O. himself refers to K.'s identifying *choraka* as aniseed (ibid.: 441).
92. Olivelle 2013: 543. O. thinks it is K.'s suggestion, but actually K. was simply following a long line of authorities, including Ghoshal (1929) and Jha (1967).
93. Bühler 1892: 75 fn32.
94. Olivelle 2013: 543.
95. Olivelle et al. 2015: 251.

are fixed' (based obviously on the contrast with the next item meaning one-sixth of the actual produce) although he was aware of the scholiast's 'taxes levied from the whole villages', did just the right thing in indicating the ambiguity by giving the Sanskrit term in brackets.

Likewise, to illustrate the point a different way: What precisely is meant about and what the reader will make of the mutual distinctions of 'assemblies, congregations, and gatherings of people' (1.13.2; O.'s rendering)? If the original terms for the three kinds of meeting – *sabhā*, *pūga*, and *jana-samavāya* – are given, they would certainly help the observant reader (when, say, he/she runs into *pūga* elsewhere), and may indeed alert the casual one (who otherwise would be wont and entitled to take all three – standard synonyms – as one and the same) to the actuality of the distinctions, whatever they may have been.

We conclude this essay in celebration with the earnest hope that that this reprint edition of Professor D.N. Jha's *Revenue System* will get the reception it deserves.

ABBREVIATIONS

AŚ : *Arthaśāstra* (Kangle 1960)
Contributions : Ghoshal 1929
EI : *Epigraphia Indica*
Introduction : Kosambi 1956
JBBRAS : *Journal of the Bombay Branch of Royal Asiatic Society*
JRAS : *Journal of the Royal Asiatic Society*
Manu : *Manusmṛiti* (Olivelle 2005)
K. : R.P. Kangle
Mbh : *Mahābhārata* (Critical Edition)
MW : Monier-Williams et al. 1899
O. : Patrick Olivelle
Rām. : *Rāmāyaṇa* (Critical Edition)
Revenue System : Jha 1967
VI : Macdonell and Keith 1912

REFERENCES TO THE FOREWORD AND AFTERWORD

Agrawala, V.S., 1953, *India as Known to Pāṇini,* 1st edn., University of Lucknow, Lucknow.

Basant, Prabhat Kumar, 2019, 'Sacred Geographies and Social Landscapes: A Study of Mānava-Dharmaśāstra', Lecture Delivered at 'Dāstān', the History Society of ARSD College, New Delhi, on 25 October 2019.

Beal, Samuel, 1875, *A Romantic Legend of Sākya Buddha from the Chinese-Sanscrit*, Trübner & Co., London.

Bhandarkar, D.R., 1904, 'Epigraphic Notes and Questions', *JBBRAS* (Old Series), vol. XXI, pp. 392-412.

———, 1913, 'Epigraphic Notes and Questions (XIX, Aśoka's Rock Edict Reconsidered)', *The Indian Antiquary*, vol. XLII, pp. 255-8.

———, 1932, *Asoka*, revd. and enlgd. 2nd edn., Calcutta University, Calcutta.

Bose, Manindra Mohan, 1928, 'Asoka's Rock Edicts I, VIII, IX, and XI', *The Indian Historical Quarterly*, vol. IV, pp. 110-23.

Brereton, Joel P., 2019, 'Pāṣaṇḍa: Religious Communities in the Aśokan Inscriptions and Early Literature', in P. Olivelle (ed.), *Gṛhastha: The Householder in Ancient Indian Religious Culture*, Oxford University Press, New York, pp. 20-42.

Bühler, G., 1883, 'Beiträge zur Erklärung der Asoka-Inschriften', *Zeitschrift der Deutschen Morgenländischen Gesellschaft*, 37(1), pp. 87-108.

———, 1886, *The Laws of Manu: Translated with Extracts from Seven Commentaries*, The Clarendon Press, Oxford.

———, 1892, 'The Madhuban Copper-Plate of Harsha', Dated Samvat 25, *EI*, vol. I, pp. 67-75.

———, 1894: 'Aśoka's Rock Edicts According to the Girnar, Shāhbāzgarhī, Kālsī and Mansehra Versions', *EI*, vol. II, pp. 447-72.

Burrow, T., 1968, 'Cāṇakya and Kauṭalya', *Annals of the Bhandarkar Oriental Research Institute*, vols. 48-9, Golden Jubilee Volume 1917-1967, pp. 17-31.

Chakravarti, Adhir K., 1971, 'Sources of Slavery in Ancient Cambodia', in D.C. Sircar (ed.), *Social Life in Ancient India*, Calcutta University, Calcutta, pp. 121-42.

Chakravarti, Uma, 1985, 'Of Dasas and Karmakaras: Service Labour in Ancient India', in Utsa Patnaik and Manjari Dingwaney (eds.), *Chains of Servitude: Bondage and Slavery in India,* Sangam Books, Madras, pp. 35-75.

Chanana, Dev Raj, 1960, *Slavery in Ancient India as Depicted in Pali and Sanskrit Texts*, People's Publishing House, New Delhi.

Chattopadhyaya, B.D., 1995, 'State and Economy in North India: Fourth Century to Twelfth Century', in R. Thapar (ed.), *Recent Perspectives of Early Indian History*, Popular Prakashan, Bombay, pp. 309-46.

Chattopadhyaya, Debiprasad, 1993, *What is Living and What is Dead in Indian Philosophy*, 3rd edn., People's Publishing House, New Delhi.

Cohen, G.A., 1978, *Karl Marx's Theory of History: A Defence*, Expanded edition (2000), Princeton University Press, Princeton.

Doniger, Wendy and Brian K. Smith, 1991, *The Laws of Manu: With an Introduction and Notes*, Penguin, London.

Ganapati Sastri, T., 1924-5, *The Arthaśāstra of Kauṭalya, with the Commentary Śrīmūla of Mahāmahopādhyāya T. Gaṇapati Śāstrī*, 3 pts., The Superintendent, Government Press, Trivandrum.

Ghoshal, U.N., 1929, *Contributions to the History of the Hindu Revenue System*, Calcutta University, Calcutta.

———, 1930, *The Agrarian System in Ancient India*, Calcutta University, Calcutta.

Gokhale, B.G., 1968, 'Review of Jha 1967', *The American Historical Review*, 73(5), pp. 1603-4.

Jha, D.N. 1967, *Revenue System in Post-Maurya and Gupta Times*, Punthi Pustak, Calcutta.

———, 1971, 'Land Revenue in the Maurya and Gupta Periods', in idem, *Studies in Early Indian Economic History*, Anupama Publications, Delhi. 1980, pp. 53-73 (rpt. from Sharma, ed., 1971).

Kane, P.V., 1941, *History of Dharmaśāstra*, vol. II, pt. I, Bhandarkar Oriental Research Institute, Poona.

Kangle, R.P., 1960, *The Kauṭilīya Arthaśāstra*, pt. I: *A Critical Edition with a Glossary*, University of Bombay, Bombay.

———, 1963, *The Kauṭilīya Arthaśāstra*, pt. II: *An English Translation with Critical and Explanatory Notes*, University of Bombay, Bombay.

———, 1965: *The Kauṭilīya Arthaśāstra*, pt. III: *A Study*, Motilal Banarsidass, Delhi (rpt. 1992).

Kosambi, D.D., 1952, 'Ancient Kosala and Magadha', *JBBRAS* (New Series), vol. XXVII, pt. II, pp. 180-213.

———, 1956, *An Introduction to the Study of Indian History*, Popular Book Depot, Bombay.

———, 1964: 'The Autochthonous Element in the Mahabharata', *Journal of American Oriental Society*, vol. LXXXIV, pp. 31-44.

———, 1978-9: 'The Line of *Arthaśāstra* Teachers', in B.D. Chattopadhyaya (ed.), *Combined Methods in Indology and Other Writings*, Oxford University Press, New Delhi, 2002, pp. 260-78 (rpt. from *The Indian Historical Review*, vol. 5, nos. 1-2, July 1978-Janurary 1979, pp. 1-15).

Legge, James (tr.), 1886, *A Record of Buddhistic Kingdoms, Being an Account by the Chinese Monk Fā-hien or His Travels in India and Ceylon (A.D. 399-414)*, The Clarendon Press, Oxford.

Mazumdar, B.P., 1971, 'Land Revenue in Early Medieval North India (*c.* 600-1200 A.D.)', in Sharma (ed.), pp. 20-32.

Macdonell, A.A. and A.B. Keith, 1912, *Vedic Index of Names and Subjects*, vols. I and II, John Murray, Albemarle Street, W.; for the Govt. of India, London.

McClish, Mark, 2019, *The History of the Arthaśāstra: Sovereignty and Sacred Law in Ancient India*, Cambridge University Press: Cambridge.

Monier-Williams, M., E. Leumann, C. Cappeller and Other Scholars, 1899, *A Sanskrit-English Dictionary*, 2nd edn., The Clarendon Press, Oxford (rpt. 1960).

Moreland, W.H., 1929, *The Agrarian System of Moslem India*, W. Heffer & Sons, Cambridge.

Nath, Pran, 1929, *A Study in the Economic Condition of Ancient India*, The Royal Asiatic Society, London.

Olivelle, Patrick, 2005 (With the editorial assistance of Suman Olivelle), *Manu's Code of Law: A Critical Edition and Translation of the Mānava-Dharmaśāstra*, Oxford University Press, New York.

———, 2006, *Ascetics and Brahmins: Studies in Ideologies and Institutions*, Anthem Press, London and New York, 2011 edn.

———, 2013, *King, Governance and Law in Ancient India: Kauṭilya's Arthaśāstra: A New Annotated Translation,* Oxford University Press, New York.

———, 2019, *Yajnavalkya: A Treatise on Dharma*, Murty Classical Library, Harvard University Press, Cambridge.

Olivelle, Patrick, David Brick and Mark McClish, 2015, *A Sanskrit Dictionary of Law and Statecraft*, Primus Books, New Delhi (rpt. 2017).

Pollock, Sheldon, 2011, 'Crisis in the Classics', *Social Research*, 78(1), Spring 2011, pp. 21-48.

Rawlinson, H.G., 1920, Preface, in R.G. Bhandarkar, *A Peep into the Early History of India: From the Foundation of the Maurya Dynasty to the Downfall of the Imperial Gupta Dynasty (322 B.C.-circa 500 A.C.)* (D.B. Taraporevala Sons, Bombay), pp. i-iv. The book was first published in the form of an article in 1900 in the *Journal of Bombay Branch of Royal Asiatic Society*, vol. XX.

Rocher, Ludo, 1972, Review of Jha 1967, *Indo-Iranian Journal*, 13(4), 1971 (1972), pp. 287-9.

Sahu, B.P., 1997, 'Introduction', in B.P. Sahu (ed.), *Land System and Rural Society in Early India*, Manohar, New Delhi, 1997, pp. 1-58.

Scharfe, Hartmut, 1993, *Investigations in Kauṭalya's Manual of Political Science*, Harrassowitz Verlag, Wiesbaden.

Schlingloff, Dieter, 2013, *Fortified Cities of Ancient India: A Comparative Study*, Anthem Press, London.

Shamasastry, R., 1924-5, *Index Verborum to the Published Texts of the Kautiliya Arthasastra*, 3 pts., Government Branch Press, Mysore.

Shamasastry, R., 1956, *Kauṭilya's Arthaśāstra*, 5th end., Sri Raghuveer Printing Press, Mysore.

Sharma, R.S., 1959, *Aspects of Political Ideas and Institutions in Ancient India*. Motilal Banarsidass, Delhi.

———, 1965, *Indian Feudalism: c. 300-1200*, Calcutta University: Calcutta.

Sharma, R.S. (ed.), 1971, *Land Revenue in India: Historical Studies*, Motilal Banarsidass, Delhi.

Sharma, R.S. and D.N. Jha, 1974, 'The Economic History of India up to AD 1200: Trends and Prospects', *Journal of the Economic and Social History of the Orient*, 17(1), pp. 48-80.

Shastri, Udayaveer, 1925: *Kauṭalīya Arthaśāstra*, with Hindi Translation, Meharchandra Lakshmandas, Lahore.

Sircar, D.C. (ed.), 1965, *Select Inscriptions Bearing on Indian History and Civilization*, vol. I: *From the Sixth Century B.C. to the Sixth Century A.D.*, 2nd revd. and enlgd. edn., Calcutta University, Calcutta.

———, 1967, *Inscriptions of Aśoka*, revd. edn., Publications Division, Ministry of Information and Broadcasting, Government of India, New Delhi.

———, (ed.), 1969, *Pracyavidya-tarangini*, Golden Jubilee Volume of the Department of Ancient Indian History and Culture, Calcutta University, Calcutta.

———, 1969a, *Landlordism and Tenancy in Ancient and Medieval India as Revealed by Epigraphic Records*. University of Lucknow, Lucknow.

———, 1980, 'Some Problems of the Study of Early Indian History', General President's Address, *Proceedings of the Indian History Congress*, vol. 41, 1980, pp. 1-15.

Smith, Vincent A., 1903: 'Tibetan Affinities of the Lichchhavis', *The Indian Antiquary*, vol. XXXII, 1903, pp. 233-6.

———, 1919, *The Oxford History of India*, The Clarendon Press, Oxford.

Spellman, John W., 1968, Review of Jha, 1967, *The Journal of Economic History*, 28(4), December 1968, pp. 638-40.

Sternbach, Ludwik, 1969, Review of Jha, 1967, *Journal of the American Oriental Society*, 89(4), October-December 1969, pp. 822-3.

Thapar, R., 1968, Review of Jha, 1967, *JRAS*, 100(02), pp. 194-5.

Thomas, F.W., 1914, 'Notes on the Edicts of Asoka', *JRAS*, 46(2), pp. 383-95.

Trautmann, Thomas R., 1968, Review of Jha, 1967, *Bulletin of the School of Oriental and African Studies*, 31(3), 1968, p. 675.

Van Buitenen, J.A.B., 1973: *The Mahābhārata*, vol. 1: *The Book of Beginning*. The University of Chicago Press, Chicago.

Yagi, Toru, 1994, 'A Note on *Bhojya*- and *Bhakṣya*', in Yasuke Ikari (ed.), *A Study of the Nīlamata: Aspects of Hinduism in Ancient Kashmir*, Kyoto University Press, Kyoto, pp. 377-97.

INDEX TO FOREWORD AND AFTERWORD